Film Adaptation in the Hollywood Studio Era

GUERRIC DEBONA, O.S.B.

UNIVERSITY OF ILLINOIS PRESS

Urbana, Chicago, and Springfield

Parts of this book have appeared in *Film Adaptation,* edited by
James Naremore © Rutgers University Press 2000.

Chapter 3 was first published as "Into Africa: Orson Welles
and *Heart of Darkness*" by Guerric DeBona, from *Cinema
Journal,* Volume 33, Issue 3, pp. 16–34. Copyright © 1994 by
the University of Texas Press. All rights reserved.

Chapter 5 was first published as "Masculinity on the Front:
John Huston's *The Red Badge of Courage* (1951) Revisited" by
Guerric DeBona, from *Cinema Journal,* Volume 42, Issue 2,
pp. 57–80. Copyright © 2003 by the University of Texas Press.
All rights reserved.

Library of Congress Cataloging-in-Publication Data
DeBona, Guerric, 1955–
Film adaptation in the Hollywood studio era / Guerric DeBona.
p.   cm.
Includes bibliographical references and index.
ISBN 978-0-252-03541-8 (cloth : alk. paper)
ISBN 978-0-252-07737-1 (pbk. : alk. paper)
1. Motion pictures—United States—History—20th century.
2. Film adaptations—History and criticism.
3. Motion pictures and literature—History and criticism.
I. Title.
PN1993.5.U6D355   2010
791.43'6—dc22   2009051094

For Jim Naremore
thoughtful mentor,
inspired scholar,
and best director

Contents

Acknowledgments

I am deeply indebted to the faculty of Indiana University for their interest and support of this project on film adaptation when I was a student there. I am especially grateful to James Naremore, Barbara Klinger, Stephen Watt, Patrick Brantlinger, Bill Burgan, Susan Gubar, Donald Gray, and Terry Martin. The Lilly Library staff at IU was unfailingly helpful with my research on the chapters dealing with Orson Welles and John Ford. Ned Comstack at the archives at the Doheny Library at the University of Southern California opened up his wealth of information about John Huston. The staff members of the Margaret Herrick Library, the Academy of Motion Picture Arts and Sciences were also gracious in helping me review the production files on MGM's *David Copperfield* and much more. I owe a big word of thanks to the editors of *Cinema Journal* for their interest in the earlier versions of chapter 3 and 5 of the present volume.

My gratitude extends to my colleagues at Saint Meinrad School of Theology for their inspiration, especially Kyle Kramer, Rick Stern, Tom Walters, Eugene Hensell, Cyprian Davis, Ryan LaMothe, and Robert Alvis. Mary Ellen Seifrig, Dan Kolb, and the staff at the Archabbey Library at St. Meinrad Archabbey provided their usual professional and speedy assistance with interlibrary loans. I am also very thankful to Archabbot Justin Duvall and the monks of St. Meinrad Archabbey for their fraternal support, as well as to my colleagues in academia elsewhere, Eileen Morgan-Zayacheck, J. Arthur Bond, Russ Coon, and Evan Davis, all of whom offered their insight and useful writing critiques along the way.

Joan Catapano, Rebecca McNulty, and Jennifer Clark have been encouraging, solicitous, and professional editors. R. Barton Palmer, together with the anonymous reviewer for the University of Illinois Press, offered me invaluable assistance on revisions of the manuscript. Fr. Thomas Gricoski, OSB lent me his enviable computer formatting skills.

Finally, my love and gratitude go to my parents, Glenn and Joan DeBona, the intrepid cineastes who taught me to love the movies and made me want to memorize *Casablanca*.

1

Is There a Novel in This Film? or The Cultural Politics of Film Adaptation

> Fidelity is here the temperamental affinity between film-maker and novelist, a deeply sympathetic under-standing. Instead of presenting itself as a substitute, the film is intended to take its place along side the book—to make a pair with it, like twin stars. This assumption, applicable only where there is genius, does not exclude the possibility that the film is a greater achievement than its literary model, as is the case of Renoir's *The River*.
>
> —André Bazin, "The Stylistics of Robert Bresson,"
> in *What is Cinema? Volume 1*

Readers of this book will quickly observe that over the last dozen years or so, adaptation studies has traversed a deep sea of formalist literary critics—or what Thomas Leitch has called "the backwaters of the academy"—and landed on the brighter shores of a discipline informed by cultural studies, reception theory, and film history. As Leitch points out, the pioneering work of critics such as Brian McFarlane, James Naremore, and Robert Stam has laid the groundwork for a shift from a field previously dominated by "fidelity criticism," but that now gestures toward a new generation of investigations of films and their literary precursor texts.[1] Adaptation studies, previously referred to as "novel into film" and originating from George Bluestone's 1957 monograph on the topic, have a long legacy in the academy and, for a variety of reasons, will undoubtedly persist in some form both inside and outside the academy. The current study, however, desires to enter more deeply into the new geography of literary adaptation by exploring this territory through the lens of cultural politics; it will do so by interrogating Hollywood's use of canonical British and American fiction during the studio era.

As I will discuss shortly, my work continues an evolving conversation on adaptation that has emerged in the last dozen years or so. This newer writing on the fate of the "novel into film," or what might be called revisionist adaptation studies, specifically concerns itself with industrial choices, audience reception, and the sociocultural environment contributing to the construction of the cinematic text. At the same time, the present investigation proceeds through case studies, historicizing the particular details of the film as a culture-text, a coordinate that is often absent even from recent adaptation literature. Indeed, we know that for the first decade of the sound era, Hollywood was an intrepid user of classical literary texts, due to numerous factors. But these industry interests would soon be displaced by a different set of audience expectations and material circumstances occurring after the Second World War. My investigation of MGM's nostalgic version of *David Copperfield* during the Great Depression, Orson Welles's use of a high-modernist author, Joseph Conrad, at the end of the 1930s for his first screenplay, John Ford's retexting of Eugene O'Neill's sea plays as a kind of middle-class art cinema, and John Huston's reinvention of Stephen Crane as an anti–cold war narrative in the midst of the American involvement in Korea begin to suggest what I will call "the politics of redeployment," or what André Bazin envisioned more than fifty years ago as adaptation as "mixed cinema."

For the nascent field of film adaptation studies emerging from English departments in American universities in the 1950s[2] and often ancillary to the close reading of texts already practiced by the New Critics after the Second World War, the answer to the question "Is there a novel in this film?" was this: "Yes; and we are going to find what's left of its essential literary character after the adaptation." Adaptation critics in those days must have viewed themselves as something like rescue workers sifting through what was left of a museum after it was hit by a great roaring tempest of mass culture: they had to sort through and pick up the well-known fragments in an effort to salvage what was left of precious cultural artifacts—the canonical author, the established text, the essential meaning of the literary source. As Linda Hutcheon has recently remarked, most of the discourse on adaptation is framed "in negative terms of loss."[3] Not surprisingly, such salvage sifting seems to go nowhere. Fidelity criticism—which Dudley Andrew has referred to as "the most frequent and tiresome discussion of adaptation"—has had its variants, ranging from art historian E. H. Gombrich's discussion of the possibility of "matching" texts to narratologist Keith Cohen's semiotics of exchange.[4] Indeed, studies that "are organized around the question of whether or not a given film is better than the book on which it is based or whether its changes were dictated by concessions to a mass audience or expressions of changing cultural mores may be accomplished and persuasive in advancing their claims about the adaptation at hand, but they are unlikely to play a leading role in advancing adaptation studies as it struggles to emerge from the disciplinary umbrella of film studies and the still more tenacious grip of literary studies."[5]

Much of the present conversation about "novel into film" may be traced to the ivy-covered walls of American literary academia on the one hand, and mid-twentieth-century Paris and the brash editorial desks of the auteurists at *Cahiers du Cinéma* on the other. In his influential essay assessing the current state of writing on adaptation, James Naremore says that the discussion tends to move back and forth between two groups, both guided by a dominant metaphor. "The Bluestone approach relies on an implicit metaphor of *translation,* which governs all investigations of how codes move across sign systems. Writing in this category usually deals with the concept of literary versus cinematic form, and it pays close attention to the problem of textual fidelity in order to identify the specific formal capabilities of the media."[6] Fidelity would become the litmus test of establishing a transparent translation between novel and film, or, more to the point, collapsing film into a literary category, a touchstone that would galvanize the interest of the academy's literati from the first glimmer of interest in the newly emerging writing on film adaptation. When discussing the adaptation of *Madame Bovary,* for instance, Bluestone says that the film "falters because it fails to pick up an author's obvious use of spatial elements, fails to rethink the novel in plastic form."[7] Based on this premise, the adaptation is only successful insofar as the film mirrors the literary quality of the source text. Bluestone's favorite metaphor is that the adaptive (filmic) text is "parasitic" on the (literary) source text. "As long as the cinema remains as omnivorous as it is for story material," Bluestone writes in his closing chapter, "its dependence on literature will continue."[8] Not coincidentally, Bluestone's analysis of film adaptation praises works that approach a literary cinema, when he adapts the "organic novel" into "a kind of paraphrase of the novel."[9] For Bluestone, visual and technical (and performance) innovations in film, such as Cinemascope, together with what he refers to as "depth-illusion" are simply accidental to the formal, literary properties of the cinematic; these advancements "will take its place with sound and color as an additional but not primary line in film structure."[10]

There have been any number of assaults on Bluestone and his legacy over the last decade, but few proposals for an actual methodology for historicizing literary adaptation out of its formalist stranglehold. It is my contention that the French auteurists grant contemporary adaptation studies a cultural and sociological perspective because they "were more apt to consider such things as audiences, historical situations, and cultural politics."[11] Where the fidelity critics rely on metaphors of translation or organic derivations of such analogies, the auteurists preferred the metaphor of *performance*. "It, too, involves questions of textual fidelity, but it emphasizes difference rather than similarities, individual styles rather than formal systems."[12] If the French auteurists, especially André Bazin, Alexandre Astruc, and François Truffaut, count heavily on a performative metaphor, then they also help us to reimagine adaptation in the present day. Indeed, Truffaut's famously strident iconoclastic essay "A Certain Tendency in French Cinema" (1954) was precisely a manifesto against *literary* stuffiness, even as Astruc and others would argue for a filmic language that showcased the *mise-en-scène* and *la caméra stylo*. In a certain sense, the French New Wave was founded on a reassessment of film adaptation; it is perhaps not coincidental that much of what Bazin has to say about film language, montage, and *la politique des auteurs* appears through his seminal analysis of adaptation in the pages of *Cahiers du Cinéma* and elsewhere. As Robert Stam has pointed out, *La Nouvelle Vague* formulated its aesthetic principles around what came to be called "*querelle de l'adaptation*."[13] The French auteurists would welcome the dissemination of the literary into something like a de-bourgeoisification of the arts through mass cultural performance. Indeed, Bazin argued in his essay "In Defense of Mixed Cinema" that adaptation was itself an instrument not for division, but for equalizing the audience. After an adaptation of a literary work, the field of reading is broadened and democratized; for Bazin, therefore, "there is no competition or substitution . . . rather the adding of a new dimension that the arts had gradually lost . . . namely a public."[14] Undoubtedly, the public had been sustained for years by Hollywood studios marketing the adaptation of a popular source text for the screen, schooling the moviegoing audience in a kind of popular film criticism that compared novel to film and required no tutelage except for a scant acquaintance with the literary source. Adaptation was destined for popular commercial interest, as Bazin would say. As John Ellis puts it, "adaptation trades upon memory of the novel, a memory that can derive from actual reading, or, as is more likely with a classic of literature, a generally circulated cultural memory. The adaptation consumes this memory, aiming to efface it with the presence of its own image."[15]

I am suggesting, then, that the French auteurists provide a window into at least three different areas that might advance our discussion of literary adaptation. As I will indicate shortly, all three of these critical practices have been applied to some extent to adaptation studies, but bringing these per-spectives together under one volume provides a much-needed and neces-sary strategic angle in this field of inquiry. First, as I will show later in this chapter, Bazin's interest in a "mixed cinema" suggests the importance of renegotiating a (formalist) binary arrangement in adaptation criticism into an intertextual space, particularly from the point of view of a Bakhtinian intertextuality, or what Robert Stam has called "the dialogics of adaptation." After all, long before Bluestone and the formalist critics attached themselves to the trope "novel into film," adaptation was not even a discipline, but a kind of popular form of "criticism" practiced by moviegoers that advanced Hollywood box office interests. In discussing adaptation, Bazin imagined that the end of adaptation was a "digest" made for an audience, asking us to think of film adaptation "in relation to commercialism, industrial modernity and democracy, and to compare it with an engraving or digest that makes the so-called original 'readily acceptable to all.'"[16] In terms of "digest," Bazin writes that "one could also understand it as a literature that has been made more accessible through cinematic adaptation, not so much because of the oversimplification that such adaptation entails . . . but rather because of the of the mode of expression itself, as if the aesthetic fat, differently emulsified were better tolerated by the consumer's mind."[17] Such commercialized strate-gies became part of redeploying classic texts in Hollywood during the studio period, using intertextual collaborators to shape the audience.

The second perspective, concerning the cultural power of the text itself, also helped to shape Bazin's thinking in those early years, but is not far from Truffaut's intuitive reaction to adaptation in the 1950s: what about the implica-tions for the literary canon in adapting "novels into film?" As Naremore and others have pointed out, at precisely the moment that Truffaut was railing against bourgeois literary adaptation, Bluestone was establishing a meth-odology that tends "to confirm the intellectual priority and formal supe-riority of canonical novels, which provide the films he discusses with their sources and with a standard of value against which their success or failure is measured."[18] Truffaut's essay is often (rightly) viewed as a manifesto of a young Turk railing against established literary conventions, but his seminal statement suggests a reassessment of the cultural value of the "literary" and its function in cinema culture. Third, if the auteurists famously lionized the director, then what about the status of the literary author of the antecedent source text and his or her relationship with the director of the filmic text? The issue of who becomes the "author" of the adapted text or, even more interestingly, how the literary author is promulgated as a discourse inside and outside the filmic text becomes yet another fascinating lens with which to examine literary adaptation.

My argument throughout this book is that the use of intertextuality, the function of cultural value, and the aura of authorship provide a significant angle with which to engage the adaptation process. I must point out that although I have been inspired by the metaphor of performance of the auteurists, this is not a sustained argument for the origins of these three strategies in the French New Wave. Nor am I claiming in any systematic way that the auteurists touched on every aspect of these three categories that I am proposing for a kind of methodological matrix for studying adaptation. But the interests of the French New Wave and the editors of *Cahiers du Cinéma* were extroverted, political, and sociological, while maintaining an interest in the cinematic text as a performance site. Bazin's overwhelming interest in the performative dynamics of the adaptive text as a "mixed cinema"—a site of commercial interest—points us in the direction of *how* and *under what conditions* texts were negotiated in Hollywood for an audience. I think that this performance metaphor necessarily offers a viable alternative to prevailing static, formalist criticism in adaptation studies. It is my hope that the present book helps to raise questions that further the advancement of the discipline by historicizing case studies within the studio period of classic Hollywood.

That said, the method I have chosen is to take four instances where American film culture has redeployed the "literary" and placed them under the lenses of intertextuality, cultural/textual power, and authorship, using them as coordinates inside a specific period in Hollywood history. In discussing George Cukor's *David Copperfield* (1935), Orson Welles's unproduced film script *Heart of Darkness* (1939), John Ford's *The Long Voyage Home* (1940), and John Huston's *The Red Badge of Courage* (1951), I am proposing a paradigm that takes seriously Naremore's suggestion "that what we need instead is a broader definition of adaptation and a sociology that takes into account the commercial apparatus, the audience, and the academic culture industry."[19] In this regard, I believe that I am responding most recently to Simone Murray's proposal for materializing the adaptation industry. For Murray, adaptation is not "an exercise in comparative textual analysis of individual books and their screen versions, but a material phenomenon produced by a system of institutional interests and actors."[20] I am interested in questions such as: how did the film industry make use of certain texts during the studio era?

My purpose in this investigation concerns the cultural politics of redeploying literary texts during one of Hollywood's most exciting and creative periods. As a methodology, I have not confined myself to one particular way of "doing adaptation criticism," but have suggested a kind of matrix for this field of study, broadly consisting of intertextuality, cultural value, and authorship. In addition to the pioneering writings of the French auteurists that recognize the performative aspects of adaptation, I have drawn from the work of more recent writers, such as James Naremore, Pierre Bourdieu, and Robert Stam, in order to advance what used to be called "novel into film." I must point out, however, that even though each of these areas have been explored individually in writing on film adaptation, as far as I can tell, this book is the first time that these strategies have been brought together in any kind of systematic way and proposed as a methodology. That is not a criticism, but an observation about purpose: I view the tactics I have been discussing as interdependent and interconnected. I have used Robert Stam's enormously helpful three-volume series that he edited with Alessandra Raengo throughout this chapter; the editors engage a plethora of essays emphasizing a range of films and texts that foregrounds Bakhtinian dialogism within a network of intertextual strategies. These volumes are, I take it, deliberately diversified in order to serve a wide range of critical interests. Julie Sanders's *Adaptation and Appropriation* (2006) devises another approach to adaptation-as-intertextuality. Striving to arrive at something of a guidebook to adaptation, which she sees as a "sub-section of the over-arching practice of intertextuality," Sanders reminds us of the important link between the dramatic and the literary when she says that "performance is an inherently adaptive art; each staging is a collaborative interpretation, one which often reworks a playscript to acknowledge contemporary concerns or issues."[21]

As far as cultural value and literary politics are concerned, Jennifer M. Jeffers uses a concept of "reterritorialization" in *Britain Colonized: Hollywood's Appropriation of British Literature* (2006) to interrogate the ways that Hollywood has appropriated and colonized British literature. Jeffers is horrified at the specter of cultural appropriation and Americanization of English literature, particularly Shakespeare, for commercial interests. She nicely explores how cultural value becomes cannibalized through cinematic commercial interests in Hollywood. Yet Jeffers's "reterritorialization" represents something like a return to Bluestone and company, although parasitic damage and the museum's literary wreckage she grieves is strictly British property.[22] Most recently, Jack Boozer has edited a collection on "authorship and adaptation" that focuses on the collateral relationship of the screenplay to the motion picture and its ties to authorship. Like Stam's collection, Boozer's text brings together a wider range of essays around class studies that serve eclectic interests of those interested in a broad spectrum of films, this time investigating how the screenplay figures into the overall dynamic of the cinematic text. Boozer acknowledges the work of poststructuralists like Michel Foucault, but rightly questions the "total erasure of the individual creative voice."[23]

These individual studies have enriched the study of adaptation. But my research indicates that bringing together at least three new approaches to adaptation studies within a historical period greatly expands our understanding of the process of materializing adaptation. Consider MGM's production of *David Copperfield.* As producer, David Selznick relied on collateral relationship a popular construction of an author, Charles Dickens, who wrote about the poor, but whose fiction garnered middle-class moral knowledge and respectability. The actors and their costumes were carefully matched with illustrations by "Phiz" that were part of a Dickensian visual vocabulary. Even the education industry had its collateral supports, as it educated students in "how to read" the film *David Copperfield.* Intertextual? Yes, clearly. But even more: such intertextual practices would guarantee the cultural value of consuming a "literary" film text, undoubtedly a shrewd move for Selznick and MGM after the implementation of the 1934 Production Code. Finally, given the ways in which Charles Dickens served MGM during the Depression in the 1930s, the question of authorship of the film is intrinsically related to both intertextuality and the hegemony of cultural value. Therefore, the author of the film is surely more Dickensian than the director, George Cukor; the film's Victorian signature only further galvanizes its canonical legibility, respectability, and prestige. Neither intertextuality, cultural value, nor authorship alone are sufficient to read literary adaptation, but taken together, these provide a wide aperture with which to see how texts have been redeployed inside a cultural nexus.

The frame of 1934 to 1951 creates a historical web of Hollywood productions that redeployed literary texts; it intentionally bookends two MGM productions, both of which might be read as utilizing to varying degrees the dynamics of intertextuality, cultural power, and authorship. Metro's adaptation of Dickens's *David Copperfield* reveals savvy production skills accessed at precisely the right time in American history, thereby bolstering cultural value; it became perhaps the best example of a prestige production in the 1930s. By contrast, the same studio's rendering of another canonical novel, Stephen Crane's *The Red Badge of Courage* in 1951, shows us an example of adaptation when cold-war panic and the aura of the canonical text lacked the cultural hegemony of previous decades. In a historical context, a discussion of adaptation of both novels not only illuminates the interplay among intertextuality, cultural value, and authorship, but this matrix discloses the crucial role these components play in American studies. Redeploying the cultural memory of a Victorian author like Charles Dickens during the Depression served the strategic advantage of a studio investing itself with the aura of prestige and credibility for the middle class, but the tactic of redeployment for a canonical author like Stephen Crane would prove much less successful fifteen years later in cold-war America, especially when John Huston chose to render the novel as something of an allegory of the fragile and debilitated post–World War II soldier, clearly stamping his own authorship on the film.

The "next generation" of adaptation critics recognizes the necessary departure from formalism, but, as Murray indicates, delineating an extensive historical or material network of adaptations could vastly expand the field. *David Copperfield* may be an example of a prestige adaptation, but no less illuminating is a study of a maverick director like Orson Welles's use of a paradigmatic modernist text at the end of the 1930s. Welles's unproduced screenplay for Joseph Conrad's *Heart of Darkness* could not be further away from *David Copperfield;* their difference expresses, once again, the various aspects of intertextuality, cultural value, and authorship. While MGM redeployed a favorite British author to negotiate class issues during the Great Depression, Welles chose as his first film a modernist novella to educate his audience: the screenplay was filled with instructions on how to see through the illusion of film and politics, and Welles was prepared to use Bell & Howell Eyemo cameras and subjective narration to illuminate the novel's dark, even racist, undercurrent. Far from using adaptation to vitiate tensions, Welles's screenplay became a kind of modernist parable against fascism similar to his previous theatrical productions of *Julius Ceasar* and *"Voodoo" Macbeth.* Therefore Welles's struggle with RKO suggests a debate that was perhaps more about ideology than style. The character of Kurtz and his obsession for power mirrors the political scene worldwide, but also forecasts a more subdued counterpart in the person of Charles Foster Kane. From the perspective of literary and cultural power, Welles's reading of a modernist text brought out its disturbing features—hardly standard fare for the late 1930s. But the proposed film version of Conrad's *Heart of Darkness* became a stunning modernist prototype, a blueprint for the future work of the great American auteur.

At the same moment that Welles was using modernist techniques to shock his audience, John Ford was advantageously deploying the literary as a signifier of his well-publicized "arty" style to promote his own prestige as a director with a distinctive technique. The adaptation of four of Eugene O'Neill's sea plays provided Ford with a venue that would allow the director to use Gregg Toland's cinematography to promote his own signature style. The authorship

of *The Long Voyage Home* was never in question: it was a self-fashioned auteur capitalizing on middlebrow German expressionism, a legacy Ford had
cultivated from Fox Studios since the 1920s.

Perhaps the most revealing thing to say about Hollywood's activity during the studio period is the enormous range of its literary adaptations, even
within the parameters of canonical literature. Indeed, the sum of these productions alone discloses the remarkable spectrum and vitality of Hollywood-
as-literary-adapter. Clearly, *David Copperfield* stands out among dozens of
literary prestige productions in the 1930s. Meanwhile, Welles's adaptation
sought to strip the middle-class audience of the pleasure of reading a film;
like Conrad, the young director was interested in getting his readers "to see."
As Welles was creating a unique style that would give him the thumbs down
for his first production at RKO, John Ford capitalized on an arty cinematography that bought him a reputation. Years later, cultural and studio politics
transformed a little novel about the Civil War into a major battle at MGM.
Himself a kind of modernist prone to think of himself as a literary adapter,
John Huston used an antiwar reflection on the Civil War not to reinforce
a romantic reading of a past domestic tragedy, but to document the present reality of the Korean War and the cold war. *The Red Badge of Courage*
is a record of intertextual misfires (using a World War II hero in the role of
cowardly soldier, for instance), canonical misreading, and the struggle for
authorship. The study of the film's adaptation is a suitable ending for a study
of Hollywood's redeployment of canonical literary texts, and the cultural
hegemony that would help shape them into film history.

I would like to think that this kind of investigation leads to others, and
where adaptation praxis serves as an instrument for an interrogation of
American film culture, raising lots of questions about ideological and institutional choices, star power, and production value during key moments in
American history. Obviously, I do not see intertextuality, cultural value, and
authorship as independent functionaries, but rather as tactics woven together
in the broader picture of cultural politics. In my view, the present text is an
effort to build upon and expand the work many of my contemporaries have
been amassing in adaptation studies over the past decade.[24] That said, I part
company with some of my colleagues in the field, though, because there is
no attempt here at a survey of adaptation, old or new, or even an attempt at
redefining the idea of "adaptation," the way Julie Sanders and Linda Hutcheon
have done. Hutcheon's *A Theory of Adaptation* (2006), Thomas Leitch's *Film
Adaptations and Its Discontents* (2007), and Sanders's work paint the landscape of adaptation astutely with examples and broad strokes. All three texts

are necessary in beginning to discover insightful and useful explorations of the contours of adaptation post-Bluestone. Having examined a representative selection of recent studies on adaptation, including Hutcheon and Sanders, Leitch says that

> The future of adaptation studies is best indicated by essays that either challenge the still prevailing model of book-into-film, a model which dictates most of the interchangeable titles of monographs and collections on film adaptations—or raise more interesting questions, questions that are more productive of further, still more probing questions. Essays that are organized around the question of whether or not a given film is better than the book on which it is based or whether its changes were dictated by concessions to a mass audience or expressions of changing cultural mores may be accomplished and persuasive in advancing their claims about the adaptation at hand, but they are unlikely to play a leading role in advancing adaptation studies. . . . They are limited not because they give incorrect answers to the questions they pose, but because those questions themselves are so limited in their general implications.[25]

I hope that the present proposed methodology and the case studies that support this system raise interesting questions to advance film adaptation, cultural history, and American studies. While all three of these strategies I have named here begin to course in and out of the various film texts I will discuss in this book, for the moment it might be useful to focus in some detail at intertextuality, cultural value, and authorship and their relationship with film adaptation.

Intertextual Strategies

Together with fidelity criticism, a modernist, literary impulse has dominated the discourse on adaptation in this country for decades. But from the early days of cinema, the film industry imagined a collateral relationship among a variety of systems surrounding the adaptation process. Indeed, Tom Gunning has shown that there were numerous intertextual adaptive strategies at work in the cinema before 1907, in which classic works such as *Ten Nights in a Ballroom, Faust, Uncle Tom's Cabin, Hamlet, Robinson Crusoe,* and *Rip Van Winkle* were deployed in what Gérard Genette has called *palimpsests,* or "references caught within an echo chamber of popular memory."[26] With an eye toward rethinking film adaptation, particularly insofar as it has opposed words and pictures, Kamilla Elliot has meticulously examined the artificial distinction drawn between visual/verbal categorizations and discovered that these assignations "break down at every level in the hybrid arts of illustrated novels and worded films."[27] At the same time, what Robert Stam has called a "dialogics of adaptation" aptly suggests a window into the film/novel debate. Stam uses Mikhail Bakhtin's concept of "dialogism" and Julia Kristeva's "intertextuality," together with Genette's "transtextuality," to advance the notion that film adaptations "are caught up in the ongoing whirl of intertextual reference and transformation, of texts generating other texts in an endless process of recycling, transformation, and transmutation, with no clear point of origin."[28]

For Stam, adaptations

> Can take an activist stance toward their source novels, inserting them into a much broader intertextual dialogism. An adaptation, in this sense, is less an attempted resuscitation of an originary world than a turn in an ongoing dialogical process. The concept of intertextual dialogism suggests that every text forms an intersection of textual surfaces. All texts are tissues of anonymous formulae, variations on those formulae, conscious and unconscious quotations, and conflations and inversions of other texts. In the broadest sense, intertexual dialogism refers to the infinite and open-ended possibilities generated by all the discursive practices of a culture, the entire matrix of communicative utterances within which the artistic text is situated, which read the text not only through recognizable influences, but also through a subtle process of dissemination.[29]

A fascinating example of intertextual dynamics in adaptation—or the "effective co-presence of two texts"[30]—is the biblical epic. Ella Shohat has shown the skewed nature of the literalist or fidelity readings in adaptation criticism as it applies to the Judeo-Christian scriptures. Hinting at the importance of intertextuality in biblical adaptations, she says that, "An imprecise and reductive discourse about cinema as merely a visual medium, then, underestimates the potential of film language to transform 'The Book' into multiple realms in which the word, images, sounds, dialogue, music and written materials all constitute, together, the complex space called cinema."[31] In a certain sense, I would suggest even further that the Bible is the *premier* test case for the adaptive text as the site of alleged fidelity of word into image. As Pamala Grace argues, "Of all films based on written texts, those about the life of Jesus may make the loudest claims of "fidelity" to their source.[32] When discussing the difference between the Old Testament and Homer, for instance, Erich Auerbach, and later, M. M. Bakhtin, see the literary claims emerging from the

Bible as utterly different than other poetic instances because scripture stories represent "Universal history, their insistent relation—a relation constantly redefined by conflicts—to a single and hidden God, who yet shows himself and who guides universal history by promise and exaction, gives these stories an entirely different perspective . . ."[33] Moreover, redeploying the New Testament as the locus of intertextuality was in place long before film culture invested in biblical spectacle, because, as one scholar puts it, "many popular images operate in tandem with an oral culture or printed text: devotional literature, Bible passages, hymns, prayers, and teaching guides."[34] In other words, devotional spectacle and popular piety prepared well for the biblical epic through collateral religious and cultural practices. When it came to a critical consideration of adaptations of the Gospels for cinema, Bazin gestured at the intertextual, indeed performative, aspects of what he referred to as "immense catechism-in-pictures" when he said that these spectacular aspects of the history of Christianity were "simply amplified variations on the Stations of the Cross or on the Musée Grévin."[35]

Because intertextual dynamics course through the biblical text in incalculable ways, fidelity to the established, written "text" has very little to do with adapting the life of Jesus. Rather, tapping into an *already* firmly established, pious visual and aural discourse was crucial to adapting the silent version of the filmed Gospels, something that the nascent American film culture learned early on. In addition to the popular devotion of the Stations of the Cross, we know the *tableaux vivants* were an essential feature of the early filmed Passion plays: they provided a verisimilitude and an aura of authenticity—and the sacred space—from one popular medium to another. The blurring of the distinction between religious space and theatrical space raises an interesting question that Thomas Leitch approaches in study of adaptation: "What is the relation between inspiration ('a religious experience') and mass entertainment?"[36] Such an inquiry provides the spine to fill out our body of discovery about intertextuality and adapting the biblical text. It is also easy to see that intertextuality provided American audiences with a complex matrix for verisimilitude, even faith—in a word, a desirable and consumable spectacle. A successful biblical adaptation will use a variety of performance media to make the Bible legible and consumable for a modern audience. I will contend here that the relationship between inspiration and mass entertainment is particularly applicable to Cecil B. DeMille's well-known adaptation of the Gospel, *The King of Kings* in 1927, which Richard Maltby's reconstructive production history has already examined from the perspective of industry censorship, demonstrating "a close and mutually supportive relationship between the liberal Protestant churches and the motion picture industry."[37] From my vantage point, though, the production still raises fascinating issues in regard to so-called fidelity to the (biblical) text and intertextuality, or the "literary" and "performance" prevalent in adaptation discussions. As I will suggest briefly, DeMille's success occurs precisely through his ability to redeploy the source text into a performance space of intertextuality: he will blur the distinction between worship and theatrical space, a celebration of "an ongoing interaction with other texts and artistic productions."[38]

Cecil B. DeMille was no stranger to the practical considerations and marketing strategies of intertextuality. As Sumiko Hagashi has shown, early in his career DeMille relied on intertextuality in advertising in adapting stage westerns such as *The Squaw Man* (1914), *The Virginian* (1914), *The Call of the North* (1914), *What's His Name* (1914), and *The Man from Home* (1914) "to address educated middle-class audiences."[39] Much of the intertextual production techniques that DeMille exploited and reinterpreted emerged from a tradition of "Victorian pictorialism" concomitant with liberal Protestant beliefs and Arnoldian concepts embedded in American culture.[40] In his first great biblical adaptation, *The Ten Commandments* (1923), DeMille was clearly attempting to imbue a religious aura to the entire production, from the way he handled publicity to the manner in which he expected the cast to behave off the set. When it came to the production evolution of *The King of Kings,* a sophisticated soundtrack allowed for the positioning of another text alongside a familiar depiction of Jesus, the disciples, and the events of the New Testament. The appropriation of music, or particularly hymns in the film, showcased a contemporary and conscious, post-Biblical ecclesial presence in the midst of an "authoritative scene," such as the use of the nonchoral version of Martin Luther's "A Mighty Fortress is Our God," after Mary Magdalene has been cleansed of her seven demons. The presence of an extremely well-known sixteenth-century hymn scored underneath a biblical sequence suggests a remarkable use of intertextuality and religious cultural cross-referencing.[41] In a certain sense, the use of recognizable Christian hymns as a coda to biblical scenes showcases an ideal faith response to those scriptural moments within the film text itself. Much like visual discourse, church hymnody helps negotiate the space between the middle-class (churchgoing) spectator and the film text. The interplay of the hymn on the scripture further galvanizes the contemporary audience into a spectacle that is not two thousand years in the past, but contemporary and ecclesial. The theater becomes a house of worship, then, mediating the space between religious and theatrical experience.

The intertextual use of other media increased Jesus' cinematic legibility and significantly erased the distinction between the performance and the worship space. We know that Gustave Doré's engravings, together with James Tissot's illustrations from the King James Version of the Bible—always a staple in every Protestant household—provided DeMille with substantial material for his sets. Taken together, these form the 276 representations of Renaissance and Victorian religious paintings that claim to comprise the film.[42] Doré would remain an artistic touchstone for DeMille's *mise-en-scène* throughout the director's career, simulating the engraver's landscape and lighting techniques.[43] More important, though, DeMille tapped into the Doré illustrations of the Bible as a way of accessing genteel American culture that was familiar with the *Doré Bible* in the nineteenth century. As contemporary movie reviewer, Mordaunt Hall, wrote in the *New York Times* on April 20, 1927, *The King of Kings* traces the past masters, now animated by film technology, and that "one of the most beautiful scenes in this production is that of the Last Supper. It is strikingly like the old paintings of this subject, but here the figures come to life." Indeed the scene of the Last Supper is a remarkably lit classical composition, a set-piece that might well substitute for a modest devotional painting in any pious Christian home. As the scene opens, DeMille simply lets the action unfold without titles until Jesus stands, now enshrined in an aura of celestial light. Then there is a three-quarter shot as Jesus breaks the bread, followed by the title, a direct quotation from Luke 22:19: "Take, eat—this is My body which is given for you. This do in remembrance of Me." He then offers the cup, with a quotation from Matthew 26:27–28: "This is My blood of the New Testament—which is shed for many unto the remission of sins. Drink ye all of it!"

In many ways, the Last Supper sequence is iconic of the crafty use of intertextuality in *The King of Kings,* because the scene accesses not a strictly literary source but one distilled from the performance currents of many strands of the popular (Christian) religious imagination. Moreover, The Last Supper sequence remains notable not only for revealing the visual discourse functioning in a crucial intertextual moment, but also for reminding us how intertitles operate as proclamations to authenticity. As Bruce Babington and Peter William Evans explain, "This extreme iconicity and familiarity of gesture finds its perfect expression in the *tableauxesque* style of the film, the constant stasis of compositions and poses deriving from the Victorian spectacular theatre with its tradition of creating living representations of famous paintings. The effect is compounded by silent film's need of intertitles, so that Christ's words are not given, as in the sound films, in the distinctive grain of the actor's voice but in the written form, predetermined and authoritative, qualities underlined even more by DeMille's quoting at the bottom of the frame the Gospel sources of the titles."[44]

DeMille cleverly weaves some "natural" dialogue in *The King of Kings,* and this language has a special relationship with the word of the biblical text deployed throughout the film. Indeed, the overall effect of scriptural/ original dialogue might be expressed, as Thomas Leitch reads biblical adaptations, through the lens of Mikhail Bakhtin. Leitch says that "Scriptural texts are the model for all texts seeking to exercise unquestioned authority rather than an invitation to playfully creative adaptation or an assimilation to new language or new media." From the perspective of an analysis of the intertextual contours of *The King of Kings,* then, we might say that the direct quotes from the Bible offer us what Bakhtin calls an "authoritative discourse" that "binds us, quite independent of any power it might have to persuade us internally."[45] Clearly, the Bible stands as an authority beyond all others, especially in the American Protestant tradition. But the screenwriters have peppered the script with abundant nonscriptual quotations as well. Therefore DeMille gains a "moral or rhetorical authority for incidents he and his screenwriters have transformed beyond recognition or created out of whole cloth. . . . Such transplanting of scriptural tags suggests that DeMille is treating the Gospel narrative as multiple text not because it exists in more than one telling but because it is divisible into microtexts, any one of which is available to authenticate any other, or indeed any invented incident like the curing of Mark that might be added to the story."[46] Finally, the presence of intertitles are themselves a very interesting intertextual feature that has only recently been rigorously investigated from the point of view of reexamining the novel/film debate, thanks to Elliott's work on words and images of illustrated novels and their relationship with early films.[47]

The intertextual strategy in *King of Kings* grants the film—and the image of Jesus—credibility, authority, and what Walter Benjamin might have called an "aura." "In permitting the reproduction to meet the beholder or listener in his own particular situation," says Benjamin in "The Work of Art in the Age of Mechanical Reproduction," "it reactivates the object reproduced."[48] Therefore the most significant way that DeMille established an aura around Jesus was not through fidelity to the biblical text, but by an intertextual dynamic that drew discursively from existing images already present in American film and religious culture in the late 1920s. Even further, in addition to the use of intertextual multiple media, drawing from various forms of *tableux vivants* to lend credibility to the film adaptation, DeMille introduced a significant use of narrative point of view into *The King of Kings* as well, which also lends legibility to the aura and person of Jesus. The Oberammergau Passion narratives, and the significant early film biblical adaptations of the New Testament such as *The Manger and the Cross* (1912) and the biblical sequence of D. W. Griffith's *Intolerance* (1916), photographed Christ flatly and objectively, as if he were part of a historical tapestry. But DeMille's camera dynamic allowed for formerly distant and historical figures to take on a new, subjective narrative life. As Sumiko Higashi notes, "By moving his camera in for medium close-ups and close-ups, DeMille humanized biblical characters and thereby bridged the gap between macrocosm and microcosm in historical representations."[49] In Benjamin's terms, then, although the portrait of Christ has been detached from its historical and ecclesial setting, mass cultural reproduction has allowed for "a renewal of mankind"[50] in the cinema, one that clearly delighted both Paramount and the box office.

An aspect of this point of view sequence is worth a closer look. In photographing the audience's first encounter with Jesus, roughly fifteen minutes into the film, DeMille drew from classical and popular portraiture of Jesus that looked directly at the spectator. Our original encounter with Christ occurs through the eyes of a blind girl, whose sight is restored. As she gradually sees, so does the audience; we encounter the face of Christ directly. DeMille would work point of view in *The King of Kings* to his distinct advantage, deploying subjective camera shots in order to collude with his audience's piety. DeMille might have had in mind any number of religious representations of Jesus that look directly at the viewer. But we know that Bruce Barton, an adviser on *King of Kings* and author of the best-selling book on images of Jesus, favored hyper-masculine images of Christ.[51] Barton's *The Young Man's Christ* (1914), for instance, used as a frontispiece Darius Cobb's *The Master* (1914), in which Jesus has very strong masculine features and large piercing eyes that look directly at the spectator. As Richard Maltby points out, works like Barton's *The Man Nobody Knows* (1925) were normative expressions of liberal Protestant discourse, expressing Christ's humanity, and echoed elsewhere by Harry Emerson Fosdick and others who "centered their belief in a reconstructed, therapeutic version of the New Testament, exalted Jesus as a healthy personality."[52] In drawing from Barton and a range of material to establish an on-camera, full facial representation of Jesus, DeMille was not simply introducing a character, but evoking a performative religious experience—or perhaps, more to the point, confirming one.

Adapting the Bible into the "authentic Jesus," then, ratifies an expectant, devotional aura in the spectator. As David Morgan puts it, "Likeness as physical resemblance amounts to seeing what one presumes should be there and ignoring or forgetting what in fact is. In other words, people believe an image looks like Jesus because they conform the image's features to their expectations about him."[53] In retrospect, it seems clear that the mechanical reproduction of Jesus on film in the 1920s bestowed on Christ a certain kind of authenticity, transforming the place of exhibition as well from a theater to a kind of sacred space. DeMille's biblical epic becomes a clear instance of what Benjamin calls the ability of mass culture and technology to "put the copy of the original into situations which would be out of reach for the original itself."[54]

Intertextual strategies worked well for DeMille in adapting the biblical text, beginning with *The Ten Commandments* and coursing through *The King of Kings*. Drawing from a wide spectrum of intertextual resources, DeMille negotiated what Roland Barthes would call a "readerly" text or, as Higashi describes it, "a usable past for social classes that, unlike the cultural elite, were unambiguous regarding the use of popular culture as a representation of their religious views . . . *The Ten Commandments*, with separate narratives set in the biblical past and the present, marks a transitional point in that the director produced highbrow art at the same time that he addressed spectators who would have disapproved of the modernity of his early Jazz Age films."[55]

That DeMille maintained a great deal of control over the use of intertextuality seems clear, and in *The King of Kings* this dynamic is nowhere more evidenced than in the potentially problematic area of star performance. Intertextuality in biblical adaptations must remain relatively transparent, simply evocative, or else these characters would threaten to turn the text into a self-conscious narrative, a parody or pastiche. (One thinks, for instance, of the transcendently awkward fifteen seconds toward the end of George Stevens's 1965 production of *The Greatest Story Ever Told* when John Wayne, cast as the centurion at the foot of the cross, announces in a completely identifiably "John Wayne" cadence to the audience familiar with his star image and roles in other pictures: "This *truly* was the Son of God.") The casting decisions made for all adaptations are crucial, but more embarrassing in the case of biblical films if the star image threatens to overwhelm the character around whom there may be a complicated and established visual and historical discourse. Intertextual strategies involving casting are important because they implicate the actors not only in previous roles but, as Naremore tells us, with "narratives written about the actor in publicity and biography and thus becomes a global category."[56] To this end, DeMille went to great lengths to suppress the star image of H. B. Warner, making him wear a veil on his face when he traveled to the Paramount lot to shoot the film. Warner and Dorothy Cumming (as the Mother of Jesus) had to sign a contract that prohibited them from taking parts for the next five years that might smudge their sacred status. They were told they could not engage in any unwholesome activities during the shooting itself, including playing cards and riding in sports cars.

At the same time, the star image as an intertextual performance text worked well for DeMille in casting the actress to play Mary Magdalene. Jacqueline Logan, a former Ziegfeld girl at the peak of her career, is described in the intertitle commentary of *The King of Kings* as one who "laughed at God and man." Scantily clad, even, I imagine, for a first-century harlot, she is associated with exotic wild animals, such as the zebras that pull her racing chariot, as well as the pet leopard she cuddles in the palace. The emperor says to her shortly after the beginning of the film, "Mary, if thou will give thy kisses to a beast, why not me?" Sometime later, when she encounters Jesus, the famous Mary Magdalene becomes transfixed by his gaze. What follows is a fascinating series of double exposures exemplifying the seven deadly sins. Embarrassed by her bare midriff and uncovered head, the repentant Magdalene covers herself and then sits at Christ's feet. Finally, the sequence closes with the soundtrack playing an instrumental version of the classic religious hymn, "Franconia" ("Blessed are the Pure at Heart").

Several texts converge here, including Logan's star image. This sequence, I would argue, resembles something like a domestication scene and begins to suggest the wider cultural spectrum of religious attitudes in the late 1920s, as well as DeMille's narrative strategy in adapting biblical epics for prudish (and religious) American audiences. Jesus casts out Mary's seven sins but subdues her sexual and vital energy, including making her virtually speechless for the rest of the film. If Mary was associated with wild beasts, bold action, and aggressive conversations before she met Christ, her encounter with Him has left her utterly domesticated: she has been tamed by Jesus. Like the mother of Jesus, whom we also glimpse in the home at Nazareth and who is accompanied by peaceful doves, Mary Magdalene becomes a veiled and docile matron, submissive and passively mute. Any previous hint of a sexual past has not only been cleansed but erased. Therefore Jesus figures into DeMille's narrative as the one whose patriarchal gaze has de-eroticized and domesticated the female spectacle into a neutral space. Because Mary also inhabits a star image text of a former Ziegfeld girl and exotic Hollywood starlet, Jesus subdues the wild erotic associations with popular culture as well. Yet it is easy to see, however, that DeMille has it both ways. This kind of (hyper-masculine) Jesus would certainly appeal to the moral majority in the 1920s, with its temperance reformers, its cultural and religious conservatives, its patriarchal hegemony. But at the same time, the same Mary who has been cleansed also treated us first to the sumptuousness of her body and her extravagant energy, together with the more prurient aspects of the cinema. Lest we enjoy any guilty pleasures in the theatrical spectacle, Jesus is there to cleanse us all from our respective sins. In a curious sort of way, this sequence is a strange and bizarre version of Laura Mulvey's version of the so-called "male gaze" writ large. But DeMille has stretched the boundaries of the biblical text once again, and availed himself of an intertextual environment for artistic and commercial success.

Cultural Value

The Arnoldian idea that poetry is disinterested could not ring more falsely when examining the politics of film adaptation, which is never far from complex ideological and social formations like the canon and literary prestige. Indeed, fidelity adaptation critics have been especially naïve about the ways respectable literary taste—canonical literature—might function politically and ideologically. The literary critics of a modernist bent and who melded into adaptation studies in the 1950s and 1960s would attempt to mutate mass culture into a literary cinema, thereby preserving its appeal to certain highbrow audiences. Fidelity criticism has simply perpetuated a bifurcating social practice that has had its origins in the early days of American film culture as a way of cementing class and cultural distinctions. With a desire to preserve essentialist readings of key literary texts, much of the fidelity discourse of adaptation gleaned from the American literary establishment had conservative underpinnings. As formalist critics galvanized around highbrow, canonical literature and an Arnoldian aesthetic, they would necessarily maintain a binary, even adversarial, relationship with novel/film—the "literary versus the cinematic"—preserving the integrity of the written, source text over and against its filmic adaptation. This modernist position was particularly endemic to the literary establishment in English departments across the country, out of which Bluestone and fidelity critics were creating a new industry of adaptation criticism. "English professors have traditionally been suspicious of mass-produced narratives from Hollywood," says Naremore, "which seem to threaten or debase the values of both 'organic' popular culture and high literary culture."[57] The appeal to organic and high culture is evidenced well enough in Bluestone but also part of the literary establishment in the 1950s when *Novels into Film* first appeared. As Gerald Graff points out in his account of *Professing Literature,* the New Critics, firmly ensconced in the academy by the mid-twentieth century, "operated within the internal structure of literary works themselves" and had something of an 'ax to grind' against the technocratic tendencies of modern mass civilization."[58] The New Critics legacy emerged from I. A. Richards, Cleanth Brooks, and T. S. Eliot himself, all of whom celebrated an attention to form, paradox, and ambiguity.[59]

From Bluestone's perspective, it is the novel and not the film that has the capacity to inhabit moral density and complexity, or what Matthew Arnold referred to in *Culture and Anarchy* (1869) as "the care for sweetness and light, spontaneity of consciousness." Along these same lines, Eliot's "Tradition and the Individual Talent" (1920) praised Canto XV of Dante's *Inferno* because the emotional effect occurs not solely from feeling but "is obtained by considerable complexity of detail." As an inheritor of the Arnoldian and modernist tradition, Bluestone appears to fear the danger of film's "mutating," vulgarizing effect on the novel when the adaptation fails to attain the complexity of the original. Such distinctions between highbrow and lowbrow culture are echoed in all sorts of ways. For example, conservative sociologist Ernst Van den Haag, who bitterly critiqued comedian Lenny Bruce's nightclub routine as "a sort of verbal diarrhea," notes the process of popular culture's vulgarization of highbrow culture, which sounds a great deal like Bluestone's parasitic metaphors of adaptation of novel into film: "Corruption of past high culture by popular culture takes numerous forms, starting with direct adulteration. Bach candied by Stokowski, Bizet coarsened by Rodgers and Hammerstein. . . . Freud vulgarized into columns of newspaper correspondence advice (how to be happy though well-adjusted). Corruption also takes the form of mutilation and condensation . . . works are cut, condensed, simplified and rewritten until all possibilities of unfamiliar or esthetic experience are strained out. . . ."[60]

The formalist or literary analysis of "novel into film" becomes more striking when compared to other critics who preceded Bluestone with an intertextual interest and an awareness of institutional and cultural politics as a dense sociological web, interconnecting and defining the practice of film adaptation. These critics were not interested in fetishizing the formal convergence of the novel and film like the adaptation critics did in the American academy, especially in the 1960s and 1970s. Almost two decades before *Novels into Film* appeared, Margaret Farrand Thorp's *America at the Movies* (1939) was published, offering an insightful look at Hollywood's ability to interest "different audiences at different levels."[61] Thorp reads American film culture as a kind of superhighway into which many roads are traversing and intersecting:

commodity culture, popular and classical music, the fashion industry, education, nationalism, and even the Hays Office—often deployed so exclusively by adaptation theorists such as Bluestone to show textual corruption.[62] In recognizing how film might operate discursively, primarily negotiating tensions for middle-class audiences, Thorp handles such diverse topics as the interaction between the Official Joan Crawford Club and cinema fashions. Thorp sees films in a heteroglossic environment, as "great promoters also of collateral reading," alluding to the significant historical relationship Hollywood had with canonical literature, very visible in 1930s America, especially with the educational system. Bookmarks at public libraries that advertised current literary adaptations were only one of the many clever devices used to create a collateral relationship between film and literature. As early as the later 1920s, for instance, Mary Allen Abbott, together with Max Herzberg and the National Council of the Teachers of English, were publishing numerous and long-running "Photoplay Appreciations" for students in American high schools studying classic works of fictions or drama.[63]

Thorp perceptively observes that a study of movies made from literature is the place where young American film audiences get their first critical edge. "Quite without intention the movies have influenced [literature and theater] also at another point, in technique. The contemporary theater is indebted to the cinema for some of its experiments with scenes of different levels, sudden black outs, spot lights that select now one group of characters and now another on a complex stage."[64] Thorp reminds us that as early as 1923, Cleveland launched its first "bookmark," which was inserted each week into a book circulating in the library promoting a film. For example, the mark would be placed in a book currently adapted for the screen (*Union Pacific*, 1939) and would also recommend historical works such as Edwin L. Sabin's *Building the Pacific Railway* (1919) or works of fiction like Zane Grey's *The Union Pacific Trail* (1918). Encouraged by the success of the bookmarks and genuinely enthusiastic about the movies, the Cleveland Library went on to other inventions. They arranged display placards with stills from the picture, information about the book from which the film was drawn, and a shelf of books on a related topic.[65]

In the light of the heteroglossic environment in which discursive texts receive cultural value, we find an alternative method for adaptation studies. This praxis is clarified when we examine texts as cultural capital rather than essentialist, canonical texts. Drawing from the interpretive communities they inhabit, some texts are granted a greater or lesser hegemony based on their cultural capital, or canonization as a prestige product. Pierre Bourdieu makes the relation between literary value and the economic system more explicit when he employs the term *symbolic capital*—or, a "double discourse of value," by which, according to Bourdieu, "symbolic goods are a two-faced reality, a commodity and a symbolic object: their specifically cultural value and their commercial value remain relatively independent although the economic sanction may come to reinforce their cultural consecration."[66] Bourdieu's idea of symbolic or cultural capital is useful for a discussion of the canonical in adaptation because, "The consecrated authors who dominate the field of production also dominate the market; they are not only the most expensive or the most profitable but also the most readable and the most acceptable because they have become part of 'general culture' through a process of familiarization which may or may not have been accompanied by specific teaching. This means that through them, the strategies directed against their domination always additionally hit the distinguished consumers of their distinctive products."[67]

As has been well documented, the use of the canonical was a shrewd marketing tool in early cinema. From the point of view of American film culture, we know that one of the main causes in the shift from primitive to classical cinema involved a change in influences from the other arts, shifting from an initial close imitation of vaudeville to a greater dependence on short fiction, novels, and legitimate drama.[68] These literary sources were often heavily weighted by the aura of canonical value. Consider the case of the so-called "prestige production," which reached its peak in the 1930s but has had a long history of associations with the film industry, extending back to the early days of silent cinema. Such prestige productions provide us with a gateway into a collaborative, political environment, a shaping of a text that stretches beyond the imagined borders of fidelity criticism. The use of film adaptations, often deployed from established canonical texts, famous historical moments, or religious episodes coincided early on with some form of pressure—legal, economic, or moral—exerted on the industry. As William Uricchio and Roberta Pearson have observed in excellent and superb detail, the industry was well advised to start producing "literary qualities," particularly Shakespeare, beginning in 1908, mostly for financial reasons. The 1907 *Ben Hur* copyright decision made adaptation of the Bard "not only respectable but free" and provided a guaranteed market for European exports. "From 1908 to 1913 the American film industry produced at least thirty-six fifteen minute Shakespearean films, while importing a great many more foreign Shakespeare productions."[69] These prestige productions had a distinct advantage in accessing popular taste disguised as high art. Indeed, audiences who might have been lured to the theater because they were consuming literary prestige, readymade highbrow culture at the movies, could also thrill to "duels, illicit romances, murders—as the rankest cheap melodrama."[70]

Not surprisingly, the interest in canonical adaptation expanded in early film culture, and for a variety of reasons. According to Eileen Bowser, there were a number of companies investing in literary products. Vitagraph produced *Julius Caesar, Richard III, Romeo and Juliet,* and *Macbeth* in 1908 and then went on to film *King Lear* and *A Midsummer Night's Dream* the following year. Kalem made *As You Like It* in 1908, while Selig filmed *The Merry Wives of Windsor* two years later. The independent company Thanhouser made not only productions of Shakespeare and other classics, but also filmed versions of Ibsen's *The Lady from the Sea, Pillars of Society,* and *A Doll's House* in 1911.[71] There were some companies, like Biograph, that only made a few "quality films," and when they did so they were literary adaptations of authors such as Shakespeare, Tolstoy, Dickens, Browning, and Hugo.[72]

Literary prestige provided early cinema with respectability, an aura that was notoriously absent from the nickelodeon. Despite the trade presses' indications to the contrary, the adaptation of canonical texts would, for the most part, lure "the better classes" to the theater, liberating them from the guilty pleasure of cinematic viewing. As Lawrence Levine has pointed out, "Even when Shakespeare penetrated to the very heart of mass culture in the form of films and radio and television programs, it was almost always as a means of gaining prestige for the producer, director, and actors."[73] At the same time, though, much evidence suggests that "there were convergent textual expressions of Shakespeare, while at the same time incorporating signifiers that connoted a more restricted, or distinctive, Shakespeare."[74] There was something for everyone in adapting a canonical literary figure like Shakespeare; clearly, these productions were not just for the purpose of edifying the audiences. Indeed, the film industry was tapping into a deep well of class interest and highbrow literary culture and, together with other forms of mass culture, negotiating prestige entertainment for middlebrow and lowbrow audiences. Parenthetically, one interesting exception remains Vitagraph's *Julius Caesar,* which received a great deal of attention because of its violence and scantily clad actors that virtually haunted William Fox, the president of the Moving Picture Exhibitors' Association in the midst of New York's Mayor McClellan's hearings on the morality of moving pictures in December 1908.[75] In fact, *The Nickelodeon* published an article "On Filming a Classic" on January 7, 1911, that justified the use of canonical literature as viable material for cinematic exhibition, saying that the

"Classic" is here used in a rather loose and unrestricted sense, as it generally is used by adherents of the photoplay, meaning vaguely a kind of piece
that is laid in a bygone era and one which aims to evoke some kind of poetic
and idealistic illusion differing from that illusion of mere reality with which
photoplays are ordinarily concerned. "Costume play," "historical piece," "poetic drama," variously conveys a similar idea. Often the subject is one that is
already known to the drama and universally admired, or it may be an adaptation from some story of poetry or fiction, or taken from the pages of history
or the Bible. . . . It is needless to say that such subjects are the hardest kind
to present. They demand an expensive outlay of costumes and scenic effects,
deep and careful research into the manners and customs of the era depicted
. . . faultless photography, and above all a Producer . . . who shall . . . possess
the eye of an artist and the mind of a poet.[76]

How then did the classic function historically for Hollywood's textual
adaptations, and under what conditions? The test case for canonical value
in adaptation was the 1930s, which would mine Shakespeare and nineteenth-
century European and British classical literature, together with prize-winning
contemporary authors. These kinds of adaptations (with authors like Charles
Dickens, Leo Tolstoy, and contemporary novelists like Pearl S. Buck), according to Tino Balio, were "far and away the most popular production trend of
the decade," with about half the films produced from 1934 to 1939 designated
"prestige pictures."[77] Their popularity owed something to the elasticity of the
prestige picture itself, which encompassed several genres.[78] But the aura of the
canonical undoubtedly served as a self-corrective to the industry, which was
moving toward regulation by implementing the well-known Motion Picture
Production Code in 1930 and then a revised version of the same regulations
under Joseph Breen in 1934.

The redeployment of canonical texts as adaptations in the 1930s harkened
back to the days of the "literary qualities" in the early days of cinema. At
the turn of the century, as in the 1930s, the canonical purchased for the film
industry an aura of respectability. Canonical books are invariably linked to
middle-class cultural formations; they are what Charles Altieri calls "ideological banners for social groups." In the context of Hollywood during the
Great Depression and the era of self-regulation in the industry, canonical texts
were valued highly because they were marks of legitimacy for the likes of the
Legion of Decency: "social groups propose them as forms of self-definition,
and they engage other proponents to test limitations while exposing the con-
tradictions and incapacities of competing groups."[79] As Jane Tompkins has
shown, Hawthorne and other canonical works are in place because the groups

that put them there are "the most culturally influential."[80] Therefore, as Barbara Herrnstein Smith says, "all value is radically contingent, being neither a fixed attribute, an inherent quality, or an objective property of things but, rather, an effect of multiple, continuously changing, and continuously interacting variables or, to put this another way, the product of the dynamics of a system, specifically an *economic* system."[81] Prestige productions were a matter of shrewd economic interest, fueled by readable texts and guaranteed by ideological formations. As André Bazin would indicate in his early, important essay, "Adaptation, or Cinema as Digest" (1948), "Most of the films that are based on novels merely usurp their title, even though a good lawyer could probably prove that these movies have an indirect value, since it has been shown that the sale of a book always increases after it has been adapted to the screen. And the original work can only profit from such an exposure."[82]

In the 1930s, producers like Irving Thalberg and David O. Selznick functioned as brokers for symbolic capital for middle-class audiences in America. Thalberg managed to combine MGM's star glamour with literary property to secure prestige productions. "Irving Thalberg looked to the theater for story ideas and talent to make his prestige pictures."[83] He produced the screen version of Eugene O'Neill's *Anna Christie* staring Greta Garbo and later showcased the glamorous Swedish actress in *Grand Hotel,* based on a best-selling novel and, shortly thereafter, a popular play. The combination of star power and literary prestige worked well for MGM throughout the decade, with Selznick taking the lead to secure proven literary capital for the studio. More important, adapting canonical fiction and plays from proven authors allowed the 1930s audience to consume cultural value and authority, to stratify itself in a cultural economy, to purchase what Bourdieu calls "cultural distinction" based on "taste." "Taste classifies, and it classifies the classifier. Social subjects, classified by their classifications, distinguish themselves by their classifications, distinguish themselves by the distinctions they make, between the beautiful and the ugly, the distinguished and the vulgar, in which their position in the objective classification is expressed or betrayed."[84]

Again, the advent of the Production Code in the 1930s, as well as the economic conditions during the Great Depression, worked in no small measure to transform the movies into a "literary cinema" of respectability, much like the "literary qualities" functioned in an earlier age to initiate an age of moral reform at the movies. Even those Depression-era audiences who were militating against vulgarized, depraved mass culture would permit themselves to consume a work based on a canonical text like Dickens or Tolstoy for the purposes of moral education and edification. Bourdieu points out that, "in cultural consumption, the main opposition, by overall capital value, is between practices designated by their rarity as distinguished, those of the fractions richest in both economic and cultural capital, and the practices socially identified as vulgar because they are both easy and common, those of the fractions poorest in these respects. In the intermediate position the practices are perceived as pretentious, because of the manifest discrepancy between ambition and possibilities."[85]

In retrospect, we can speculate that Bluestone, the formalist critics, and those who subscribe to the fidelity school of "novel into film" are the dutiful inheritors of the 1930s legacy of respectable, literary cinema. The film adaptation discourse that appeared in the 1950s in the academy simply reinforced prestige text's cultural value. Indeed, Bluestone seems to love William Wellman's *The Ox-Bow Incident* (1943) precisely because it is a moral "classic prototype of the serious western,"[86] managing somehow to transform one of the popular staples of Hollywood mass culture into highbrow literary property, an art film, with high-modernist qualities all its own.

The Politics of Authorship

Authorship has emerged as a singularly crucial point of departure for a fruitful discussion on adaptation, especially after the writings of Roland Barthes and Michel Foucault and, more recently, with the fate of the auteur and its implication for cultural politics.[87] In the words of Mireia Aragay, "a redefined notion of auteurism has become a central focus in recent writing on adaptation."[88] Who is the author of a particular work once it has been adapted? Although Roland Barthes famously announced the "Death of the Author" in his landmark 1967 essay by saying that the reader had to free the text from the confines of the author—"a text's unity lies not in its origins . . . but its destination"—the authors of many adapted works were liberated by a profound stylistic shift in American film culture some decades earlier, by the time of the Second World War.[89] If the 1930s were the site of significant redeployment of the literary canon for adaptation, by the 1950s the opposite would be true. The era of the Great Depression was nurtured by a love affair for adapting classic literary texts for the screen that invariably cultivated a prestigious partnership with the author of the written text. Indeed, the typical 1930s film teaser trailers for prestige adaptations usually showcased the famous novel or play and its author, recalling fond memories of reading a particular writer when in the throes of childhood, thereby creating an alliance of the source text with the production value of the movie. Needless to say, feature literary films in the 1930s benefited from intertextual authorial references, snippets of famous memorable dialogues from notable novels and plays, exotic set pieces for historical adaptations.

But as has been observed elsewhere, by the onset of World War II, Hollywood turned to sources other than canonical fiction or even prize-winning authors for its source material. With the advent of new, faster film stock that made cinematography more dynamic and dramatically flexible, an interest in more realistic settings on the part of audiences, together with an industry concern for the loss of the oversees market, Hollywood would start mining extracanonical material for its source texts for feature films. John Huston's breakthrough film, *The Maltese Falcon* (1941), often said to be the point of departure for the nascent film noir genre, would set the tone for the next several decades by using noncanonical fiction for adaptation. The interest in popular fiction and the tensions surrounding canonicity became only too clear to Huston ten years later when he adapted Stephen Crane's *The Red Badge of Courage*. Indeed, the years that encompassed *films noir* and other films of the 1940s and 1950s were far from those that prized prestige texts so highly valued by producers like Thalberg. On the contrary, canonical authority, like the Production Code itself, would lose its hegemony by the 1950s, replaced by more popular (or pulp) fiction, and establish other genre conventions, such as melodrama and detective fiction. The atmosphere after the Second World War was an environment in which "The movies seem no longer to need the authority of a sanctioned literary work, and can now promote their own rebellious independence by choosing works of popular literary culture outside the respected literary mainstream, works that often provide enough intellectual space for the filmmaker to do what he or she wishes to do in filmic form."[90] To be sure, the gradual collapse of the Production Code would expand the use of noncanonical texts, pulp fiction, and original screenplays. But the rise of the director, or what Leitch has called the "adapter as auteur," would succeed to a great degree precisely in displacing the authorship of the source text to the director himself. For reasons that must be obvious, canonical texts and their authors only serve to outstrip the director's power to "re-author" the film. In his famous 1967 interview with Francois Truffaut, Alfred Hitchcock said that, "There's been a lot of talk about the way Hollywood directors distort literary masterpieces. I'll have no part of that! What I do is to read a story only once, and if I like the basic idea, I just forget all about the book and start to create cinema."[91]

The case of Hitchcock is instructive, as explained by Leitch, who examines the director in the context of the way in which "adapters establish themselves as *auteurs* outside the film industry and the academy."[92] Hitchcock spent his career "wresting authorship" away from the source text. He accomplished the setting of his imprint on a work not only by imbuing the film with his own unique style, but by procuring lesser-known authors like the detective novelist Cornell Woolrich for his adaptations. Also, Hitchcock established his own signature in his well-known cameo appearances in his films, which contributed to his own stamp of ownership on the new (filmic) text. Well aware of the struggle for authorial power, or the "matching" between the source text and the film that would invariably face any adaptation, Hitchcock

> Methodically avoided literary cachet as an area in which he could not successfully compete and instead embraced a generic identification that he was able to promote through his carefully crafted public image, as well as his films. His success in turning his own corporeal presence into a trademark in his cameo appearances, his witty end-papers to *Alfred Hitchcock Presents* and the *Alfred Hitchcock Hour,* the monthly mystery magazine and the board game to which he lent his name and image, even the signature eight-stoke silhouette with which he often signed autographs established him as the quintessential directorial brand name, an auteur capable of eclipsing authors whose claim to authority was simply less powerful.[93]

Writing in the late 1960s, Peter Wollen would read the rise of the auteur not defined as one "simply in command of a performance of a pre-existing text. . . . The director does not subordinate himself to another author; his source is only a pretext, which provides catalysts, scenes, which fuse with his own preoccupations to produce a radically new work. Thus the manifest process of performance, the treatment of a new subject, conceals the latent production of a quite new text, the production of a director as auteur."[94] Based on our previous discussion of cultural value, the emergence of the auteur, strategically submerging the source text, seems counterintuitive, because adaptation would seem to suggest an exploitation of the very text that is being buried. After all, showcasing the canonical and classical aura of the novel was vital to the prestige film in the 1930s. But the key dynamic in understanding the struggle for authorship in adaptation lies precisely in comprehending the shift from an interest in the text to the director as new author, after the Second World War. To secure the definitive signature of authorship—the "name above the title," as Frank Capra subtitled his autobiography—a director *had* to find a less than memorable source text. Rather than the canonical status of a given text enhancing the production value of the film, then, the reverse became true in the postwar years and after. "If it had been written by a lesser author," Stanley Kubrick once said in an interview for *Der Spiegel,* "it might have been a better film."[95]

The careers of Hitchcock and, as Leitch argues, Stanley Kubrick and Walt Disney as well, remind us that the site of authorship is marked by what Pierre Bourdieu refers to as a field of cultural production that is "structured by the distribution of available positions and by the objective characteristics of the agents occupying them."[96] The struggle between the author of the source text and the agent adapting that written text is what Bourdieu calls "position takings" within the "space of creative works." As Randal Johnson interprets Bourdieu, the dynamic of this cultural field "is based on the struggles between these positions, a struggle often expressed in the conflict between the orthodoxy of established traditions and the heretical challenge of new modes of cultural practice, manifested as *prises de position* or position takings. . . . The space of position takings can only be defined as a system of differential stances in relation to other possible position takings, past and present."[97] In terms of the cultural and political value of authorship, then, the position takings of Disney are most notable for the brand and signature that eventually emerged in the struggle to develop a new mode of cultural practice: the family feature film. The Disney brand became synonymous with an *established signature*—"Walt Disney Presents"—for family entertainment and safe programming.[98]

As I suggested earlier, an important and well-known struggle for authorship and its relationship to the source text significantly began to unfold in the post–World War II years in France with the writings of André Bazin, the influential journal *Cahiers du Cinéma,* and Truffaut's provocative essay on the politics of authorship and adaptation, "Une Certaine Tendance du cinéma francais." As Robert Stam points out, there are a number of ways to approach the intersection between literature and the French New Wave, but "the question of adaptation stands at the point of convergence of a number of crucial issues: cinematic specificity, modernist reflexivity, and inter-art and inter-semiotic relations," all of which are intricately connected.[99] Truffaut argued in his celebrated 1954 essay in *Cahiers* that French "Tradition of Quality" cinema was suffering under the weight of the literary, of "psychological realism," particularly influenced by canonical texts. "A film is no longer made in France that the authors do not believe they are re-making *Madame Bovary.*" Instead, Truffaut valorizes Jean Renoir, Robert Bresson, and Max Ophüls, among others, as "*auteurs* who often write their dialogue and some of them themselves invent the stories they direct."[100] Truffaut was not railing against adaptation as such, but anticipating a new way of reinventing the *literary as performance* in the cinema. As Dudley Andrew reminds us: "like Bazin, Truffaut looked upon adaptation not as a monolithic practice to be avoided, but as an instructive barometer for the age. The cinema *d'auteur* that he advocated was not to be pitted against a cinema of adaptation; rather one method of adaptation was to be pitted against another. In this instance adaptation was the battleground even though it prepared the way for a stylistic revolution, the New Wave, which would for the most part avoid famous literary sources."[101]

At the same time, Bazin says that the "literary" cannot be dismissed outright because, as in the case of Italian neo-realism, these films are indebted to literary origins, particularly a close relationship with the formalist experiments of American modern novelists William Faulkner, John Dos Passos, and Ernest Hemingway.[102] Indeed, the early French auteurist critics of the late 1940s were searching for *la caméra-stylo,* a way of writing that would become the equivalent of the literary—and make film on par with the other arts. In his landmark essay of 1948, "The Birth of a New Avant Garde: *La Caméra-Stylo,*" originally published *in L'Ecran francais,* Alexandre Astruc said that, "the cinema is quite simply becoming a means of expression, just as all the arts have been before it, and in particular, painting and the novel. After having been successfully a fairground attraction, an amusement analogous to Boulevard Theater, or a means of preserving the images of an era, it is gradually becoming a language. By language, I mean a form in which and by which an artist can express his thoughts, however abstract they may be, or translate his obsessions exactly as he does in the contemporary essay or novel."[103]

Much of what the auteurists were defining in the mid-twentieth century in France was, of course, already articulated by eighteenth- and nineteenth-century romantic notions of authorship, in which the author's unique qualities of personal expression, genius, and imagination produced a work through a version of what William Wordsworth once referred to in the "Preface" to the second edition of the *Lyrical Ballads* as "a spontaneous overflow of powerful feelings." Therefore the editors of *Cahiers du Cinéma* adored great, structured feelings in American directors like Nicholas Ray and the imagination—"*l'invention*"—of a film like Ray's *The Lusty Men* (1952), and "especially the search for a certain breadth of modern gesture and an anxiety about life, a perpetual disquiet that is paralleled in the characters; and lastly his taste for paroxysm, which imparts something of the feverish and impermanent to the most tranquil of moments."[104] Whether spontaneous or not, the director as author was for the auteurist critics the definitive interpreter of the adapted text, whose vibrant imagination eclipsed the bourgeois (classical) literary antecedent, devoured the source text, and, far from translating it into a "mutation," transformed it into his own likeness through what Wollen refers to as "the manifest process of performance."[105]

The French New Wave was operating out of a romantic and modernist impulse, then, stripped of any allegiance to previously established canonical categories. For Truffaut, of course, the point seemed to be precisely anticanonical, rallying against the adaptation of "quality novels" by Jean Aurenche and Pierre Bost. Yet how possible would it be to dismiss established fiction? Truffaut's revolutionary manifesto appeared to eschew the literary altogether, but that was an imprudent conclusion, at least as far as Bazin was concerned. More significantly, however, the French auteurists like Truffaut were overturning what they believed were stuffy literary *conventions,* imbued with bourgeois "psychological realism" and the related readership and spectatorship around which such values were structured. At the same time—and Truffaut is much like his mentor Hitchcock in this regard—*la caméra-stylo* would never waver far from a partnership with some kind of literary text, albeit those robbed of a canonical aura. As Naremore reminds us, "One of the best-kept secrets of the New Wave filmmakers was that many of their own films were based on books; the sources they chose, however, where often lowbrow, and when they adapted 'serious' works or wrote essays about film adaptations (such as Bazin's famous essay on *Diary of a Country Priest*), they make sure that the *auteur* would seem more important than the author."[106] Always the balanced cineaste, Bazin would qualify his support of the auteur when he says that *la politique des auteurs* "hold and defend an essential critical truth that the cinema needs more than the other arts, precisely because an act of true artistic creation is more uncertain and vulnerable in the cinema than elsewhere." But its exclusive practice means a potential negation of the film "to the benefit of praise of its *auteur. . . .* This does not mean one has to deny the role of the *auteur,* but simply give him back the preposition without which the noun *auteur* remains but a halting concept. *Auteur,* yes, but what *of? . . .*"[107]

Bazin was acutely aware that cinema had its own language of authorship, and the role of the author/director would dominate his philosophical, ethical, and cinematic interests for his professional career. After all, the auteurists of *Cahiers du Cinéma* would take their lead from his *politque des auteurs,* albeit with their own personal slant on the issue. But while arguing for the genius of authorship, Bazin would also propose an "Ontologie de l'Image Photographique," saying that "all the arts are based on the presence of man, only photography derives an advantage from his absence."[108] Such a position represents something of a metaphysical and dialectical counterpoint to the romantic view that art has its origins in the mind of the poet-author, or as Wordsworth put it, poetry drawn "from emotion recollected in tranquility." Bazin, according to Dudley Andrew, was suspicious of the editors' vocabulary at *Cahiers,* and to end with an investigation of the auteur alone was "to stop inquiring of the cinema . . . for despite his commitment to the integral humanism of Rossellini and Renoir, no one was more adept than he at teasing out the multiple strands woven into any film experience. The author may have been primary for him, but only as a tortion in the knot of technology, film language, genre, cultural precedent and so forth. . . ."[109] Remarkably, these observations about the relationship between the author and the text came to Bazin shortly after the Second World War—somewhat earlier than the founding moments of *Cahiers du Cinéma* in 1951 and not as a direct response to Truffaut's essay extolling authorship without literature. In his essay "Adaptation, or Cinema as Digest," published in July 1948 in *Esprit,* for instance, Bazin said that "the ferocious defense of literary works is, to a certain extent, aesthetically justified; but we must also be aware that it rests on a rather recent, individualistic conception of the 'author' and of the 'work,' a conception that was far from being ethically rigorous in the seventeenth century and that started to become legally defined only at the end of the eighteenth."[110] Contextualizing cinema within the history of art, Bazin here reminds us of the modern construction of authorship, a critical stance that he would work out more fully in future essays. Shortly before his death, Bazin would publish in April 1957 something of a personally clarifying essay on authorship for *Cahiers du Cinéma,* on *"la politique des auteurs."*

These discussions about authorship and debates around the auteur in the 1950s in France formed and crystallized around an evolving discourse about the *la politique des auteurs* and, indeed, what was viewed as the "supposedly transcendent qualities of *mise-en-scène.*"[111] Indeed, in a certain sense, the *mise-en-scène* was the site of authorial reconstruction and performance, the place where the "literary" was transformed imaginatively into the purely cinematic. The *mise-en-scène* freed the director from matching the source text with its filmic adaptation by allowing him to cast a unique and personal *écriture,* a new work. Alexandre Astruc would express his concept of *mise-en-scène* as the director's way of transforming what obsesses him, "as a means of making the spectacle one's own—but then what artist doesn't know that what is seen matters less, not than the way of seeing, but than a particular way of needing to see and to show."[112] In the hands of the right kind of director, a true auteur, pulp fiction became luminous and energetic, leaving the director's stylistic imprint indelibly behind. "Given the fact that in Hollywood the director often had no more than token control over choice of subject, the cast, the quality of the dialogue, all the weight of creativity, all the evidence of personal expression and statement had to be found in the *mis-en-scène,* the visual orchestration of the story, the rhythm of the action, the plasticity and dynamism of the image, the pace and causality introduced through the editing."[113] Therefore when CinemaScope appeared in 1953, it was perceived by the auteurists as a crowning achievement of a long process that now inaugurated what Jacques Rivette would call "*L'age des metteurs en scène.*" It was the *mise-en-scène* that made "total cinema" possible.[114]

With an overwhelming emphasis on performance rather than the literary, then, the editors of *Cahiers* fostered timely discussions around authorship; *la politique des auteurs* allows us to consider the ways in which the standardized literary canon and its authors, once so crucial to the cultural practice after the implementation of the Production Code at one point in the history of American film culture, would be by and large displaced by an evolution in film stylistics, an emphasis on performance brought on by the New Wave.

At this point, I would like to suggest that the two approaches of the formalists and the auteurists are exemplified in a brief look at John Ford's adaptation of John Steinbeck's *The Grapes of Wrath* (1940). Bluestone's analysis of the film remains typical of the metaphor of translation and an exaltation of literary cinema. But Ford becomes an interesting example of someone who succeeded with prestige literary adaptations but later became valorized as a director's director, an auteur who devoured the antecedent text together with its literary author. In Bluestone's reading, however, the novel and the film easily collapse into one another. The fidelity critic's best friend is a novel that "serves as precise directions for the actor. There is nothing here which cannot be turned into images of physical reality."[115] If there are deletions and compressions of time for the sake of plot, these are fine when the "images are clean and precise." Bluestone is not alone in his interpretation. Similar takes on the novel's adaptation occurred decades after *Novels into Film* was published, although some have urged that more attention be shown to the visual language of the film. Writing in 1979, for instance, Vivian C. Sobchack emphasizes the connection between themes of *The Grapes of Wrath* and visual style when she says, "The strength and immediacy of a film's visual imagery is at least equal to if not far greater than its literary content, even if its power is not acknowledged or articulated."[116] For Bluestone, the adaptation of Steinbeck's novel becomes a kind of trade-off, a successful translation because of the film's "unusual cinematographic accomplishments, its structural unity, its documentary realism. . . . If the novel is remembered for its moral anger, the film is remembered for its beauty."[117] In the tradition of Arnold and Eliot, for Bluestone it is as if there is an exchange of literary virtues that somehow makes the "mutation" between the literary and the filmic justified. In the end, the film is collapsed into the formal apparatus of the novel and we participate in its formal (literary) ends.

At the same time, Bluestone would have been well advised to pay greater heed to his own interview with Ford, who curtly told the author of *Novel into Film,* "I never read the book." Ford, of course, was mischievously articulating his own version of Hitchcock's famous line, "I just forget all about the book and start to create cinema." At least on one level, Ford was sounding the demise of the literary that had been so useful to the studios of the 1930s and then the fidelity critics a few decades later. But even further, Ford had made a career out of promoting himself as a director made for auteurists, exploiting the *mise-en-scène* in sharply identifiable ways—cinematic visual codes that the American audiences of the 1930s were learning to read and love incrementally. As I will examine in greater detail in chapter 4 of the present volume, the influence of German expressionism in the United States allowed Ford to develop a style that showcased *mise-en-scène,* foreclosing the literary (author) from his films beginning in the late 1920s and 1930s. Ironically, despite the valorization of Bluestone and the fidelity critics for *The Grapes of Wrath* and Ford's other prestige productions of the 1930s, the auteurists came to admire the director not because of his successful literary translations, but precisely because he showcased *performance,* which over and over trumped *literary translation.* "I never read the book" might well have been Ford's motto for all his films, and one taken for the director's distinct advantage. In a way, the western became the perfect performance showcase for Ford, the premiere spectacle of the *mise-en-scène* that would obliterate any trace of "translating" the literary. After he saw *Stagecoach,* for instance, Bazin said that "the art of Ford consists simply of raising characters and situations to an absolute degree of perfection."[118] In a certain sense, by becoming the new author of the text, Ford would be preparing the French editors of *Cahiers du Cinéma* to "print the legend," a myth of his own directorial aura that he had been establishing in western after western. When it came to a John Ford film, there was no question as to who was the author. He did not have to read the book, nor did we expect him to do so, even when he was adapting someone who held considerable authorial weight, such as a John Steinbeck.

Although the auteurists clearly played their crucial part in celebrating the director as author of the filmic text, there were Hollywood directors like Ford and Frank Capra, among others, who participated in what Bourdieu calls "position-takings" well before Astruc, Truffaut, and the discourse on the *politique des auteurs* that emerged years later in Europe. In Bourdieu's terms, these available positions have cultural values attached to them, and Ford himself was seizing on an opportunity already opening up in the film industry and American culture. As we will see, John Ford is only one example of the shift that Hollywood was making in the late thirties toward directorial stardom and independence, which would culminate in the approval for the Screen Directors Guild in 1940. As Thomas Schatz reminds us, it was *Stagecoach* that drew Ford into this debate when the controversy for power in the industry was at its apogee. Contrary to the usual tendency of the Hollywood features, the independently produced film for United Artists was to be known, according to the producer Walter Wanger, "as John Ford's achievement," a director's picture.[119] Read one way, then, it is possible to see that Ford's film was an example of a director exploiting performance over and against the literary. The celebrated tracking shot that dollies to a close-up of our first glimpse of the Ringo Kid was a showcase for a performer and a star-making shot for John Wayne. The stylistic qualities of *Stagecoach* were celebrated by the auteurists like Bazin as "the ideal example of the maturity of style brought to classic perfection. John Ford struck the ideal balance between social myth, historical reconstruction, psychological truth, and the traditional theme of the western *mise-en-scène*. None of these elements dominated any other. *Stagecoach* is like a wheel, so perfectly made that it remains in equilibrium on its axis in any other position."[120] Ford's stylistics imprinted his reputation as a Hollywood auteur and made it possible for a spectator to wonder whether or not he or she had to read the book, either.

2

A Victorian New Deal

Dickens, the Great Depression,
and MGM's David Copperfield *(1935)*

> It would seem that the author's name, unlike other
> proper names, does not pass from the interior of a dis-
> course to the real and exterior individual who produced
> it; instead, the name seems always to be present, marking
> off the edges of the text, revealing or at least character-
> izing, its mode of being. The author's name manifests the
> appearance of a certain discursive set and indicates the
> status of this discourse within a society and a culture.
>
> —Michel Foucault, "What is an Author?"

Like Matthew Arnold, Charles Dickens visited America twice, and no less than Arnold he shaped the nation's ideas about culture, ameliorating tensions between the Barbarians, the Philistines, and the Populace. He was loved by the people, but he also maintained a high level of literary prestige. As *The New World* newspaper commented at the time of his first visit, he "was read with pleasure over the whole immense extent of the States, from the British dominions on the north to the glades of Florida, and from the Atlantic cities to the cantonments and barracks on the Mississippi." Dickens was read even by "the hunter of buffalo in the wilds . . . with a degree of intimacy that only a friend inspires."[1] For his American reading tour in 1867–68, the attendance at his welcome was outdone only at his farewell, which was witnessed by an estimated 114,000 people. Almost immediately, he became a nineteenth-century, Anglo American classic, virtually the equal of Shakespeare.[2]

From the beginning the American discourse about Dickens was often expressed in class or ideological terms. He was an instant celebrity in part because he was a British author who wrote about democracy, and who earned a living from his talent. As the *United States Magazine* and the *Democratic Review* put it in April 1842, he was not an "aristocrat or millionaire." "As to his purse, he has to fill it from time to time by a draft on his wits, like the poorest scribbler of the tribe; and as to rank, we are rejoiced that there is no other nobility about him than the universal title of simple and glorious manhood. He is neither Prince nor Lord—but there is neither Prince nor Lord in Christendom to whom we should have awarded the ovation of such a reception."[3]

Dickens's common-man aura also owed something to his performance style, which was suited to a fairly wide range of audiences. Early in his second American tour, he performed readings of his novels for a mostly highbrow group of Boston literati, including the most famous actor of the day, Edwin Booth. A cartoon drawn by C. A. Barry, which appeared in *Harper's Weekly* on December 7, 1867, shows Dickens quietly poised behind a small lectern turning the pages of a book; with his right hand mildly gesturing as he reads, he appears to be giving a lecture, not a show. A report of the performance suggests a vaguely aristocratic occasion: "though pervaded by a touch of dandyism . . . [he was] dressed in a suit of faultless black."[4] But other, less aestheticized features of his style were equally agreeable to tradespeople and the managerial middle class. "Not a breakfast table, not a parlor, not an office, not a shop," wrote a *Chicago Tribune* columnist on December 11, 1867, "can be entered without finding Mr. Dickens and his entertainment the subject of conversation; and old jokes from 'Nickleby' and 'Pickwick' are chuckled over, as if they had only just been revealed to the world." Several contemporary observers commented on his mixture of highbrow and lowbrow appeal, his ability to turn even an intellectual assembly into comedic popular theater. For example, a Boston reviewer noted that the "polished ice of that proper community has seldom cracked so loudly and cheerily."[5] The New York intelligentsia, including what the *Evening Post* called "the best" of society—Lowell, Holmes, and Longfellow—was reportedly even more animated than the Boston Brahmins, despite their complaints about Dickens's "cockneyish accent."[6]

When Dickens departed America in 1868, at least one Shakespearean scholar complained that his performances were "sedulously low-brow. He yielded to temptation to get a cheap laugh by continually playing down to his readers."[7] Even so, he guaranteed the widest possible audience. Lawrence Levine has ranked him alongside Shakespeare and Milton as one of three "highbrow" authors who most appealed to the American middle class.[8] For this reason, he quickly became part of the American educational system (Edna Hays's detailed study of the requirements for English for college entrance exams lists *A Tale of Two Cities* and *David Copperfield* in 1880 and 1893, respectively). At the same time, he was recognized as a liberal reformer who wrote about the poor. As one contemporary remarked, his writing asserts the "idea of human equality, under the influence of the progress of which regal palaces and baronial castles of the whole world are crumbling and destined to crumble to ruin."[9] Therefore, when Dickens died in 1870, George Templeton Strong wrote in his diary that there were at least two Dickenses, because "his genius was unquestionable; his art and method were often worthy of the lowest writer of serials for Sunday papers. . . . Few men since Shakespeare have enriched the language with so many phrases that are in everyone's mouth."[10]

As Dwight MacDonald pointed out in the *Partisan Review* in 1968, Dickens has a double appeal: "superb comedy alternates with bathetic sentimentality, great descriptive prose with the most vulgar kind of theatricality."[11] Not surprisingly, every one of Dickens's novels was dramatized and six of his stories reached the American stage. Immediately after the publication of *David Copperfield* (1850) and *Dombey and Son* (1848), popular songs such as "Dora and Agnes" and "Florence" were circulated, to wide acclaim.[12] The phenomenon continued well into the twentieth century. Kenneth M. Goode's and Harford Powel's *What About Advertising?* (1927) said that Americans of the Jazz Age voted Dickens as one of "the ten greatest men in history," and rated *David Copperfield* as their favorite novel. By 1930 the "Dickens Fellowship" had increased dramatically in the United States, including such periodicals as the *American Dickensian* in New York; the *Chigwell Chronicle* in Boston, and the *Los Angeles Dickensian* and the *Blunderstone Review* in Philadelphia.

Meanwhile, the underlying form and message of Dickens's novels may have helped to shape Hollywood cinema. At least this is what Sergei Eisenstein argued when he visited the United States in the 1930s, and he later explained its implications in his famous essay, "Dickens, Griffith, and the Film Today"(1944). All of American cinema, he wrote, had grown logically out of D. W. Griffith—and Griffith, in turn, was a late-nineteenth-century provincial who was inspired by Dickens and Victorian stage melodrama: "In social attitudes Griffith was always a liberal, never departing far from the slightly sentimental humanism of the good old gentlemen and sweet old ladies of Victorian England, just as Dickens loved to picture them. His tender-hearted film morals go no higher than a level of Christian accusation of human injustice and nowhere in his films is there sounded a protest against social injustice."[13]

The very form of Griffith's work, with its parallel actions and its drive toward organic unity, was, Eisenstein noted, an outgrowth of the "structure of bourgeois society," which is "woven of irreconcilably alternating layers of 'white' and 'red,' 'rich and poor.'" In Hollywood films, these parallel lines of social class never clashed or exploded into conflict. Instead, as in Dickens's novels, they were brought together through sentimental, good-hearted conclusions in which virtue triumphed over vice. Such plot constructions were overwhelming contributions to Griffith's body of work. As Michael Pointer notes, Griffith only adapted one of Dickens's stories "from text to screen," *The Cricket on the Hearth* (published in 1845 and adapted in 1909), but the sense of melodrama and atmosphere so crucial to a film like *True Heart Susie* (1919) was a real Dickensian legacy, clearly a partial reworking of *David Copperfield*. Furthermore, in *Orphans of the Storm* (1921), "Griffith added the setting of the French Revolution in a manner that evoked the atmosphere and background of *A Tale of Two Cities* so powerfully that at times one feels the film must be from Dickens, whereas in fact only one small incident in the film is taken directly from Dickens's book."[14]

In the first half of the twentieth century, Dickens had an almost folkloric appeal for Americans—but at no point was he more important to the culture as a whole than during the Great Depression, when Roosevelt's New Deal tried to stave off revolution by introducing social reform. Cultural historian Richard H. Pells has accurately described the political situation of those years: "The Roosevelt Administration had succeeded in reducing the tension and fear which plagued the country in the early years of the depression. Through an expert use of the mass media, through the reliance on a rhetoric that was very traditional even as it introduced unprecedented reforms, through the insistence on national unity and cooperation in a time of extreme emergency, through an emphasis on order and security rather than social upheaval, the New Deal gave people the sense that their problems were at last being recognized if not yet solved."[15]

The politics of the New Deal were designed to mediate between extremes, and for that reason Dickens was particularly well suited to the times. He was a traditional yet popular British intellectual who suggested Victorian stability, and who spoke to the need for reform without revolution. There can be no question of his wide dissemination during the period. Richard B. Hovey, in recalling his education in an "average American high school" during the Great Depression, writes that Dickens was required sophomore reading and that *A Tale of Two Cities* (1859) was "nicely suited for fifteen-year olds."[16] FDR himself was known to read *A Christmas Carol* (1843) aloud every year, according to his assistant, Harry Hopkins, and that "the little book was one of his priceless possessions."[17]

In 1934, the journal *The Dickensian* announced a "DICKENS BOOM."[18] Throughout the 1930s, the American demand for Dickens and for Dickens-like historical novels surpassed even the popular enthusiasm for the detective story, probably because Dickens's Victorian England served as a way of understanding the Great Depression. James D. Hart explains this phenomenon by saying that, "A period of stress and turmoil, leading people to books both for escape and explanation, favored the revival of historical novels. In a time when to face the present or the future was unpleasant, looking backward was a comparative pleasure, affording surcease from contemporary problems and an understanding that people of other ages had weathered worse times."[19]

Dickens's best-known historical novel, *A Tale of Two Cities,* not only became standard high school reading for a generation during the Depression, but was also made into a half dozen plays and, in 1935, a major Hollywood feature for MGM. The vogue for this book is easily understood if we consider how its conservative reaction to the French Revolution could be applied to the contemporary scene. It provided adventurous escape, suggested parallels with the present, and gave many Americans a sense of childhood nostalgia for the reading of the "classics"—a nostalgia which, as Lawrence Levine notes, had been on the rise in the late 1920s.[20] At about the same moment, *A Christmas Carol* became what Paul Davis calls a "culture-text," and was eventually adapted in a variety of forms by the mass media, more than any other work in the history of English literature. This story about a family in poverty, abused by a wealthy employer, must have strongly resonated with Depression audiences. Moreover, because the story promoted the sentimental values of good-heartedness and charity, it provided a means to counteract socialist ideology and preserve a utopian faith in American enterprise.[21] Small wonder why a recent biographer of Dickens says that the author "almost single-handedly created the modern idea of Christmas."[22]

From almost their beginnings, the movies found many uses for Charles Dickens, but it is important to note that not all of them were successful.[23] In 1924, a Hollywood production of *David Copperfield* apparently confused its audience, and provoked one critic to recommend that "if Dickens is ever to be popular with the masses . . . the plays and films taken from his works should be made much clearer than they are."[24] Even so, it appears that, early on, using filmed versions of Dickens's novels helped negotiate the widest possible reception among classes. When an early film version of *A Christmas Carol* (Scrooge) was filmed as a play by Robert Paul in 1901, the publicity announced that, "as presented on Tuesday, Nov. 26th, at Sandringham before their Majesties the King and Queen, the Prince and Princess of Wales and distinguished company. Scrooge was chosen by His Majesty as the first theatrical representation to be produced before him since his accession, thus giving further proof, if such were needed, of its perennial freshness and interest for all classes."[25]

Across the ocean and almost forty years later, at the height of the New Deal, MGM and David O. Selznick produced an apparently quite faithful adaptation of *David Copperfield* that proved not only clear but enormously popular with just about everyone, earning almost a million dollars in profit during its initial release.[26] The success of the Selznick-Cukor film no doubt had something to do with its unusually effective qualities as an adaptation, or even as a work of art. It survives today as arguably the best among screen versions of Dickens, achieving what might be described as the quintessence of "Dickens-ness." But it might never have appeared at all had it not been perfectly suited to the politics and industrial conditions of its time. Indeed, *David Copperfield* is a showcase for what Robert Stam has called the complexity of "intertextual and generic negotiations" that has woven together "any number of intertexts, literary and extraliterary."[27] Undoubtedly, this intertextuality was abated by Dickens's reputation as an author of "realistic" novels, "with its connotations of democratization, stylistic dignity, and the respectful treatment of the everyday life of 'lower' social strata."[28] At this particular historical juncture, then, "Dickens-ness" served as the basis for a certain kind of charitable, largely Republican ideology that worked as a salve for hard times, without proposing any radical changes to the system. In other words, a film adaptation of Dickens could therefore respect its source and still have widespread appeal, satisfying the leaders of industry, the Arnoldian intellectuals, the respectable middle class, and the anonymous masses.

The Prestige Text

By the 1930s, the artistic production of "Charles Dickens" harbored what French sociologist Pierre Bourdieu calls "symbolic capital," which refers to the degree of accumulated prestige, celebrity, consecration, or honor and is founded on a dialectic of knowledge (*connaissance*) and recognition (*reconnaissance*).[29] In a certain sense, then, *David Copperfield* carried a kind of "charismatic" ideology during the Great Depression that, Bourdieu explains, is "the ultimate basis of belief in the value of a work of art."[30] In addition to having an ideological importance (and in Bourdieu's terms it was *precisely* because of its symbolic capital) the 1935 *David Copperfield* was an exemplary source for what Hollywood once called the "prestige production"—an idea that dates from the early days of the feature film. According to Tino Balio, the term *prestige* signified not a genre but "production values and promotion treatment. A prestige picture is typically a big-budget special based on a pre-sold property, often as not a 'classic,' tailored for top stars."[31] As I suggested earlier, by the 1930s the prestige picture was firmly established in Hollywood, and its making would become the most popular production trend of the decade, with fourteen examples listed in *Film Daily's Ten Best*. Half of the films produced between 1934 and 1939 and close to thirty of the sixty-seven pictures on *Variety's* Top-Grossing Films lists in the 1930s were prestige pictures. Compared with the total output of the majors, prestige pictures accounted for a small percentage, but compared to the total production budgets, they accounted for a lion's share. Moreover, prestige pictures played a crucial role in defining the public image of a company.

Such films were especially important to the career of David O. Selznick, who was able to reap financial and aesthetic dividends from overtly literary capital. But according to Selznick's biographer, David Thomson, interest in *David Copperfield* was not at all great at MGM. "With so much required of sets and costumes, and with such quantities of plot and caprices of character, classic novels appeared to be unlikely movie material. People at Metro predicted that the picture would only play in England or in those few places where reading flourished."[32] Thomas Schatz's profile of MGM during this period says that the studio's New York office disliked "highbrow period pieces and costume dramas that were not only costly but were deemed a bit much for the average viewer."[33] Selznick later recalled that besides the obvious cost of the film, the biggest obstacle he faced from other executives was that they could not conceive of *David Copperfield* as a star vehicle. The New York office had a point. When the movie industry had hit its rock bottom in 1933, MGM was the only major studio to make a profit, and it did so through another form of symbolic capital—star power—not literary prestige. Literary capital, the studio realized, was unpredictable. In Bourdieu's terms, authority based on prestige is "purely symbolic" and may or may not imply increased economic assets.

It would be up to David Selznick to persuade the studio executives at MGM that *David Copperfield* had strong cultural capital for the movie-going public. He was convinced that the Dickens project and the classics in general had a wide appeal. Selznick's previous experience at RKO would inform his production interests at MGM, and his shrewd assessment of American film culture would help usher in what Tino Balio has called "the second wave of prestige pictures in 1934."[34] Selznick was clearly experimenting with his production interests while at RKO, possibly taking his lead from the man he would eventually join at MGM as a unit producer in 1933, Irving Thalberg, who once wrote in the *Saturday Evening Post* that "the intelligent producer will go on experimenting—which in pictures means going on spending—until he believes in his own mind that he has made the best possible product."[35] Therefore, Selznick appears to have arrived at an interest in the classics just at the moment when Depression America (and evidently the producer himself) was changing its tastes toward a more conservative, even Arnoldian, bend. Selznick's success as a producer had to owe something to his enviable ability to read American culture as if it were a weather barometer. Interestingly enough, when he was vice president in charge of production at RKO, Selznick produced *King Kong* in 1933, which Tom Doherty argues exhibits the "racial paranoia and forbidden lure of miscegenation."[36] At the same time, however, he initiated a few months later (coproduced by Merian C. Cooper) the first successful literary prestige picture in ten years and one of the most successful films in the 1930s, an adaptation of Louisa May Alcott's *Little Women* (1933), starring Katherine Hepburn.

By the time he got to MGM, Selznick had seized the moment. In a memo to Loew's sales and distribution offices in February 1934, he argued that "there is no question in my mind that the public has finally decided to accept the classics as motion picture fare."[37] *David Copperfield* would begin production on September 27, 1934. Although he resigned to become an independent producer in June 1935, Selznick stayed with the studio until that next December and would bring two other classics to MGM, both of which carried star power *and* literary prestige. The next was Tolstoy's *Anna Karenina* (also released in 1935, six months after *David Copperfield*), a star vehicle for Greta Garbo (and a reprise of the same role she played in 1927's *Love*, with John Gilbert). And that film was closely followed in the same year by an adaptation of another Dickens novel, *A Tale of Two Cities*, which starred Ronald Coleman. Besides giving MGM an aura of middle-class respectability, canonical authors like Dickens and Tolstoy also enabled the studio to achieve product differentiation and to expand its distribution and exhibition. According to Thomas Schatz, "Both were sizable hits, grossing over $2 million a piece, and were further evidence of Selznick's confidence and his sensibilities as a prestige-level producer. They also solidified MGM's commitment to lavish adaptations of literary classics. Thalberg later claimed that it was the success of *Copperfield* that encouraged him to do *Mutiny on the Bounty,* a project that Mayer had nixed when Walter Wanger asked to produce it in 1933. Thalberg's adaptation of the Nordhoff and Hall epic, released in 1935, grossed well over $4 million—MGM's biggest hit since *Ben-Hur* a decade earlier."[38]

The recognition of *David Copperfield*'s cultural value would also prove profitable for reception by British audiences. Therefore on March 17, 1934, Selznick sent a telegram to Arthur Loew in the Metro offices in New York urging that *David Copperfield* would "add hundreds of thousands of dollars to British empire gross while still giving us [a] picture that would be as good for this country, and at the same time do wonders for [the] entire standing of our British company."[39] When the picture was finally released on January 18, 1935, and opened in New York, the critics of the day were aware of its allure to a British audience; one review noted that *Copperfield*'s "production values are evident. It is obvious that money was spent lavishly. MGM has produced prestige building entertainment—something for the British lion and Leo to exult over."[40] Schatz notes that *David Copperfield* cost $1,069,254 to produce; 25 percent of the film's $2.8 million gross came from Commonwealth countries, and that *A Tale of Two Cities* took in 31 percent of its $2.4 million gross.[41]

This British angle had been exploited throughout the production of *David Copperfield,* which employed British actors and an extensively researched preproduction team headed by Natalie Bucknell. Before shooting or even casting began, Selznick took his crew to Britain for a month. He also hired a much-respected British novelist, Hugh Walpole, to collaborate with Howard Estabrook on the screenplay for the film (Walpole made a cameo appearance as the Vicar), and in the trailer, Selznick had Lionel Barrymore introduce Walpole as "the distinguished author of *Captain Nicholas, Vanessa* and other great successes." When the film opened in London on February 28, 1935, a "Dickensian" publicity luncheon was held at the Savoy Hotel, complete with English "Victorian" dessert, "The Old Charles Dickens Trifle." But Selznick also recognized the nostalgic importance of *David Copperfield* for middle-class American boys who grew up in the early twentieth century. In press releases, he claimed that his father had read the book aloud to him, and recorded that throughout the production he "lugged with me everyplace the old-fashioned, red-leather copy of *David Copperfield* which my father had given me." (Joseph Mankiewicz scoffed at this idea, saying that the famous producer never read anything but a synopsis. Ben Hecht once told Selznick, "the trouble with you, David, is that you did all your reading before you were twelve.") Selznick also made an astute assessment of both market forces and American cultural hegemony. Literary prestige was associated in some quarters with respectability and wealth, and such prestige had long been used as a way of "reforming" films seen by the vulgar masses. Frank Dyer, vice president of the Motion Picture Production Corporation, had remarked in 1910 that "when the works of Dickens and Victor Hugo, the poems of Browning, the plays of Shakespeare and stories from the Bible are used as a basis for moving pictures, no fair-minded man can deny that the art is being developed along the right lines."[42]

Certainly it was no accident that Selznick's devoted attention to authors like Tolstoy and Dickens coincided with the most puritanical era of the Hollywood censorship code. With some exceptions, the industry during this period was unlikely to risk an adaptation of contemporary novels, especially realistic American fiction. *Harrison's Reports* (April 18, 1931) wrote that Dreiser's *An American Tragedy* (1925), "with its shameless wallowings in the sex gutters, its debauchery and insistent dwelling on the baser sides of human nature, would seem impossible of conversion into anything resembling wholesome or appealing entertainment for the majority of picture followers."[43] Post–World War I writers like Ernest Hemingway, William Faulkner, and Sinclair Lewis consciously rejected their repressive nineteenth-century predecessors and turned toward a modernist idiom. Indeed a novel like Lewis's *Main Street* (1920) or *Babbitt* (1922) hardly presented a flattering portrait of contemporary American culture and surely lacked the safe, nostalgic appeal of a Victorian "coming of age" novel. The industry was at a difficult juncture for adapting novels that were often seen as experimental. Toward the end of his tenure as president of the Motion Picture Producers and Distributors of America (MPPDA), Will Hays went on record lamenting the ubiquitous repercussions occurring over an adaptation of Faulkner's *Sanctuary*.[44] During the days of the Hays Code, the industry solved the problem of adapting difficult contemporary texts by using what Richard Maltby calls "pre-tested" material, because "adaptation from Broadway successes, best-selling novels and non-fiction, and short stories from mass-circulation magazines offered the best guarantee of commercial success, substantially outweighing the cost of their acquisition."[45] By the 1930s and the implementation of the new Production Code, the industry sought relief from the pressure brought by the Legion of Decency through literary prestige productions, and so launched its Better Pictures Campaign of 1934. In a retrospective article called "Producers Aim Classics," the *Motion Picture Herald* observed in 1936: "An increasing demand for better pictures, crystallized in the Legion of Decency movement in 1934, led to the voluntary adoption by the industry of higher standards of production and the resultant success of a group of literary masterpieces, so-called, made into pictures has been so great that today a larger number of the 'million dollar' productions than ever before are built around notable literary successes, either old or new."[46]

These classics would nevertheless undergo the scrutiny of the Breen Office and the Production Code of 1934. Even the so-called classics were not guaranteed approval by the PCA. Bringing Tolstoy's *Anna Karenina* to the screen would eventually prove to be a tough road for Selznick, who had to carefully excise the overt traces of Anna's moral and sexual transgressions, something the Breen Office regarded as applicable even to a literary classic. According to the annual PCA report for 1934, even a novel like *Anna Karenina* would not be "exempted from the text of the code." At one point, Selznick wondered how much more they could cut out of the script and still have a film.[47] Additionally, Garbo's star power, a big selling feature for the studio, would be somewhat compromised for the Legion of Decency because of her previous sexy and provocative roles, not least of which was Jesuit Daniel Lord's assessment of the "libel of an odd but eventually heroic and Catholic queen" in *Queen Christiana*.[48] The steamy 1927 version of *Anna Karenina* with Garbo and Gilbert probably did not go unnoticed by the more zealous members of the Legion of Decency, even though the ending was changed. Fortunately for Selznick and MGM, *David Copperfield* was another matter altogether and, ironically, it was as if the very lack of overt star power helped to negotiate the film's reception with audiences. To adapt Dickens into a Hollywood movie in the early 1930s was to give comfort to the numerous supporters of the Legion of Decency and members of a general film boycott, who were disturbed by contemporary depictions of sexuality and violence; it was, in fact, a way to acquire a kind of moral prestige.[49] (As William Dean Howells, himself present at one of Dickens's reading tours, had said after reading *David Copperfield*, the novel was a "tasteful" book, without excessive sexual references.)

The Breen Office played a large role in shaping Hollywood's choice of fiction, but Dickens was also a safe author in American schools, and the educational community itself was publishing a number of pedagogical tools for high school film appreciation that could further shape the audience for Selznick's film. Already by 1928, Mary Allen Abbott's *Motion Picture Preferences for Different School Grades* (Columbia University Press) had appeared. In 1933, Edgar Dale's *How to Appreciate Motion Pictures: A Manual of Motion Picture Criticism Prepared for High School Students* was published by MacMillan. *Teaching Motion Picture Appreciation,* by Elizabeth Watson Pollard

(Ohio State University Press) and *How to Judge Motion Pictures* (Scholastic) were brought out the following year. But perhaps the most significant secondary educational contribution to the study of film in the 1930s was Dr. William Lewin's monograph, *Photoplay Appreciation in American High Schools* (1935). Based on Lewin's institutional self-study, new classroom units of "photoplay appreciation" were being adopted. The result was the long-running series *Photoplay Studies on Moving Picture Plays.* Under the general editorship of Max J. Herzberg, each volume featured a discussion of a particular film geared for students. A number, such as Mary Allen Abbott's *David Copperfield* (1935), even featured a teacher's manual. The series was designed as an introduction to both the film and the novel or play, and it contained study questions. Some of the casebooks, such as the one on *A Tale of Two Cities* (December 1935), also promoted an essay contest.

As Steve Wurtzler remarks regarding the emerging relationship between the film industry and the American school system, "Such an informal partnership benefited the film industry. Prestige garnered through producing a literary adaptation might be redoubled in those communities in which some temporary relationship could be developed between theater owner and local school system." This arrangement occurred, for instance, with the New Haven, Connecticut, high schools and the local theater when the students were sent to view Dickens's "masterpiece" *David Copperfield* when the film opened in January 1935.[50] The establishment of a strong link between American schools and Hollywood could only strengthen the moral weight of Dickens for Hollywood and, more generally, create a justification for classic literary adaptations. Wurtzler says that, "the release of Hollywood adaptations of literary classics and the incorporation of filmgoing into the school curriculum thus represented a convergence of commercial and educational interests. Hollywood's entrance into the English curriculum during the mid-1930s also provided a culturally valorized rationale for movie attendance in the immediate aftermath of widely publicized critiques of the roles movies played in the lives of American children."[51]

By the time of the release of *David Copperfield,* there were already *Photoplay Studies* on a number of feature films: *Treasure Island, Great Expectations,* and *The Little Minister.* The *Photoplay Studies* were clearly a promotional device backed by movie studios, but on a scholarly level they were intelligently written. They contained thorough historical background, biographical information about authors, and detailed accounts of individual productions, bibliographies, and filmographies. One of the important functions they provided was to valorize the film as an adaptation. Mary Allen Abbott's volume on *David Copperfield* includes a number of facts students should know about the locale, the period, the costumes, and the characters before they viewed the movie. She advises them: "If possible, before seeing the motion picture, read the book. Read as rapidly as possible. Do not read the footnotes. After seeing the film, however, you may want to use them in a more leisurely reading. As preparation for the film, read as rapidly as possible. Read for the stories, since in Dickens' novels there are always several stories, and read for what you can learn about the characters."[52]

Abbott shapes the book as a "popular classic," but she seems to use it only as a touchstone, a guide to characterization in the film. Far from "matching" the novel with the film, she tells the students that they should "be prepared to enjoy the screen play (supposing you do enjoy it) as a separate art form." She even stresses that "the producer, the director and writer of the screenplay, Hugh Walpole," are the most significant persons for students of Dickens to remember.[53]

Abbott's *Photoplay* study of *David Copperfield* is particularly good at describing the details of the production, an emphasis Wurtzler says was there in part to "demystify the film production process. . . . Within the film-education movement, such a demystification was mobilized to fulfill a pedagogical function and to foster shared standards for evaluation." The ingenious instructions on the screenplay and cinematography (meant for older students) discuss "screen continuity as compared to the book." Abbott tells students of the meticulous research MGM exerted in order to replicate the historical period: they hired ten research workers in England; they sent photographers to Yarmouth, Blunderstone, Dover, Canterbury, and London; and they matched "Phiz's" (Halbot Knight Browne) drawings to the character's costumes. In addition to teaching the students about the fascinating history of *David Copperfield*'s production, Abbott goes on to talk about George Cukor's style, Oliver T. Marsh's cinematography, and even the editing techniques of Robert J. Kern. She asks the students to be attentive to close-ups, which might be there "to emphasize some important object in the narrative," as in Murdstone's turning the key in the lock after he has beaten David. A close-up can also be used "to connect two scene-sequences," as in the shot of David's birth and of his father's grave. To high school seniors, Abbott offers certain challenges, inviting them to compare the specific details of the movie with the book. She concludes that they will "learn more about the differences between novel and drama by analyzing a single scene from *David Copperfield* than by hours of studying abstract principles of dramatic construction."[54]

The *Photoplay Study Guides* were responsible for educating thousands of students not only about *David Copperfield* and other novels and plays, but also about film and production. Wurtzler says that some film educators incorporated motion-magazines into the school curriculum as a way to further "demystify" film production. In her article on "Increasing Motion Picture Appreciation Among Youth," Elizabeth Watson Pollard wrote that the students "should discuss how sounds and settings are faked in order to dull the fright and intense excitement which stir children too deeply."[55] Wurtzler observes that, "at many U.S. Schools, as the 1930s progressed, film-education efforts even included exercises in student film production, as described in articles such as Elias Kats's 'Making Movies in the Classroom' (1936), Kerry Smith and Irene Lemon's 'Learning Through Film-Making' (1937), and William G. Hart's 'Possibilities in the Use of the School Newsreel' (1938). But, although filmmaking was increasingly incorporated into the curriculum, the primary site of educators' intervention was imagined as the orchestrated discussion, reading, research, and writing surrounding student moviegoing."[56]

The result was a kind of fusion between Hollywood and other aspects of the culture industry, and a rise of popular art into respectability. Throughout the process, Charles Dickens functioned as a mediating influence. Again and again, Dickens is portrayed in the guide as an author who healed social divisions, bridged the divide between elite and popular, and promoted concern for others. When the *Teacher's Manual* (also by Abbott) was issued as a companion to the guide, it quoted Ashley Thorndike's *Literature in a Changing Age* to the effect that Dickens was "the great democrat" who wrote "not primarily for those who are acquainted with the best that has been known and said." But the manual later observed that there was a highbrow, discriminating audience for Dickens, of which students could aspire to be part. Teachers of *David Copperfield* were told that Dickens offered a meeting point for two worlds: "the connoisseur . . . and those in a school group who have never willingly read any good novels before."[57]

David in America

Whatever its ideological, educational, or profit motives, there can be no doubt that the Selznick film version of *David Copperfield* works splendidly as an example of the art of adaptation, not because of an essentialist "fidelity" discourse, but because of the experience of "heteroglossia," which, in Bakhtin's language, "permits a multiplicity of social voices and a wide variety of their links and interrelationships (always more or less dialogized)."[58] In this regard, the alliance between the U.S. curriculum and the film industry discloses the porous relationship between the source and the adaptive text. Indeed, as Wurtzler puts it, the *Study Guide for David Copperfield* "exposes the convergence of distinct institutional interests surrounding film and filmgoing during the height of the U.S. studio system. . . . The decision to adapt from one medium to another provided the opportunity to incorporate not only a text, but also the medium itself into pre-existing curricular standards."[59] It appears as if those who assembled the *Study Guides* were intuitively aware of multiple resources that converged around the space of the adaptive text. In this regard, Abbott's thoughtful attention to the visual details in *Copperfield* is worth special notice, confirming Eisenstein's later observation that Dickens created "extraordinary plasticity" and that the "optical quality" in his fiction provided cinema with "parents and pedigree . . . a past."[60] And yet Dickens was not the only source of the film's images. As I have indicated in the previous chapter, until very recently, and as a general rule, writing about film adaptation tends to think of the "precursor text" in purely literary terms in the tradition of George Bluestone, not recognizing that every movie is conditioned by a large set of influences from other media. Brian McFarlane and Robert Stam are among those who remind us of the intertextual issues at stake in adaptation. "The stress on fidelity to the original undervalues other aspects of the film's intertextuality,"[61] says McFarlane. And for Stam it is Bakhtinian "dialogism" that helps us overcome the "dyadic source/adaptation model which excludes not only all sorts of supplementary texts but also the dialogical responds of the reader/spectator."[62]

Some adaptation "fidelity" criticism obviously stems from Eisenstein's classic reading of Dickens and Griffith in literary, rather than visual, terms. Recently, however, scholars such as Rhoda Flaxman and Kamilla Elliott have scrutinized the visual language in Victorian literature and its relationship with film culture. When Elliott discusses the "interart" discourse in adaptation and the cinematic Victorian novel, she says that, "the assertion that film derived its visuality primarily from nineteenth-century novels is at best dubious. It is highly unlikely that film, with its more tangible visual roots in nineteenth-century photography, magic lanterns shows, public spectacles, theater, painting, *tableaux vivants*, and optical toys, required such an ancestor to discover visuality. While novel and film scholars protest that the novel engaged in a peculiar type of visuality unique to itself and to film, art historians have demonstrated repeatedly that any such 'cinematic' propensities in Victorian novels can be more (chrono)logically traced to visual and dramatic media prior to and contemporaneous with these novels."[63]

Analyzing nineteenth-century novels such as *Vanity Fair* (1848), as well as its "prose pictures" and illustrations, even the fate of intertitles in early screen adaptations, Elliott goes on to problematize traditional ways of viewing adaptation from a purely literary antecedent. She wants to locate "ways to navigate between the visual and the verbal within as well as between signs and arts, down to the visual-aural and signifier-signified splits running within signs themselves."[64] Therefore, we should keep in mind that the film of *David Copperfield,* even more than most Hollywood adaptations of nineteenth-century literature, was based not simply on a written text (however "plastic" or pictorial) but also on what Carol T. Christ and John O. Jordan have recently called the "Victorian visual imagination." After all, these critics observe, Dickens painted pictures with words with the considerable help of Phiz, and Dickensian illustration eventually became a small industry unto itself. This industry, and the whole of Victorian visual representation, was crucially important for MGM. One hundred years before *David Copperfield* flashed across American movie theaters, the 1836 edition of the *Spectator* referred to Dickens in superlative terms, comparing him to the illustrator who would become his other collaborator: "Boz is the Cruikshank of writers."[65]

J. Hillis Miller has observed that much of the interdisciplinary interest in nineteenth-century novels and their illustrations as "multimedia collaborative productions," which combined "two kinds of signs," has been fueled by film studies. Miller has two very influential essays in mind in his discussion, Eisenstein's "Word and Image" (originally published in 1938 as "Montage 1938") and Walter Benjamin's "The Work of Art in the Age of Mechanical Reproduction"(1936).[66] Angela Dalle Vacche notes in her own analysis of cinema and painting that "by blurring the distinction between high art and popular culture, the cinema has always had a tendency to challenge not just painting in isolation but rather the whole system of the arts, thus disclosing the possibility of new configurations, hierarchies, alliances, and hostilities."[67] From the point of view of adaptation studies, then, the studio's strategic use of nineteenth-century Victorian iconography in bringing Dickens to the screen helped collapse the false dichotomy between the source/adaptive text of *David Copperfield*. David Bordwell has drawn attention to the use of visual sources in film adaptation, beginning with early film uses of *tableaux vivants*, some of which were used to create the *mise-en-scène* of the film.[68] The Selznick unit also made elaborate use of every other kind of visual record of the period.[69] The Phiz illustrations, for example, were meticulously paired to the actors, and were used as guides for set designers Merrill Pye and Edwin B. Willis. (Compare Phiz's illustration for the interior of the parish church in chapter 2 with the church we see in the film.) Perhaps unknowingly, in deploying the visual discourse associated with *David Copperfield* so closely to the actors, Selznick and his collaborators were further narrowing the gap between the novel and the film for his audience. After the film debut, Margaret Lloyd perceptively wrote in the *Christian Science Monitor* (February 2, 1935) that "every reader creates his own picture as he reads, and thereafter he is adverse to accepting any other . . . was it the preparation of 'Drawings by Phiz' that allows us to accept the immortal characters as they are now presented?" That presentation was almost certainly enhanced by a production that thrived on character actors matched as illustrations rather than star power. In a way, each of the performers are triumphs of an acting ensemble, neatly collapsed and matched into Phiz's illustrations and Dickens's terse characterization and dialogue. The potential dissonance of a big screen "acting persona" clashing with the reader's own "picture as he reads" was a risk that was utterly eliminated. Therefore it would appear as if yet another dyadic divide has been crossed in adapting *David Copperfield,* this time between static, pictorial representation and performance space.

On another level, the film undoubtedly owes much of its visual success to director George Cukor, who remarked that "I don't believe in 'correcting' Dickens, saving him and all that. I just had to go with the vitality of the thing."[70] The "vitality" of which Cukor speaks is as much a matter of performance as of language, and Cukor's work is notable for the way it selectively borrows conventions from the pantomime style of acting in nineteenth-century theater. As one small example of the technique, notice the early scene when David and Peggoty ride off in a horse-drawn carriage while Murdstone and David's mother remain behind on the roadside: the mother waves goodbye and then raises her hand to her brow in a pretty gesture of Victorian sentiment, as if she were posing for a picture; meanwhile, the tall, dark Murdstone gazes down at her like a stage villain about to gain possession of a porcelain doll. All the performances of the large cast have this same lively eccentricity (abetted by the costumes of Dolly Tree) that seems "Dickensian" without ever lapsing into a feeling of parody. Surely one of the most impressive achievements of the sort is Lennox Pawle in the role of Mr. Dick—a sublime and saintly fool, unlike anything in the history of American movies, who seems to have stepped out of a childish but surreal cartoon.

At the same time, both Cukor and the script writers have managed to subordinate the Dickens text to the classical Hollywood style, which by the mid-thirties had reached its most restrained paradigm. In a way, Cukor and MGM rewrote Dickens into another idiom—and this, Eisenstein's seminal essay on Dickens and montage notwithstanding—was no easy task.[71] As J. Hillis Miller has argued, the novel *David Copperfield* calls the "reader's attention to the distance between the present condition of the narrator and that of the past self."[72] Its subjective narrative technique (closer to Wordsworth than to Proust), together with its multiple plots and its sheer size (it resembles what Henry James famously called a "loose baggy monster"), was hardly an ideal for the modernized, sleek narratives of Hollywood of the 1930s. Much of the film's apparent faithfulness therefore depends on its clever use of the "author" as a purely discursive function. The idea of "Charles Dickens," so thoroughly assimilated into American life, enabled Selznick, Cukor, and MGM to convert *David Copperfield* into a style that is "omniscient, highly communicative, and only moderately self-conscious."[73] Ultimately, the production relies upon the idea of a storyteller named "Charles Dickens," who, in Foucault's language, "seems always to be present, marking off the edges of the text, revealing, or at least characterizing, its mode of being."[74]

Of all the problems raised in redeploying *David Copperfield* into a Hollywood movie in the 1930s, surely the narrative technique was the most formidable. Yet, from the very start of the film, Hollywood is able to appropriate and adapt the first-person narration in the novel to an omniscient form. The formal appropriation begins with what Gérard Genette calls a "paratext," which "enables a text to become a book and to be offered as such to its readers and, more generally, to the public."[75] The first shot is therefore of the book itself, showing an epigraph from *David Copperfield*'s revised *Preface* of 1869 with Dickens's signature: "Like many fond parents, I have in my heart of hearts, a favorite child, and his name is David Copperfield." Next we see a brief shot of the opening lines of the novel: "To begin my life with the beginning of my life, I recall that I was born." Then, with the opening of the film proper, we see a pastoral image of a line of trees, and Betsey Trotwood moving through an establishing shot of the Copperfield cottage at Blunderstone in Suffolk. In this sequence, the words of the author meld with those of the first-person narrator, and finally with the dramatized action. The resulting effect is what Richard Maltby describes as a typical device in classic Hollywood movies: restricted, overt acts of narration at the beginning, which give way to the "screen world."[76] This particular film presents us with the author, "Charles Dickens," who seems to endorse the visual project with his very signature; it is his reflections that begin to negotiate the audience from a novel into a film. Dickens's revised 1869 *Preface* gives him (and us) a critical distance on his whole body of work—David Copperfield is his favorite child, among a myriad of characters brimming over his house of fiction, resembling something like the choked Micawber residence in the novel itself. Given Dickens's reputation as an author in 1930s America, the *Preface* could not have been a more brilliant rhetorical strategy. The voice-over gathers readers into moviegoing space, as we are invited to traverse the body of Dickens's fiction together while settling on this special, "favorite child." In collapsing the private reader into a public audience, it combines the complex, semi-autobiographical elements of the novel with Hollywood conventions of temporal and spatial coherence, or with what David Bordwell refers to as "the centrality of the invisible observer."[77] Equally important, by transferring the first-person narration into a highly communicative omniscient narration, it invites the audience to think of "Charles Dickens" as the ultimate creator of the cinematic space.

Remarkably, the film gives us the emotive force of a first-person account without resorting to any further voice-over narration. Even without the ever-present novelistic "I," this version of *David Copperfield* is quite lyrical, partly because of the India ink expressiveness of Oliver Marsh's black-and-white cinematography, which sets the action in a traditional Hollywood framing. As A. Lindsley Lane said in *American Cinematographer* in 1935, the camera stimulates, through its choice of subject matter and set-up, the sense of "being at the most vital part of the experience—at the most advantageous point of perception."[78] That "most advantageous point" in the novel is David himself, whose consciousness becomes a kind of filter for our own emotive experience and impressions. In the film, Marsh and Cukor give us a highly personalized form of dramatic *showing* rather than telling. The opening action, for example, positions us as secret sharers of David Copperfield's private life. We follow Betsey to the window of the cottage, where she sees her nephew's wife in the living room. With her, we trespass the boundaries of a gate and a window, and then we peek into a domestic space and spy on a grieving woman. Here and elsewhere, the film does not so much abandon the subjective edge of the novel as it fully dramatizes the subjective experience of the characters' actions. From the moment we lay eyes on David as a gurgling infant, the camera pays him loving attention, selecting him out of a crowded parlor. Soon afterward we begin seeing close-ups of his reactions in almost every sequence; we view his world apart from the adults (as he makes eye contact with other children, say, in the church service) and we are introduced to important characters through him (our first glimpse of Murdstone, for instance, is a point-of-view shot from David's perspective).

David Copperfield as a novel relies as much on the central character's memory as it does on his direct sense of perception. Consider the beginning of chapter 2 ("I Observe"): "The first objects that assume a distinct presence before me, as I look far back, into the blank of my infancy, are my mother with her pretty hair and youthful shape, and Peggotty with no shape at all, and eyes so dark that they seemed to darken their whole neighborhood in her face." The mature narrator's intense but recollected impression of the other characters produces a slightly hallucinatory realism, and it seems to invite the Freudian interpretation that some twentieth-century critics have applied to the novel. As Walter Allen has remarked, there is "a singular purity in the [narrator's] drawing of the adult characters as they are seen through the boy's eyes. They are, in fact, a boy's characters: fabulous beings, drawn not critically but in wonder."[79] The film captures this effect largely through the performance of the actors, beginning with the high-strung, emotive Freddie Bartholomew as David. Cast by Selznick as an unknown, the ten-year-old Bartholomew seems a hyper-aware British waif, and Cukor structures the early portion of the film around his awestruck, declamatory reactions to almost everything—such as when we first meet him at his father's grave: "Poor father! How lonely and dark it must be for him at night while we're at home by the fire." Especially in the early scenes, David views the world "in wonder," innocently commenting on the mystery of death, on the cruel abuse of the Murdstones, or on the love he has for his mother; he is both a sensitive plant and a judge of what he sees, embodying something of the double vision of the novel itself.

Inevitably, the film is more tightly organized than the novel, more directly focused on the hermeneutic problem of what will ultimately happen to David. And yet it conveys some of the discursive complexity of its source, which has an ability to split the narrative viewpoint among the young David, the mature David, and the "implied author." For example, there are moments in the film when we know more than David does—as when his mother is secretly engaged to Murdstone. (The nuptial arrangement is signaled to us by Peggotty, who speaks to Mrs. Copperfield in a *sotto voce,* sardonic tone while David is playing a piano in the background: "Did ya have a pleasant evening, Mum? . . . the stranger makes an agreeable change.") There are also moments when the *mise-en-scène* and the montage serve to comment overtly and somewhat archly on the characters, in a fashion similar to omniscient novels. Notice, for instance, David's encounter with Dora at "The Enchanted Bird" ballet. David dotes on the beautiful young woman while we occasionally see the action onstage from her point of view. When the stage "hunter" takes aim at the Bird, Dora reacts with the sort of wide-eyed innocence we associate with David as a child. "Can he be so cruel as to shoot her?" she asks. David answers, "Sometimes, love is cruel." Dora calls out, "Be careful! Be careful!" At that, the Bird flies away, and Dora cries, "she's escaped! She's escaped!" David responds, "Please Miss Spendlow, may I call?" A medium shot shows the two young people standing up excitedly, while the ballet continues in the background. "Perhaps," Dora says, "if my aunts permit." The repeated cutting between the stage and the box during this scene tends to confirm what Eisenstein observed about parallel montage in Dickens himself: a bourgeois courtship is resolved into an "organic" synthesis, which is framed in a single shot at the end. But throughout the exchange between Dora and David, the action on the stage also serves as a metaphor for David's cautious, stylized pursuit of a mate. Dora herself is dressed rather like a bird, complete with a large feather fan, and her nervous, flighty behavior (skillfully executed by Maureen O'Sullivan, who seems both guileless and seductive) only intensifies the comparison. All the while, the matrons at her side snuggle up near her like two nervous hens protecting their young.

As I have already suggested, the film's ability to "match" the actors with the characters in the novel is nothing less than uncanny, and has often been remarked upon. Besides Lennox Pawle as Mr. Dick, among the most brilliant performances are W. C. Fields as Wilkins Micawber (Selznick originally had in mind Charles Laughton, but the dailies showed an "innately sinister and self-pitying" character, and so he was replaced with Fields's "élan and slapstick verve"[80]), Edna May Oliver as Aunt Betsey, and Roland Young as Uriah Heep. But somewhat like the novel, the film also works on a more sophisticated level to establish a strong bond between the audience and a gallery of colorful figures who are seen through the eyes of both the young and the older David. Here, once again, the film creates a kind of "double vision." People who seem to have finished their roles—Micawber, the Peggottys, Aunt Betsey, Mr. Dick, Uriah Heep—reappear during the second half, when the mature David returns to the scenes of his childhood. On a more theoretical level, the film establishes what Peter Brooks calls "the work of repetition as the binding of energies" to create a coherent plot and a strong relationship with the characters for the audience, much like Dickens's fiction. "Repetition is clearly a major operative principle of the system, shaping energy, giving it perceptible form, form that the text and the reader can work with in the construction of thematic wholes and narrative orders. Repetition conceived as binding, the creation of cohesion . . . may allow us to see how the text and the reader put energy into forms where it can be mastered, both by the logics set in motion by the plot, and by interpretive effort."[81] When we view the second portion of the film, we feel a kind of nostalgia not directly from the literary source text but from the earlier portions of the reinvented filmic text; hence our feeling of the "rightness" and inevitability of the characterizations is partly confirmed by our delight in seeing old faces again, watching them perform their familiar turns. This feeling of nostalgia, however, pervades the entire narrative, despite the fact that the early episodes are shadowed by trauma and loss. Herbert Stothart's sentimental musical score helps considerably, but it is significant that the music we hear during the opening credits is composed of traditional Christmas songs, such as "The First Noel." Before it even begins, the film invites its audience to think of *A Christmas Carol,* a story that, by the 1930s, had become part of the seasonal American ritual, invoking primal images of family homecomings and acts of Christian charity. Much of the Depression audience who saw the film was probably also engaged in another kind of nostalgic journey: a return to a generalized idea of Dickens, who had been part of their upbringing and introduced them into this film from the very start. Perhaps, too, some of them thought of the film's bygone setting as a realistic depiction of a utopian world inhabited by their ancestors.

Dickens Redeployed

I began this chapter by equating Dickens with Matthew Arnold, and I would now like to return to that equation, because an "Arnoldian" ideology informs both the liberal culture of Victorian England and the Selznick adaptation of *David Copperfield;* indeed this is one reason the film appears so profoundly true to its source. In saying this I do not mean to suggest that anyone at MGM had actually read *Culture and Anarchy* or that the studio had a conscious desire to make use of Arnold's ideas, even in a secondhand way. My point is simply that *David Copperfield,* like other pictures Selznick and Cukor had made together, offers a kind of Arnoldian narrative about how the divisions of social class can be overcome through learning and generosity of feeling.

If the American Establishment was undergoing a process of self-evaluation during the 1930s—and if Hollywood itself was aspiring to a certain respectability and sophistication—Selznick and Cukor helped the process along by creating an imaginary world in which lowbrow and highbrow could meet and sometimes even marry. Their 1933 film, *Dinner at Eight,* seats the "Barbarians" and the "Populace" at the same dinner table. (The famous closing sequence resolves potentially explosive class tensions through a comic touch: matronly Marie Dressler, playing an aristocrat, stops in her tracks and does a double take when sexy Jean Harlow, playing a gold digger, remarks that she has just been reading a book.) The Selznick-Cukor adaptation of Louisa May Alcott's *Little Women* at RKO in 1933 goes even further. Bryn Mawr–educated Katherine Hepburn plays Jo Marsh, a self-taught young woman from the provinces, and the seamless fit between actor and role is rather like the synthesis achieved by the plot, in which a popular writer marries a cultivated German professor. At the level of the acting, the film allows a country girl to acquire a Boston-Brahmin accent, and at the level of story, it shows us a hard-working, self-sacrificing heroine who finds a cultivated spouse. In Cukor's closing sequence, Jo and her family are celebrating in their house in the country when the German professor appears at the door in midst of a rainstorm. Cukor neatly poses the couple on either side of the threshold, illustrating the divide between Germanic high culture and provincial Americana. The couple's subsequent announcement of their intention to wed gives Hollywood's utopian romance, or what Stanley Cavell calls its "pursuit of happiness," an Arnoldian twist—a sense of love and success being achieved through the acquisition of taste.

David Copperfield strongly resembles *Little Women* in its ability to mediate potential class conflicts. David's twin goals in *David Copperfield,* not unlike Jo's in *Little Women,* are the Arnoldian ideals of harmonious marriage and moral education. Here we should recall that Arnold ties his notion of cultural "perfection" to a process of socialization. "The individual is required," he writes in *Culture and Anarchy,* "under pain of being stunted and enfeebled in his own development if he disobeys, to carry to others along with him in his march towards perfection, to be continually doing all he can to enlarge and increase the volume of the human stream sweeping thitherward."[82] The Hollywood film of love and marriage, and especially the typical Selznick film of this period, has a similar project in mind. Jo in *Little Women,* for example, must find a proper mate to accompany her "development." At first she seems doomed to choose between a provincial husband and spinsterhood as a writer, but eventually she finds a way to move out of her lonely (in Arnoldian terms, "indifferent") self and join the larger community. In effect, her good taste not only enables her to acquire a proper lover but also to become a socially responsible person. In similar fashion, the ennobled David Copperfield eventually becomes disillusioned by Dora's superficiality and carelessness; his combined sentiment and taste—his sweetness and light—enable him to take up the more useful but equally sophisticated responsibilities of a mature union with Agnes.

David's achievement of Arnoldian perfection is made possible because he seems to embody every level of the society—the neglected poor, the decent middle class, and the polished aristocracy. His childhood fall out of comfortable circumstances and his youthful, practical education among the working poor shape his adult decisions, particularly his final unmasking of Heep's embezzlement; but he also has an inherent refinement that enables him to become a kind of artist. Freddie Bartholomew's ability to convey this last quality is especially important. In a brilliant discussion of Hollywood in the 1930s, Charles Eckert has written about the "specter" of impoverished childhood during the Great Depression: "The most persistent specter that the depression offered to those who had come through the crash with some or most of their fortunes intact was . . . that of a small child dressed in welfare clothing, looking, as he was usually depicted, like a gaunt Jackie Coogan, but unsmiling, unresponsive, pausing to stare through the windows of cafeterias or grocery stores, his legs noticeably thin and his stomach slightly swollen."[83]

Significantly, L. B. Mayer had initially approved Selznick's proposal for a film of *David Copperfield* because he thought it might make a good vehicle for Jackie Cooper, the MGM equivalent to Jackie Coogan, who had scored great success as a working-class kid in *The Champ* (1931). Freddie Bartholomew is an altogether more appropriate choice, precisely because he is an upper-class type—a fragile child who speaks with exquisite English diction and who represents the fear of falling downward on the social scale. (He was once again used in 1937—in MGM's highly effective adaptation of Rudyard Kipling's *Captains Courageous*—in which he literally falls from a luxury liner into a fishing boat.)

No less than the darling child of the 1930s, Shirley Temple, Dickens's nineteenth-century waifs helped Americans emerging from the Great Depression to imagine how they might be ultimately redeemed through talent, work, and charity. Oliver Twist finds his wealthy grandfather; Tiny Tim finally gets a middle-class home and health care. More important, however, a character such as David Copperfield is able to transcend contradiction and conflict by reforming his own social class: he is born into a solid bourgeois family, he becomes an orphan, and he moves upward again toward a "classless" world informed by what Arnold calls a "general humane spirit." Early in the film, Cukor positions him in a composition similar to Jo's fateful doorway sequence at the end of *Little Women*: emerging from his house to greet his mother and Mr. Murdstone, he stands on the threshold, neatly posed between Murdstone and Nurse Peggotty. The two adult figures represent two aspects of Victorian capitalism—the masculine, industrialized, "public" world, managed by the businessman, and the feminine, domesticated, "private" world, guarded by the nurse. During the course of the film, David negotiates and reconciles these tensions by acquiring wide experience and humane learning and by becoming a sort of aristocrat of moral discrimination.

From the beginning, David has delicate manners—he is certainly one of the most polite children in cinema history—yet he is attracted to Peggotty's atavistic world of folk culture. Early on, Peggotty takes him to Yarmouth, where Dan Peggotty (Lionel Barrymore) and Ham (John Buckler) continually refer to him as Master Davey. In an impressive scene, he plays on the beach with Little Emily (Fay Chaldecott), when the young girl suddenly runs off, dangerously straddling the dock overlooking the wild sea. To show us the girl's exhilaration, Cukor positions the camera in an unusually high angle behind her head. Ecstatically, she holds up her hands while David, refusing to walk on the wharf toward her, calls to her frantically; she then skips un-harmed toward David and tells him, "that's fun, dancing near the edge." The contrast between Little Emily's spontaneity and David's reserve points to a more profound difference between the naturalized folk and the cultivated middle class. Yarmouth is an instinctive, oral culture, filled with Cockney accents and the sounds of the harsh sea, but David's new household is a stiff, quiet realm governed by Murdstone, who reads to his wife and beats David when he cannot perform mathematical calculations.

When Matthew Arnold describes the antithesis of perfection, he is describ-ing Murdstone, the abusive, tyrannical keeper of keys, whose "bondage to machinery" and lack of "harmonious expansion of human nature" is related to his "inaptitude for seeing more than one side of a thing" and his "intense energetic absorption in the particular pursuit" he is intent in following.[84] The folk community at Yarmouth, however, has its own flaws. Little Emily's fitful display of fancy and her later involvement with David's dashing schoolboy idol, James Steerforth (Hugh Williams), are symptomatic of what Arnold de-scribes as a lack of "social" conscience. Steerforth, an aristocratic, Arnoldian "Barbarian" if ever there was one, seemingly compelled by "the habit of doing as one likes," eventually succumbs to his own atavistic instincts and is swal-lowed up by the sea. The mutual hatred that Peggotty and the Murdstones have for one another is only the clearest of many examples in the film of polarized classes who are guided by what Arnold terms "class spirit."

The first step in David's true education is his forced movement away from this divided experience at Yarmouth and Blunderstone into the "general expansion" of London, where he encounters his tutor and guardian, Mr. Micawber. In many respects, Micawber represents a comic mixture of class traits: he is both gentleman and con man, both literate and impoverished, both verbal and acrobatic. After eluding his creditors on the streets of London, he does a tricky balancing act on the rooftops overlooking St. Paul's Cathedral, then descends through a skylight into his home with a flood of elaborate language, announcing, "in short, I have arrived." As the star who incarnates Micawber, W. C. Fields achieves a similar kind of reconciliation of opposites. He had been a brilliant vaudeville juggler and one of the best of the silent comedians, but he became known in the sound era for his sardonic verbal wit. He often played a trickster who could move between classes. As a dandified, bogus professor or an articulate drunk, he could negotiate between slapstick and epigram. In the role of the verbose, acrobatic Micawber, he draws on the whole range of his abilities, meanwhile slightly anticipating what James Agee called the "fiendishly funny and incisive white-collar comedies" of his later career.[85] He therefore takes on a certain resemblance to Dickens himself, who could please diverse audiences with his performances.

But Micawber is in one sense a social failure and his relationship with David is short-lived. David's most important guide is his Aunt Betsey Trotwood, and it seems fitting that he arrives at her doorstep in Dover after having lost all of his money and most of his clothes. With the assistance of the blissfully cuckoo Mr. Dick, Betsy takes the boy in, gives him a dose of homemade medicine, and puts him to bed, where he prays not only for himself but for all homeless boys. Like a newborn child, he is given a bath, fed by hand, and wrapped in blankets. Mr. Dick tells him grotesque stories about the beheading of Charles I, but then casts the deciding vote in favor of his proper upbringing by saying, "have him measured for a suit of clothes directly."

After a superbly articulate and melodramatic showdown with the Murdstones, Aunt Betsey takes charge of her nephew's life, and in this role she is vividly contrasted with the dour, heavily eyebrowed Jane Murdstone. Both are eccentric spinsters who dislike boys, but Betsey quickly becomes lovable (in one moving sequence, she rigidly holds back her affection for the helpless David, and then embraces him warmly). Jane undergoes no such metamorphosis. "Of all the boys in the world, I believe this one is the worst," she says of David, and she clings tenaciously to her imagined class superiority. She sarcastically thanks Betsey for her "very grrrrreat politeness," though she regards her as being "either intoxicated or mad." By contrast, Aunt Betsey shows compassion for outsiders like Mr. Dick and David, and she undergoes growth and development from a strict spinster into a loving parent figure. In Arnoldian terms, she manifests "an inward spiritual activity, having for its characters increased sweetness, increased light, increased life, increased sympathy."[86]

David, who, as he says, has been "slighted and taught nothing," is now ready for the process of rebuilding and instruction. At Dover, he shows the first signs of social responsibility and universal charity by praying for others less fortunate than himself. Aunt Betsey tells him that he must go to school at Canterbury because of his duty to others: "you have to be educated, Davey, and take your place in the world." In her final words to the boy, she insists that he cultivate a humane spirit to accompany his gentlemanly learning: "You must make us proud, Davey. Never be mean in anything. Never be false. Never be cruel. Avoid these three vices and I can always be hopeful of you." Eventually, as he moves toward the larger and more prosperous community (a community to which he seems always to have rightly belonged), David is given the opportunity to show his moral responsibility. At the Wickfield household, his foil is not a Victorian captain of industry or a provincial capitalist like Murdstone but a character from the petty bourgeoisie—the accountant Uriah Heep, who has none of David's polish, and who is literally twisted with class resentment. As they discuss who will take over Mr. Wickfield's business, Heep says: "I am a very 'umble person, I'm well aware. My mother's 'umble. We live in a 'umble abode . . . my father's former calling was 'umble."

David's frank and apparently unworldly innocence is contrasted with Heep's hypocrisy and villainy. Oliver Marsh emphasizes the melodramatic conflict by lighting Heep's eyes in horror-movie style, and at one point, when Heep leaves David, the young man wipes his hand in disgust, as if he fears contamination. That gesture is a sign of David's newly acquired social and moral superiority. Heep tells us, "I have no wish to rise above my place," and from the point of view of the film's ideological project, he *must* stay where he is, representing a kind of rough beast. He functions as a scapegoat for all the social evils David has encountered—a man who has attempted to rise above his status without possessing an aestheticized sensitivity and a humane education.

The villainous Heep was well suited to MGM's conservative ethos during this period; for in the last analysis, the superbly crafted film version of *David Copperfield* is less about the fantasy of moving upward into the prosperous middle class than about the desire to make the economy's ruling elite behave in humane fashion. Its hero is a man of high taste and simple virtue who falls undeservedly into the world of the poor, and who returns from that world to expose a vulgar financial manipulator. Such a hero was especially useful in the 1930s, when the gulf between the classes was quite visible, when the more prosperous sectors of the economy needed to develop a sort of bourgeois noblesse oblige, and when, as we have seen, one of England's greatest novelists became one Hollywood's most employable talents.

3

Into Africa

Orson Welles and Heart of Darkness

Since cinema pretends to be an art
it should be, above all, film and not the sequel to
another, more literary, medium of expression.
—Orson Welles, interview with
Cahiers du Cinéma (1964)

"I think I'm made for Conrad," Orson Welles told Peter Bogdanovich about his 1939 unproduced adaptation of Joseph Conrad's *Heart of Darkness*. "My script was terribly loyal to Conrad. And I think that, the minute anybody does that, they're going to have a smash on their hands."[1] RKO studio chief George Schaefer must have agreed. To Schaefer, who first enticed Welles with an amazing guarantee of artistic freedom, and perhaps even to Nelson Rockefeller, who by 1938 controlled that studio, Welles's cinematic rendition of Conrad seemed like the ideal project. Welles had already successfully adapted *Heart of Darkness* as a radio drama in 1938 for the Mercury Theater. Captivated by Welles's dazzling New York theatrical reputation and infamous *War of the Worlds* broadcast, Schaefer was insistent on retaining well-known literary people for the studio. But, as is well known, Welles's version of Conrad's famous 1899 novella never made it into production. Despite the arrival of the celebrated *Wunderkind* in Hollywood, *Heart of Darkness* "got the discard" and was, according to *Hollywood Variety* (January 9, 1940) "overboard" for RKO.

Yet *Heart of Darkness* is exemplary in an investigation for adaptation precisely because of its failure to become a Hollywood movie. Indeed, we might say that Welles's first film project remains a fascinating case for the study of literary modernism, film history, and adaptation because it looks back to a founding moment of modernist literature, bringing it into a new context.

As others have noted, *Heart of Darkness* would include a radically subjective narrative technique, a cast of character types foreshadowing the style of 1940s film noir, a naturalistic African setting, and an unorthodox introduction that instructed the audience on how to view the film. In adapting Conrad, Welles would draw from a discourse of what has become one of the most infamous examples of the modernist experiment with the "primitive," while inflecting it with his own unique style. I will suggest here that Welles's *Heart of Darkness* treats Conrad's theme of primitivism self-consciously, revealing its underlying racism and misogyny. In essence, Welles exposes the darker, ambivalent side of modernism itself, disclosing what Fredric Jameson has called Conrad's "schizophrenic writing" or "the preconditions of Conrad's modernism," which is "found in the increasing fragmentation both of the rationalized external world and of the colonized psyche alike."[2] Welles's *Heart of Darkness* works, then, to problematize the "invisible" classical Hollywood narrative, blurring the traditional, bifurcating paradigm of what Robert B. Ray has perceptively identified as the variations worked by American ideology around an "opposition of natural man versus civilized man."[3]

We are in an enviable position to make an assessment of Welles's interpretation of *Heart of Darkness,* because the critical literature on Conrad's original work has been experiencing something of a renaissance over the last several decades.[4] Briefly stated, canonical readings have traditionally followed a "mythic" interpretation of Conrad's story of Marlow's quest for Kurtz in the Belgian Congo as a modernist exploration, or what Albert J. Guerard has called a "journey within the self." In Guerard's interpretation—and later, Ian Watt's—Conrad deploys primitivism in order to ground the tale's meaning in psychological categories.[5] But revisionist studies, increasingly well known, such as those by Edward Said, Chinua Achebe, and Marianna Torgovnick, link *Heart of Darkness* to a broader, more historicized, social function of nineteenth-century white European culture that regarded the African as the primitive Other.[6] Thus, Conrad's text has attained an ambivalent status in recent years, causing literary critic Perry Meisel to rightly position the novella as *the* exemplary witness of modernism's paradoxical nature, which provides "as many advantages as it does restrictions."[7]

In making *Heart of Darkness* into a movie, Welles would probably be expected to transfer the enormously influential canonical reading of Conrad's story to the screen, the well-known formal and thematic schema widely popular in classical Hollywood films of the 1930s, like *King Kong* (1933), which exploit the savage versus the civilized.[8] But by contrast, Welles adapted Conrad's text in such a way as to bring out a modernist ambivalence, or an inclination to render what Meisel calls "modernism as metacriticism."[9] In so doing, Welles gave *Heart of Darkness* a complex, contemporary significance. This version of *Heart of Darkness* was designed as a late-1930s allegory about fascism, but it is also a critique of the Hollywood culture industry. With its depiction of a proto-fascist "hero," its controversial treatment of racial issues, and its misogynist "love interest," *Heart of Darkness* would have departed from what Robert Sklar has called a "post-Depression mythology," refusing to depict the kind of world that Hollywood filmmakers regarded as a "patriotic duty."[10] But Welles, whose politics were shaped by the left-wing aesthetics of Popular Front narrative, went further, depriving the film of a controlling ideological point of view so necessary for Hollywood classical discourse, and demythologized the story itself.[11]

Hollywood, as everyone knows, has never favored modernist narratives. And Robert L. Carringer has claimed that Conrad's Marlow stories, in particular, do not adapt easily to the screen.[12] Welles thought differently, for his version of *Heart of Darkness* would have been governed by an incredibly elaborate narrative technique, involving not only a subjective camera and off-screen narration, but also a series of reflected images as Marlow traveled up the river looking for Kurtz.[13] That Welles himself at one point intended to play both the atavistic Kurtz and the civilized Marlow may show that the young radio and theatrical celebrity–turned Hollywood director was somewhat sympathetic to Conrad's psychological themes. Yet much of the screenplay suggests a departure from traditional forms of representation. Although the studio wanted a film based strongly on what it called "Welles and the girl," for example, Welles stressed that his project was "definitely NOT 'love in the tropics.' . . . Everyone and everything is just a bit off normal, just a little oblique—all this being the result of the strange nature of their work—that is, operating as exploiters in surroundings not healthy for a white man."[14]

Welles hints here at just a few of the many unconventional aspects of the screenplay. That "Everyone and everything is just a bit off normal," especially the narration, is evinced from the very start of the film script. Indeed, even the heavily protected, classical opposition between narrator and audience was toyed with in the extraordinary introduction to *Heart of Darkness,* which is composed of four separate sequences involving direct address.[15] Moreover, until recently, historians have said little about the fact that Welles's proposed first film for RKO was shockingly unorthodox in its treatment of racial themes, and, according to the script, was intended to show sexual relations between a white man and what Welles described as a "real black type."[16] These radically unusual features—"surroundings not healthy for a white man"—may have had as much to do with RKO's cancellation of the project as the financial problems Welles encountered. Therefore the studio's rejection of the script has left us with some lingering questions, not only about its production history itself but about the fate of Orson Welles as an adapter of "novels into film," an interpreter of literary modernism.

Welles the Modernist

I propose that the first of these queries concerns the script's origins, which Jonathan Rosenbaum has rightly suggested in his brief but pioneering foray into the *Heart of Darkness* script for *Film Comment* in 1972, lie in Welles's radio and theater career.[17] Indeed, in discussing Welles's radio history, David Thomson says that "There has never been a moviemaker who was more shaped and driven by radio—nor a director who had mined his own ambiguous soul in radio first."[18] Although we know that Conrad's portrait of a seaman, Marlow, narrating the horrific adventures of his journey into the Belgian Congo, was first adapted as a radio drama, the prelude to Welles's interest in *Heart of Darkness* and its first-person narration originates from adapting Charles Dickens for the airwaves. I have already argued the importance of Dickens to 1930s American (film) culture in the previous chapter, but we can also say that Welles became a kind of broker for "Boz" for the enormous venue of popular radio drama. In 1938, CBS introduced "First Person Singular," a program for which Welles adapted four of Dickens's novels (*A Tale of Two Cities, Oliver Twist, The Pickwick Papers,* and *A Christmas Carol*) into radio plays. Contrary to most of their original written form, Welles adapted the scripts as subjective narration, sometimes with multiple voices. For Marguerite Rippy, Welles was becoming increasingly interested in first-person narration during the late 1930s; he clearly intuited something that radio offered and that the theater did not:

> Following *Dracula* and *Treasure Island, A Tale of Two Cities* was the third text to be adapted by Welles in the series. It was an ideal choice for "First Person Singular," since it both fulfilled Welles's interest in the collapse of narrated time and offered a variety of possibilities for experimentation with the retellings of the story in first-person narration. . . . The performance actually split the narration evenly among Manette, Lorry, and Carton, thereby fragmenting the listener's identification and creating a sense of three competing "authors" of this tale—two of whom, Manette and Carton, were played by Welles. . . . Finally, it offered Welles a chance to explore his lifelong personal and professional interest in doubling.[19]

Welles was attracted to multiple narrations telling a single story, a technique that would most obviously repeat itself most famously in *Citizen Kane*. But in adapting Charles Dickens for the radio, Welles was clearly, if momentarily, disengaging from the aesthetics of the theater in order to capitalize on a subjective, narrational technique that made the story more personal and intimate—something radio shared with prose fiction. In an article for *Radio Annual* (1939), Welles said that "the less a radio drama resembles a play the better it is likely to be. This is not to indicate for one moment that radio drama is a lesser thing. It must be, however, drastically different. . . . And so we find that radio drama is more akin to the form of the novel, to story telling, than to anything else of which it is convenient to think."[20] Although Welles had redeployed Dickens for Depression-era America on the radio, modernist novelists like Conrad would be an obvious choice for narrational experimentation; *Heart of Darkness* represented a kind of arch-text of the journey narrative that ends with inexplicable horror. As Marlow describes in his account of the voyage to the heart of the Congo to find Kurtz: "Going up that river was like traveling back to the earliest beginnings of the world, when vegetation rioted on the earth and the big trees were kings. An empty stream, a great silence, an impenetrable forest. The air was warm, thick, heavy, sluggish. There was no joy in the brilliance of sunshine. The long stretches of the waterway ran on, deserted, into the gloom of overshadowed distances. . . . It was the stillness of an implacable force brooding over an inscrutable intention."[21]

The novella is what James Naremore describes as "both an experimental narrative and an adventure story derived from the 'sensation' literature of the mid-Victorian period."[22] When it was performed as a radio drama (for Mercury Theater on the Air) on November 6, 1938, *Heart of Darkness* would obviously exploit the subjective features of Conrad's "boxed" narrative frame. But the proposed film version of the novella would do even more than the radio play, even as it harkened back to the multiple narrations found in the Dickensian adaptations for "The First-Person Singular" series. As Rippy observes, "With Welles playing Kurtz as well as Marlow, the narrative visually splits an aural narrative that is singular. This strategy clearly recalls his adaptation of *A Tale of Two Cities*, in which radio directly transmits the 'I' to the listener, but also extends the first-person perspective to more than one central narrator (Manette, Carton, and Lorry). The use of the camera to evoke the aural, however, adds a layer of complexity to the structure itself, and to the act of filming."[23]

As Robert Spadoni argues, Conrad's novella was perfect for maximizing the first-person narration for the radio and then film, because the formal strategy begged an interest in creating a personal relationship with the audience. "The novel itself is more 'radiophonic' than many others Welles might have chosen. Much of this tale's radiophony emanates from the voice of its teller." Subjectivity, as Welles imagined it, became an interface for the reader/audience and the written text: "In the transition from printed to radio text, Marlow's tale becomes literally an oral narrative and thus gains a primal immediacy that suits the evocation of a primal world. The novel overlays levels of narration with bands of sensory experience that become less real as they converge on the heart of darkness."[24] Moreover, for Spadoni the transition from radio to film was made to order, precisely because of the narrational features Welles used in the radio version of *Heart of Darkness*. It is as if Welles took Conrad's famous injunction drawn from the preface to *The Nigger of the "Narcissus"* (1897) and made it his underlying strategy in adapting the novella first into a radio drama, then into a film: "My task what I am trying to achieve is by the power of the written word to make you hear, to make you feel—it is, before all, to make you see."[25] As Spadoni goes on to say, "To fashion a *Heart of Darkness* for radio is to strip away one of these bands and to concretize the next one down: now we just listen and 'see.' . . . The transition from radio to film text peels away the next sensory layer and transfers the meaning of Marlow's tale to its kernel: now we just see."[26]

Welles may have had another way of "seeing through radio" in mind, as well. The radio adaptation of *Heart of Darkness* suggests Welles's political leanings, already shaped around the Popular Front, together with left-wing causes of various kinds—among them, his public support for social equality and involvement with the Federal Theater Project; these activities would be listed more than a decade later in the infamous 1950 blacklist report, *Red Channels: The Report of Communist Influence in Radio and Television.*[27] The broadcast of *Heart of Darkness* occurred only a week after Welles's most famous and notorious radio production of *The War of The Worlds,* the result of which—mass panic in some parts of the country—begin to suggest the power of radio and technology to bridge the national consciousness. As Michael Denning has suggested, the famous broadcast became part of an antifascist rally in the context of the 1930s "Cultural Front."[28] Read along these lines, Welles was exploring through mass culture the power of demagoguery to control the vast population of radio listeners in Depression-era America. Conrad's novella was an obvious choice for Welles during his Popular Front period, not only because of his interest in its modernist narrational features, but because of the text's exploration of narcissism and idolatry in the toxic figure of Kurtz, a kind of emblem of the modern human subject in moral devolution. By the late thirties, Kurtz in *Heart of Darkness,* together with some other early key characters in modernist fiction, had already come to represent a series of allegorical flashpoints of modern disintegration, representative of what Ricardo J. Quinones acknowledges as the "evolution of a negative typology," forecast in the twentieth century. Characters like Kurtz in Conrad's *Heart of Darkness* or Aschenbach in Thomas Mann's *Death in Venice* "revealed cosmic emptiness behind human experience, of the unresponsiveness of alien surroundings that seriously questions humanistic ideals or simple endeavor, and the dissolution of the known, ordinary, solid world."[29] Decades before Welles wrote the screenplay of *Heart of Darkness,* Kurtz became a signifier for the high modernism of T. S. Eliot of everything that was wrong with contemporary society. "Mistah Kurtz—he dead." was the epigraph Eliot chose for his 1925 poem, "The Hollow Men."

While interpreting literary modernism in the midst of the Great Depression and a world plagued with fascist aggression, Welles appears to have drawn on the formal features of Conrad's novella to develop a self-conscious awareness on the part of the listening audience, something he learned from working with Archibald MacLeish, according to Michael Denning and Judith E. Smith. "Using radio to voice concerns about the threat of European fascism invited authors to reinflect radio's own formulas as a means of dramatizing political concerns. . . . MacLeish's inventive use of a radio announcer who was not in control of the action—a striking departure from formula radio, where normally the characters controlled the plot—as a strategy to dramatize the threat of fascism."[30] Within the context of the Popular Front of the late 1930s, MacLeish's *The Fall of the City* was broadcast on April 11, 1937, for CBS and was not only the first play in verse written for the radio, but had the largest cast—more than two hundred—of any drama for the airwaves until that time. As an antifascist allegory, *The Fall of the City* portrays a populace renouncing their freedom:

> Freedom's for fools
> Force is the eternity
> Freedom has eaten our strength and corrupted our virtues.
> Men must be ruled.[31]

Welles, who played the part of the narrator in MacLeish's broadcast, looks at the fascist dictator who has conquered the city. The narrator gazes into the open visor of the armor-clad victor and tells the audience:

There is no one
No one at all
No one.
The helmet is hollow.
The metal is empty.
The armor is empty.
I tell you there is no
One at all there.[32]

MacLeish reminds listeners that yet another "hollow man" has appeared on the modern stage. Drawing significantly from his experience with *The Fall of the City*, Welles was able to revisit the politically antifascist implications of first-person narration in *The War of the Worlds* on the radio. This tactic was something he also returned to in his production of a contemporary radio version of *Julius Caesar* with a "commentary" by the leading political radio reporter of the day, H. V. Kaltenborn's, who supplemented his reportage during the play by reading passages from Plutarch's *Lives of Noble Grecians and Romans*.[33] Kaltenborn was a fascinating choice because the radio audience would have associated him with the grim reports he was sending from the war-torn fascist conflict occurring during the Spanish Civil War. Further, with music by Marc Blitzstein, the radio adaptation of *Julius Caesar* itself reminds us of the interest Welles had in experimenting with different kinds of narrations in adaptation, and the provocative use of subjectivity. When he adapted the Shakespeare play for the stage less than a year before, its antifascist, allegorical implications were vivid enough, but the chance to educate the audience through narration was less possible in live theater. As I will suggest later in this chapter, Welles discovered a kind of Brechtian model to educate this theatrical audience. But radio always held out the possibility of subjective narration for Welles, for personalizing mass culture with an indelible, personal encounter with the listener, a quality that was not only important to him personally but an increasingly evocative aesthetic unfolding in mass culture. For instance, Welles spoke enthusiastically about the way in which the close-up could personalize film language. Under the right circumstances, radio had the possibility of communicating to millions in an intimate way, something like the way Bing Crosby, and later Frank Sinatra, were able to do in revolutionizing the sexy style in the popular American ballad. According to Naremore, when Welles surveyed the way in which most radio plays were broadcast, he "wanted to eliminate the 'impersonal' quality of such programs, which treated the listener like an eavesdropper. The radio, he recognized, was an intimate piece of living-room furniture, and as a result the 'invisible audience should never be considered collectively, but individually.' "[34] To listen to a recording of *The War of the Worlds* broadcast now is to understand Welles's ability to convey the personal urgency of a narrator who becomes the witness to the horror of mass alien invasion, while inextricably connected to the terror of his listeners. Indeed, at least on one level, the mass panic resulting from that notorious broadcast owed to the intimate reality of the narration itself, personally expressing a national tragedy evolving in living rooms across America.[35]

That individual, subjective style also helped Welles vitiate between highbrow and lowbrow cultures when adapting cultural literary capital like the classics. In a certain sense, Welles was able to take the two giants of literary culture—Shakespeare and Dickens—and reinterpret them through the lens of modernist subjectivity and narrative experimentation, sometimes for political ends, but always through democratic means—the radio. As Jean-Pierre Berthomé and François Thomas say, "the Welles of stage and radio was essentially an adapter, a specialty that he carried over into film . . ."[36] As Welles himself would affirm, "radio is a popular, democratic machine for disseminating information and entertainment. . . . The Highbrows are still sniffing at it. But when television comes—and I understand it is not far off—they will be the first, in all probability, to hail [radio] as a new art form."[37] With Conrad, he took the process into a further exploration of personal consciousness and awareness in a recognizable part of an emerging political discourse in the 1930s, "an antifascist radio aesthetic."[38]

At the same time, the answers to the often perplexing issues involving Welles's first screenplay might lie not only on the airways, but on the stage as well. Brian Neve reminds us of the crucial relationship between the New York political theater of the 1930s and the Hollywood directors who came to light in the early 1940s.[39] It seems plain that Welles's connection with the political left on the New York stage helped determine his adaptation of Conrad's novella for RKO. That the Federal Theater, together with Welles's activities in an antifascist radio aesthetic, should serve as a foundation for *Heart of Darkness* is even clearer when we consider what is perhaps Welles's most inventive work for the stage, the so-called "*Voodoo*" *Macbeth,* which premiered at the Lafayette Theater in New York on April 14, 1936. Much of Welles's exploration of cultural alterations in Shakespeare—the whole drama took place in Haiti, circa 1820—seems a rehearsal for the racial experimentation in *Heart of Darkness.*[40] In retrospect, it appears that Welles was working within an evolving tradition of *Macbeth* adaptations within a pattern of what Richard France calls "preternatural barbarism." Indeed, by the time of Welles's production in the mid-1930s, for instance, Robert Edmond Jones's 1921 staging of the play mounted three huge atavistic masks over the action, transversed by backlights. In 1935, Vera Komissarzhevsky changed the witches into "scavengers" robbing dead soldiers. Invariably, "in Welles's hands the natural world ceases to exist entirely, and all is pure sorcery."[41] France describes the "primitive aural violence" that recalled "an immemorial evil" in an equally evocative set:

> Visually, the jungle and palace were counterpoints to each other, eventually blending in the final scene when the jungle's encroachment on civilization was complete. The jungle was represented by a luridly painted backdrop, but the palace setting was solidly three dimensional and provided for a fluidity of movement—up and down, through and around—that afforded the utmost flexibility. The most prominent feature of this expressionist structure was a multi-stored tower crowned by a practical roof. The tower was connected to the palace by a bridge, which could be used either for a passage or as a gateway over the center entrance. When in place, the portable thrown faced the courtyard, flanked by the great arched gateway. This setting was, however, preeminently a habitat for the witches, who, like so many insects, infested it, immune from all repellents.[42]

As Naremore has pointed out, every time Welles adapted *Macbeth* (the other famous example was in the 1948 film for Republic pictures), "his basic strategy was much the same: he gave it a primitive, exotic setting, and tried to eradicate its Renaissance manners."[43] The expressionist quality of the film—arguably "the purest example of expressionism in the American cinema"—only emphasized the primitive atmosphere all the more, far from the political concerns of Jacobean England.[44] Undoubtedly, the ominous presence of the witches who dominated the 1936 production had the effect of casting a spell on the audience as well, according to Brooks Atkinson: "ship the witches into the rank and fever-stricken echoes, stuff a gleaming naked witch doctor into the cauldron, hold up Negro masks in the baleful light—and there you have a witches' scene that is logical and stunning and a triumph of the theatre art."[45] The setting of the stage play exemplifies the juxtaposition between civilization and the encroaching jungle, an ancient terror that threatens to overwhelm the kingly (and Godly) order. Naremore reminds us that, in contrast to traditional productions of *Macbeth,* which may emphasize a psychological dimension of the play, and the overall interest in the human subject making a tragic choice, Welles's adaptation focused on the primitive, the savage world that threatens to overtake humanity, the chaos that urgently pries its way through the doors of civilization. Welles "set *Macbeth* in the heart of darkness, emphasizing not psychology but rather the struggle between a ruthless desire for power and a rudimentary, elemental need to maintain order."[46] Just at the end of the first act, for instance, the stage directions in the script indicate that the primitive is encroaching on the king:

> The three Witches are seen huddled on the wall. Under their chant has come a rapid throb of drums. This reaches a crescendo under a new voice that is Hecate's, loud and rasping. He is seen suddenly at the very top of the tower, leaning over the throned Macbeth below. The light of an angry dawn flames brighter behind him as he speaks. The courtyard is in shadows. The cripples are strange shapes in the gateway. Hecate and the three Witches are birds of prey.
>
> Hecate: I'll drain him dray as hay.
> Sleep shall neither night nor day
> Hang upon his penthouse lid.
> (Drums stop.)
> He shall live a man forbid.
> (A thump of the drum on the last syllable of "forbid.")[47]

In his adaptation of *Macbeth*, Welles anticipated his reading of *Heart of Darkness* as the encounter with the very depths of power and its disastrous effects on the human person. It drove Kurtz to scribble "Exterminate the beasts," and, in Welles's script:

> KURTZ: I'm a great man, Marlow—really great. Greater than great men before me. I know the strength of the enemy. Its terrible weakness. The meek—you and the rest of the millions—the poor in spirit, I hate you—but I know you for my betters—without knowing why you are except that yours is the Kingdom of Heaven, except that you shall inherit the earth. Don't mistake me. I haven't gone moral on my death bed. I'm above morality. No. I've climbed higher than other men and seen farther. I'm the first absolute dictator. The first complete success. I've known what others try to get. I've gotten it in the one place in the world where it would be got. I'm the man on top. The one man. All the rest are six feet underground where I buried them. That's the game. Bury the rest of them alive. Stay on top of yourself. I won the game, but the winner loses too. He's all alone and he goes mad.[48]

This is clearly a religious discourse—a perverse version of Matthew's Gospel account of the Sermon on the Mount—run amok; its fascistic implications are hard to miss. As in his use of Conrad, Welles's redeployment of Shakespeare in pre–World War II America highlighted political concerns; they were never far from his theatrical inventions and motivations. In September 1937, Welles and John Houseman published what became a famous manifesto in the *Daily Worker,* saying that "when the Mercury Theater opens its doors early in November, we believe another step will have been taken towards a real People's Theatre in America." In the context of the 1930s, Welles and Houseman formed part of a constellation of playwrights, actors, designers, and directors who tried to speak relatively popular idioms and to address themselves to political issues of the day.[49] It is important to remember that Welles's adaptation of an overtly fascistic *Julius Caesar,* which had its debut at the Mercury Theatre on November 11, 1937, was subtitled "The Death of a Dictator," and reminds us that the depiction of "the horror" of Kurtz in the Congo was not Welles's first attempt at an allegory of fascism brought into a contemporary idiom.

Throughout the thirties, Welles also demonstrated a remarkable affinity with other radical elements of contemporary theater, particularly as articulated by Bertolt Brecht. I hasten to add that I do not wish to draw too fine a parallel here between Welles and Brecht, because any overt Brechtian influence on Welles's corpus remains to be demonstrated. On the other hand, Brecht and Welles were connected in certain ways, and Barbara Leaming, Welles's biographer, has lamented when she says that Welles's "expressly Brechtian aspirations have been consistently overlooked."[50] More recently, however, Simon Callow has suggested that when Welles was interviewed by the *New York Post* in 1937 about his interpretation of *Caesar,* he comes close to a Brechtian aesthetic: "I believe in the factual theater. People should not be fooled. They should know that they are in the theater, and with that knowledge, they may be taken to any height of which the magic of words and light is capable of taking them. This is a return to the Elizabethan and the Greek theatre. To achieve that simplicity, that wholesomeness, to force the audience into giving the play the same creative attention that a mediaeval crowd gave a juggler on a box in a market, you have to enchant." With the "attention of the audience, the clarity and simplicity of the staging, the frankness of the theatricality," Callow reckons that Welles approaches something like a Brechtian stance in his theatrical aesthetics, which, as has been critically noted, bore very little resemblance to his own production of *Julius Caesar.*[51]

It also appears as if Welles had some tangential relationship with Brecht throughout the 1930s. We might recall, for example, that Welles was almost the director of *Galileo,* and that the WPA production of *The Cradle Will Rock* was dedicated by Marc Blitzstein to "Bert Brecht."[52] Returning to Welles's "Introduction" to the *Heart of Darkness,* we see that his technique was not only a compelling, magical game, but a kind of didactic lesson, "intended to instruct and acquaint the audience as amusingly as possible with the special technique used in *Heart of Darkness.*" Welles here suggests a Brechtian inspiration, if not an overt borrowing: "The idea is that the spectator should be put in a position where he can make comparisons about everything that influences the way in which human beings behave."[53] Once again, Welles's interest in making the audience see—certainly a Brechtian interest—was part of Welles's adaptive strategy from his days on the radio and the production of plays in "The First Person Singular." As Richard France suggests, Welles's appropriation of modernism accentuated some key features throughout his career in the theater, especially the way he used classic texts to critique contemporary culture: "In his assimilation of the modernist spirit, Welles became imbued with many of its formal devices, which he used to give such productions as *Julius Caesar* intellectual and motive qualities that surpassed anything previously seen on the American stage. Perhaps the closest analogy between his adaptation of *Caesar* and the use of classic drama to illuminate contemporary social and political concerns can be found in the work of Bertolt Brecht, whose adaptation of Marlowe's Edward II (written in collaboration with Leon Feuchtwanger) has to do with the feudal struggle for power."[54]

"To Make You See . . ."

No wonder Welles thought he was "made for Conrad." The opening shots of *Heart of Darkness* make it clear that Welles's project was as a redeployment of Conrad's story into a movie that would educate us in a Brechtian aesthetic, a "complex seeing." Welles's prologue makes us feel a tension between what Brecht would call dramatic theater and epic theater. If dramatic theater "implicates the spectator in a stage situation, wearing down his capacity for action," then epic theater "turns the spectator into an observer, but arouses his capacity for action."[55] Welles's strategy is not so different. At certain levels his film would have employed an astonishingly non-mimetic aesthetic: the self-conscious use of first-person narration functions precisely to educate the audience into thinking what Brecht called "above the flow" as opposed to thinking from "within the flow." Surprisingly enough, the prologue initially seemed in line not only in Welles's aesthetics, but in George Schaefer's new conception for RKO. A very unconventional narrative for Hollywood, Welles's adaptation was seen by the studio as an opportunity to promote the prestige aura of Conrad's novella, "the kind of literary property which carried special weight with Schaefer."[56] Further, the quality of audience participation in *Heart of Darkness* was originally described in Welles's September 15 synopsis for RKO as a "selling angle": "Not only the stars and the story but the *audience* plays a key part in this film. The story is hypnotically fascinating to the audience which is going to find itself shocked into tension, compelled to fascinated watching by this strange story. It will be a definite experience."[57]

Schaefer, a bit like Selznick a few years before, was looking for literary capital to redefine the studio through a prestige author like Joseph Conrad. But he was also counting on trading on Welles's celebrity status. According to Simon Callow, Schaefer wanted a picture that would access Welles's "notoriety" after *The War of the Worlds* broadcast, "distinctively Wellesian: flamboyant, ambitious, and controversial. . . . If, as Welles promised, *Heart of Darkness* would be innovative and provocative, as well as being Prestige Work, then he would back it. It would define the new RKO as nothing else could."[58]

In retrospect, *Heart of Darkness* was probably less a literary prestige work typical of the 1930s than a modernist phenomenon in the hands of great cinematic innovation. With his first venture into Hollywood, Welles had an interest in experimenting with multiple ideas, already emerging as part of his aesthetics from his work in radio and theater. As Simon Callow argues, "Welles was simultaneously trying to reinvent the camera, do justice to a great story, make a film that was highly entertaining and politically provocative, and provide himself with several very interesting roles."[59] A more detailed examination of the film's introduction delineates its relationship to Welles's earlier work in the theater, a curious mixture between the teacher and the magician—indeed, between didacticism and illusionism. The introductory sequence as a whole also recalls Welles's modernist interest in subjectivity and narrative invention from his previous adaptations on radio. Frank Brady has called attention to the controversial nature of the first image in *Heart of Darkness,* which was a shot of a darkened screen that brightens, by iris, to the inside of a bird cage, looking out. Welles tells the audience: "The big hole in the middle there is my mouth. You play the part of a canary. I'm asking you to sing and you refuse. That's the plot. I offer you an olive."[60] As Sarah Kozloff reminds us, there have always been prejudices against voice-over narration in the American fiction film.[61] The formal qualities that Welles envisioned for the film would reposition a Hollywood audience who would necessarily be challenged by the ideological implications of radical subjectivity. Mike Cormack has examined the relationship between cinematography and ideology in the 1930s and says that in those somewhat rare moments when direct address does occur, it is usually deployed "to enforce ideological subjectivity, rather than to question it."[62] In addition to the somewhat bizarre experiments in direct address and camera angles in Welles's script, the opening point of view shot in the first sequence was troubling to the Breen Office, particularly so because of its smoking gun fired at the audience. That sequence has received commentary from several critics and suggests an important link between narrative point of view, ideology, and Welles's experimentation with narration elsewhere. It might be useful, then, to consider the other components of the prologue, as well as the introduction as whole.

After the first sequence, the second presents us with a convict's-eye view in jail. The prisoner's point of view merges with the camera as we are taken by Welles's voice-over through the very slow process of the preparation for electrocution:

> WELLES: Sit down! (Camera pans around, taking in clock but not fo-
> cusing on it, and confronts witnesses. Then lowers a couple of feet to
> height of sitting position.)
> WELLES: Feet! (More sound to match. Then attendant rises slightly and
> looks above camera, somewhat to the side.)
> WELLES: Straps! (Attendants move into frame, make adjustments. They
> are very close to camera. Sound of straps being fastened.)
> FIRST ATTENDANT: Yes, sir.
> (First attendant straightens and moves out of scene. Second attendant
> rises and does the same.)
> WELLES: Fasten the head cap! (Sound to match.)
> WELLES (quietly): Prisoner doesn't want blindfold. (Raising his voice.)
> Have you anything to say? (pause)
> WELLES: All right, Joe, take it on the minute.
> As the camera pans to the electrician, then to the clock moving to-
> wards 12:00, the ticking gets increasingly louder until the long hand
> gets to 12:00, when Welles gives the final order:
> WELLES: All right.[63]
> Then there is the sound of the current being turned on while the
> screen goes into a blinding red stain. Camera blurring its focus at
> the same time, moves quickly to electrician whose outline distorts
> terribly, melts into dirty violet, and sound of current magnified into
> terrific metallic ring which completes sound, dies as we FADE OUT.

Using color, sound effects, aggressive camera techniques, and first-person direct address, the second episode would have been a remarkable piece of cinema for many reasons. Like the sequence preceding it, the electrocution scene emphasizes the subjective potential of cinematic narration. Additionally, the first and the second sequences complement one another, establishing a dialectical rhythm that is repeated throughout the prologue and then in the body of the film itself. In the script, therefore, the voice of Marlow forms the voice of experience or knowledge, which is joined with the demonstrative or expressive detail of the camera. As if to prepare the audience for the dialectic of experience and demonstration to follow, Welles breaks into the introduction at the end of the second sequence in order to establish his point:

> Ladies and Gentlemen, there is no cause for alarm. This is only a motion picture. Of course, you haven't committed murder and believe me, I wouldn't electrocute you for the world. Give yourself your right name, again, please. It might help. All right, now, I think you see what I mean. You're not going to see this picture—this picture is going to happen to you.

Here is the magician showing us his bag of tricks. And the tension between demonstration/experience, discourse/story, telling/showing, continues through the next two sequences. Welles explains that "the camera is your eye," and then he introduces a startling effect:

> A human eye appears, completely filling lens of camera on the screen. Our camera moves toward the eye until it completely fills the screen. As the eye is moving towards us, a sky full of clouds fades into the pupil of the eye. The outline of the eye, the lashes and then the pupil become too large for the screen. By this time all we see is the sky full of clouds.

Welles links the third sequence directly with the fourth:

> The camera pans down from the sky to a golf course, only to be interrupted by Welles's voice: "Keep your eye on the ball." The ball winds up in the rough, as Welles himself moves into a medium shot and says (looking straight into the lens) "Now, if you're doing this right, this is what you ought to look like to me."

Once again, Welles interrupts the introduction in order to remind the audience of the subjective "play" at work. The concluding sequence fully demonstrates what the earlier episodes have been indicating all along. Beginning with the projection booth, the camera pans down, taking in the orchestra floor of the theater, which is dimly lighted by the reflected light of the screen.

The audience is composed of motion picture cameras, then Welles tells the audience, "I hope you get the idea." At last, "a human eye appears on left side of screen. Then an 'equal' sign appears next to it the capital 'I.' Finally, the eye winks and we DISSOLVE."

After examining the prologue, it seems to me that it suggests a kind of dialectic of subjectivity and expressivity inherent throughout the film and which, by extension, recalls Conrad's own modernist representation of Marlow and the Congo.[64] It is not by accident, then, that Welles, even years later, recalled the crucial importance of paying attention to the original book. "There's never been a Conrad movie, for the simple reason that nobody's ever done it as written."[65] Needless to say, Welles's injunction was not an accolade for George Bluestone and the fidelity critics of "novels into film," but a plea for a radical modernist style that yields to the enlightenment of the spectator. Evidently determined to adapt *Heart of Darkness* "as written," Welles's prologue here reminds us of Conrad's aesthetics, the modernist urgency to see into the depth of darkness. "That—and no more, and it is everything. If I succeed, you shall find there according to your deserts: encouragement, consolation, fear, charm—all you demand; and, perhaps, also that glimpse of truth for which you have forgotten to ask."[66]

There are a number of additional theoretical issues that seem to surface as a result of the controversial prologue, which eventually complicated the project for Schaefer, whose limited experience as head of production taught him to regard the script's potential "guardedly" and as "very unusual."[67] The most obvious is the one I have already suggested: the introductory sequences tend to deconstruct the illusionistic technique in the body of the film. Like the story from which it is adapted, Welles's version of *Heart of Darkness* would present us with Marlow's subjective point of view, but it would begin with a preface about subjectivity itself. Welles's intention to map our spectatorial desires, driving us to know more and more about the character of Marlow, is worth recalling: it is "always sustaining, yet never fulfilled." In fact, Welles's interest in radical subjectivity soon had to be explained as something of a mystery to the executives at RKO: "As Welles develops his method, we will be able to talk about it but it is still somewhat in the experimental stage so he doesn't wish to mention it until we can find a convenient formula to express its meaning."[68] In a certain sense, Hollywood was not only dealing with Welles's peculiar inventiveness, or even encountering the emergent, liberal Popular Front narrative Welles gleaned from the Federal Theater and his work on radio; no, the industry was confronting the radical side of literary modernism itself. The advent of modernist practices in Hollywood becomes highlighted in the issues surrounding Welles's redeployment of Conrad's text and a careful scrutinizing of the politics of adaptation surrounding its genesis. For while Selznick, Goldwyn, and other producers labored over the particulars of adapting literary Victorian costume dramas in the late 1930s, the task fell to Schaefer to attempt to negotiate Hollywood with new, liberal directors like Welles, who were shaped by the New York avant-garde. Thus, with the arrival of Orson Welles in Hollywood, his rendition of *Heart of Darkness* became one of the test-cases on the limits of literary adaptation and, even beyond that, the transformation of the auteur into cultural capital.

I have indicated that the most intriguing aspect of the prologue is an attempt to educate the audience. Can we speculate on further implications of the introductory sequence in *Heart of Darkness?* The prologue is a pedagogical moment—indeed a Brechtian moment—rare in Hollywood movies, serving as a caveat against the dangers of illusionism. After receiving instruction, we arrive, fully initiated, at the final equation: eye = "I." As Brady describes the rest of the introductory sequence: "a human eye, Magritte-like, with clouds reflected in it, filling the entire scene and then transposing into the view of a golfer who hits a ball; an interior of a motion picture theater seen from Welles's perspective on the screen, so that all the members of the audience are cameras."[69] Thus educated, we are prepared for the remainder of the story. For Jonathan Rosenbaum, then, the introduction "serves the ingenious function of disclosing the playful and gimmicky aspects of the technique before the story begins, thus clearing the way for its uses as a serious narrative device," which "seems based on an attraction-repulsion principle that is not only much more complex, but unlike Montgomery—[*Lady in the Lake,* 1946] organically related to the concerns of plot. Thus while we are trapped within Marlow's circumscribed gaze as he travels through a studio-built Africa, leaving awed reports about the power and grandeur of Kurtz, we are gradually lured into wanting to share Kurtz's vision instead."[70]

I concur with Rosenbaum's assessment that the introduction functions as an advanced, indeed cajoling, indication of the subjective consciousness and is "organically related to plot." But it seems to me that we might take this one step further and suggest that if Welles maintains a modernist interest in integrating form and content, he problematizes an "organic" reading as well. For rather than presenting us with an ambiguous identification with character, the didactic function of the introduction might deliver us from *any* identification with a single point of view. As we have seen, in "The First Person Singular" radio plays Welles already fragmented and personalized a Dickensian stable narration, but with the adaptation of Conrad, the inventive screenplay launches subjectivity for political ends as well. The prologue, then, becomes a unique expression of subjectivity in its attempt to free us from racial ideas of the primitive: that Marlow's colonial encounter with the atavistic darkness depends on an insistence on racial difference, or what Abdul R. JanMohamed has famously called "the economy of the Manichean allegory."[71] As Robert Young explains in *White Mythologies,* "the same constitutes itself through a form of negativity in relation to the other, producing all knowledge by appropriating and subverting the other within itself."[72] Thus, by *exposing* the knowing subject through self-conscious, didactic narration, Welles has complicated *Heart of Darkness,* even as it has become the most complicated and most ambiguous of texts over the years, with Conrad himself being called either a deeply conservative racist on the one hand, or anti-imperialist on the other. As Patrick Brantlinger reminds us, "*Heart of Darkness* offers a powerful critique of at least some manifestations of imperialism and racism as it simultaneously presents that critique in ways that can be characterized only as imperialist or racist."[73] That Welles would problematize modernist "alterity"—what Edward Said calls Marlow's Western appetite to consume the primitive—is evinced in the remainder of the script as well, and further suggests an extremely complex—and contemporary—reading of Conrad's "will to style."[74]

If Welles designed the prologue as a polemical way to read film, then we might say that the remainder of *Heart of Darkness* tried to offer a kind of politically engaged mystery show. According to Welles's description in an RKO press release, "*Heart of Darkness* was the story of an ordinary guy (Marlow) thrown into the company of evil men. They are of a flabby type, representing every variety of the Fascist mentality and morality. They are the vicious but not very intelligent class of person, which is now attempting to take control of the world."

The subjective narration in *Heart of Darkness* would be a key element in Welles's strategy "to make us see." But there is more. As is well known, Welles called the film "an attack on Nazism," in which the audience would not simply see the action, but, like the prologue, participate directly with it.[75] Initially at least, Welles intended to play Marlow, who both introduces and closes the story in a framed narrative. For most of the film we would experience only the voice of Marlow. In order to accomplish this end, Welles wanted to use subjective shots from Marlow's point of view, photographed with hand-held, Eyemo cameras. In addition to equipping the camera with a double finder, which would enable both the director and the cameraman to follow the action, the production crew would use a gyroscope that prefigured the modern-day steadicam, plus a trick calibrating device for a "feather wipe." Welles would deploy a number of long takes in the film, and the longest sequence would run a full twelve minutes.

That such a nontraditional Hollywood film project was approved by RKO in the first place is an indication of just how much Welles functioned not only as the broker of cultural capital but as an example of symbolic goods himself. The subjective narration was indeed a "selling angle," especially because Welles himself was to play both parts. What other project—or director— could live up to RKO's roaring headlines in the trade press? "Just signed! Orson Welles . . .—brilliant actor and director, to make one picture a year . . . and WHAT a picture is planned for his first."[76] So saying, an extensive cast was planned.[77] As promised by Welles, both the characters and the cultural detail contributed to unambiguous fascistic references. Meanwhile, the company men were all Germans, and Kurtz, like Welles's portrait of Caesar just a few years earlier, was plainly an analogue to Hitler. When Kurtz says, "I have another world to conquer," and when he remarks that "there's a man in Europe trying to do what I've done in the jungle. He will fail," the film is articulating what Rosenbaum has noted as the parallels between Kurtz and Hitler, most of which concern racist ideology.[78] Additionally, the scenes in the jungle were to be elaborate, an evocation of the primitive that was somewhat reminiscent of the *"Voodoo" Macbeth* just a few years earlier; in fact, Welles did "enormous research in aboriginal, Stone Age cultures in order to reproduce what the story called for."[79] As the production files indicate, Welles carefully examined footage from early Hollywood "jungle" films. Evidently, he wanted to ensure an authentic setting, while also saving the studio time and money. The studio records also show that Welles and his staff attempted to buy elaborate jungle sequences from such films as *Congorilla, Wajan, Baboona,* and *Isle of Bali.* Of particular interest seems to have been the marvelous hippo sequence from the 1929 silent version of *The Four Feathers.* Welles later recalled that he was so concerned with realistic detail that he had seriously considered shooting *Heart of Darkness* on location, such as in Louisiana.[80]

With technical innovations (like rigging a camera with a double viewfinder and a gyroscopic head, and 40 percent of the scenes requiring special effects using pinpoint precision for editing an excessive number of feather wipes),[81] exotic and elaborate footage, a full score by Bernard Herrmann, and eighty-two days of shooting for the film, it is not difficult to imagine that the budget was to be an issue for RKO. In fact, Eddie Donahoe, the associate producer of *Heart of Darkness,* wrote to Welles in early December 1939, recommending that he talk to Schaefer about the film's fiscal possibility. According to a memo to Welles, Donahoe managed to get Welles to compare Gene Towne's estimate on *The Swiss Family Robinson* ($550,000) in order to gain a sense of the cost for *Heart of Darkness*. But Welles's film was not just another adventure movie. The total picture cost was estimated at $1,057,761 on the December 5, 1939, budget proposal. This was reevaluated at $984,620 ten days later. The staff had hoped to save money by using some stock shots. Despite a great deal of effort to adjust the cost of the film, the project was killed. The reason released to the press was the extremely large budget. Welles, according to *Hollywood Variety*, was paid $16,000 to abandon the project.[82]

Peter Bogdanovich later asked Welles if it was "as simple as that," and Welles claimed that it was.[83] But we might ask whether the budget for *Heart of Darkness* was the only burden for RKO. *Citizen Kane* would cost almost $800,000, and *The Magnificent Ambersons* more than one million. In fact, the *Heart of Darkness* project was not much more expensive than the other Mercury films. Finances aside, RKO had reason to be worried over Welles's project. The script was unquestionably modernist in its fidelity to Conrad and its use of seemingly nonmotivated, avant-garde diegetic effects was baffling for the studio. And when a mimeographed copy was sent on November 7 to budgeting and then to Schaefer in New York, the latter pondered the excessive voice-over narration and asked himself if it were wise to draw contemporary political parallels.[84] More important, after the Breen Office read the script of *Heart of Darkness,* certain prohibitions were attached that, as we might imagine, were less financial than ideological. Now the relationship between the aesthetic interests of adaptation and the Production Code is a complex one, as Richard Maltby reminds us in his own valuable exploration of adaptation in Hollywood.[85] And if we consider the strong polemical character of the script, it is not unthinkable that the Production Code's evaluation was foreseeing what it perceived to be not only a moral failure, but a potential box office flop as well. Having said this, however, it must be mentioned that the correspondence between the Breen Office and RKO intimates a strong racial component to its review of *Heart of Darkness*. These suggestions were typical of the Breen Office: "Care had to be taken," they said, "with undo gruesomeness, the realistic costumes of the natives and, in the scenes between Kurtz and the native girl, no intimation of miscegenation could be hinted."[86] The liberal Welles faced a difficult situation: how to represent Nazi racists while being censored by a protective, conservative discourse that was itself marginally racist and bigoted.

Savage Subjectivity

When we examine the aesthetic contours of *Heart of Darkness* together with its production history, it becomes clearer that this was "Welles the modernist" confronting Hollywood popular culture. This was the Welles clearly as comfortable with Conrad as with the Federal Theater's *"Voodoo" Macbeth* and the Mercury's *Caesar* attempting to radicalize a diverse, culturewide form of racial and political representation in the struggle against fascism.[87] Moreover, Welles had imagined *Heart of Darkness* as containing prolonged, interracial social involvement and sexuality. Like the novella itself, the film would expose a daring relationship at its explosive core: an African native girl—described by Conrad's Marlow as "savage and superb, wild-eyed and magnificent"[88]—with whom Kurtz forms a romantic alliance. Throughout, the film would make use of black actors as active players in the unfolding of Kurtz's decline. There was, for example, a huge cast of natives—three thousand—with "very black skin." Even more controversial, Welles had actually hoped to get a depiction of the interracial couple engaged in loving embraces on the screen past the Breen Office, as Frank Brady suggests.[89] We have only to screen any number of films representing African Americans during this period, as Thomas Cripps and Donald Bogle have done, to see that Welles's depiction of race would have been close to unimaginable in 1930s American culture, one certainly more comfortable with African Americans as maids and chauffeurs than romantic (sexual) partners.[90] Further, in his examination of depictions of race in the 1930s, Richard Dyer tells us that "it is common for oppressed groups to be represented in dominant discourses as non-active."[91] Clearly, there was nothing submissive about what either Conrad or Welles imagined in *Heart of Darkness*. Passive representation was exactly what *Heart of Darkness* was not. Everyone, including the audience, was to play a key role.

Not surprisingly, RKO was expected to be very careful to secure a non-active representation of the African natives in the Congo, and especially to avoid any black/white racial coupling or tensions. But the studio summary of September 15 on *Heart of Darkness* very definitely suggests another turn: "The natives who are subdued and slaves at the mouth of the broad river become progressively less civilized and much fiercer as the boat travels. The passengers beside the girl and the man who is telling the story, the petty and major executives of the trading company, becomes semi-hysterical. It all builds to a terrific climax in story when the man, Kurtz, is found at last. The jungle is set on fire and quenched by a storm."[92]

Heart of Darkness, with its inventive deployment of interracial sexuality and of black and white tensions that devolve into chaos, certainly foregrounds racial issues in America on the eve of World War II. But when contemplating the enormously diverse and difficult matter of race and representation, we must be careful not to condemn the Breen Office outright for what was a complex, multilevel form of cultural racism that was mirrored by popular culture.[93] Moreover, the Production Code was only one of the many ways that late-1930s eugenics became promulgated. For example, it was the paranoid fear of "the bad seed" that generated the 1939 lectures on *The Genetic Basis for Democracy,* a monograph published by the American Committee for Democracy and Intellectual Freedom, which attempted to ascertain "the correlation between bodily form and mental characteristics."[94] Christine Rosen has researched the ethical and scientific issues of selective population in the United States from 1900 to 1940 and shown how liberal mainline Protestant churches embraced the ideology of race and the new eugenics movement.[95] Indeed, even before the 1934 Production Code went into effect, Hollywood had long been obsessed with the "morale of the race," evident in such films as *Where Are My Children?* (1916). As Annette Kuhn says, "eugenics, as a set of ideas about the physical and intellectual quality of the population and its capacity for improvement through human intervention in the form of science and/or social reform, enjoyed a great vogue in the early years of this century, fuelled by concerns about the state of what was universally termed 'the race.' . . . Eugenics offered the prospect of reversing what was perceived to be a deterioration in the quality of the population."[96]

In calling our attention to racial issues, Welles's script imagines a surrealistic vision, a telescopic eye into the potential savagery lurking underneath the human subject. It was Freud's Civilization at its most discontent, as if everyone had the potential to be a Kurtz—just like Macbeth—if the thin veneer of the social order was peeled away. If we scratched the surface, one would find a primitive world lurking below, a heart of darkness that would bear the unspeakable mirror of the savage and atavistic self in all its horror. Therefore, in addition to the corrupt Kurtz, Welles's script was loaded with unsavory or unsympathetic characters. The doctor is supposed to have a "seedy and vaguely suspicious look of the quack but none of the quack's anxious desire to please." Elsa Gruner, the name Welles gave to Kurtz's lover, was supposed to "love Kurtz more than God." The cast also included "a Portuguese" who was "a malicious man," and a station manager with "bad blue blood and a club foot." Even Elsa, Kurtz's "intended" in Europe, was to be portrayed by a seductive, "exotic woman." *Heart of Darkness,* then, imagines not a stylized primitivism, but atavism out of control; it implies that given the right circumstances, the "lower classes, the 'feeble-minded,' and the 'degenerate' could breed, it was feared, at a rate which threatened the extinction of the 'best' elements of the race."[97] This adaptation was Conrad's modernism pushed to the limit: it was the Congo having its arcane, unfathomable way with the West, the "darkness" threatening to puncture the bright light of civilization. For Welles, what was beneath the skin was not fashionable, modernist primitivism, but instead contemporary fascism: racist "exploiters in surroundings not healthy for a white man."

Racial considerations notwithstanding, Welles's script also raises the fascinating matter of Hollywood's ideological control over narrative point of view. The ambiguous narrative voice in *Heart of Darkness* contributed, perhaps very substantially, to the proposed revisions of the script by the Breen Office, and it may have had something to do with the subsequent cancellation by RKO. The studio sent riders to Welles suggesting that he alter the content of the script, but the form of the picture—especially the introduction—was also controversial and worth our emphasis: "in the introductory scene, the gun could not be pointed and fired directly at the audience; the prisoner could not be shown in an electric chair that appeared to be realistic."[98]

It is easy to understand why censors might have been threatened by both the content and the form of the film. If the subject matter of *Heart of Darkness* was unconventional, then Welles's subjective technique was not typical of Hollywood, where classical discourse—with some notable exceptions—typically consists of omniscient narration that is highly communicative and only moderately self-conscious.[99] Moreover, as David Bordwell reminds us, the *syuzhet* rarely enjoys prominence in the classical Hollywood film. Instead, it is the *fabula* that consistently orders time and space, thereby constructing an "invisible observer."[100] But far from handling spatial presence as omnipresence, Welles's script, complete with a didactic, self-reflexive prologue, hints at a rupture of a *fabula* ordering from the start. As Seymour Chatman observes, "films do not frequently address the 'dear viewer' the way the literary narrator may address the 'dear reader.'"[101] Yet, Welles's introduction to *Heart of Darkness* not only makes us self-consciously aware of our relationship with the implied author, but calls our attention to the historical author as well: the well-known, indeed infamous, radio voice of Orson Welles.

Formal questions involving censorship are even more vexed than the slippery ones pertaining to content. But it is worth pondering exactly what the censors objected to in *Heart of Darkness*. It is commonplace to observe that race and ideology are benevolently—and invisibly—veiled in a *fabula* constructed classical Hollywood narrative. With Welles's instructive prologue in mind, then, we might ask if it was both the point of view shot and the (second) sequence of the prisoner in the electric chair contained in the introduction that together presented an altogether dark picture for Hollywood. At this level, we might say that the introduction to *Heart of Darkness* is as complex in form as it is in content. For Welles, like Brecht, attacked the operations of the signifier as well as the signified, attempting to engage in what Roland Barthes would later call a "writerly" practice. Through a technique that is clearly pedagogical, Welles alerts the spectator to "narrativization," which, as Stephen Heath has remarked, "is the complex operation of the film as narrative and the setting of the spectator as subject in the operation."[102] The aesthetic alternative that Welles proposed, then, ran directly counter to the imperatives of the studio system: it was an epistemological irregularity, the art of instruction rather than passive "entertainment." As if to suggest his need for a mythological necessity for Conrad's story, William Koenig, a member of the RKO story department, found the *Heart of Darkness* script incomprehensible, saying that, "there is no use looking for a story, in the screen sense of the word, here. This is not one of Mr. Conrad's best stories. He is wholly concerned here with building up a philosophical and mystical picture of a man who is a mystery to the readers of the story even at the story's end."[103] That Koenig was a principal component of the very system that Welles's version of *Heart of Darkness* undermines further suggests that aesthetics and politics relentlessly seek their own company. Far from being a vehicle for contemporary ideology, *Heart of Darkness* would be an instruction about its unmasking.

I have tried to indicate that *Heart of Darkness* seems acutely aware of the dangers of its own medium as a controlling force. Once again, we see Welles mastering Conrad's ambivalent text. Even if we grant Conrad the intention to condemn the imperialistic exploitations in the Belgian Congo during the late nineteenth century, *Heart of Darkness* nevertheless harbors the formal danger that the reader might, after all, be incorporated into the sensational, the monocular and fascistic world of Marlow himself, who, with his "geographical appetite" for maps and language, becomes our sole, colonial arbitrator in the Congo; he is the filter of "dark" experience. In the Conradian narrator's encounter with primordial Africa and in his description of Kurtz's fall into its unfathomable reaches, then, we are left with a modernist, epistemological threat, a "will to style": it engages us through point of view in a story about the survival of the West, and indeed, about the heroic endurance of its narration. *Heart of Darkness* is a racist narrative on one level because hegemonic modernism guarantees Western civilization by subordinating and objectifying the Other. And revisionist critics like Chinua Achebe and Patrick Brantlinger do well to point out that an imperialist, totalizing modernist discourse prowls at the edge of Conrad's story.

Welles's version of the novella, on the other hand, deliberately expresses a deconstructive ambivalence about Conrad, especially in the area of modernist point of view. To this end, the final moments of the prisoner's preparation for death in the introduction wonderfully and excruciatingly suggest the "will to style" of cinematic viewing. That amazing sequence serves, in fact, as an allegory of spectatorship: it is the audience who has become vicariously and quite literally wired, and, in the end "electrocuted." In addition, it is worth recalling that from the very start of the film, Welles, as mock dictator, says that he is dividing the audience in half: "you and everybody else." When Welles says, "give yourself your right name, again please," he reminds us of the potential loss of freedom in spectatorship, or what Jean-Louis Baudry would later famously call the cinema as *appareil*.[104] Welles deploys the side of Conrad's modernism that wants "to make us see"; but he rejects the other side of fascistic, racist modernism in which whiteness is validated through blackness.

Thus, as Welles has conceived it, the introduction and the subjective narrative in the "body" of *Heart of Darkness* creates a split in point of view: we would not be secret sharers in Marlow's perspective, trapped in his own vision; instead, Welles would have granted the audience an ironic distance. Having been granted a larger perspective and a point of view from the subjective voice itself, we would encounter Kurtz not as victims of the mechanical apparatus but as "educated" or skeptical viewers. To this end, the story of Marlow's adventure in the jungle is not only an allegory about fascism, but about Hollywood as well:

> ELSA: . . . You were with him—to the last.
> MARLOW'S VOICE: To the very end. I heard his very last words.
> ELSA: Repeat them. I want—I want—something—to live with.
> (The voice of Kurtz is heard again still very dimly repeating over and
>   over again his last words.)
> KURTZ'S VOICE: The horror! The horror!
> MARLOW'S VOICE (narrating): The dusk was repeating them around
>   us, like the first whisper of a rising wind.
> KURTZ'S VOICE: The horror! The horror!
> ELSA: His last word—to live with. Don't you understand? I love him—I
>   love him—I loved him!
> MARLOW'S VOICE: His last words—the last word he pronounced was
>   —your name.
> ELSA: I knew it—I was sure.
> (Elsa's eyes are filled with tears but her mouth smiles. She looks above
>   and beyond the lens of the camera.)

Marlow's meeting with Kurtz and subsequent "cover-up" (for Elsa's benefit) of "The horror! The horror!" becomes, interestingly enough, a parable about Hollywood narrative. Elsa is equated with the uninstructed viewer, duped by Marlow's ideological machinations. Her response is one of an unenlightened spectator, ultimately persuaded not by truth but by melodrama. Marlow's concluding remarks are very suggestive of Hollywood's own efforts at creating and refashioning a conservative, cultural mythology; they hauntingly recall Welles's own present struggles with the Breen Office.

> MARLOW: Should I have told her the truth?
> KURTZ'S VOICE: I want only justice.
> MARLOW: I couldn't. I couldn't tell her. It would have been too dark—
> too dark altogether—(pause). We've lost the first of the ebb—

Marlow here becomes exemplary of the classical Hollywood narrator, and interestingly enough, one of its official guardians: truth loses to romantic myth, justice to ideology, the "writerly" to the "readerly."

The story of Marlow, Kurtz, and Elsa, then, might well be our own without the twin fountains of theatricality on the one hand and didacticism on the other. It seems to me, therefore, that Welles's strategy in *Heart of Darkness* prevents us from experiencing Marlow's fate. We are instructed from the start in the dangers of spectatorship and, I would argue, in the ways of identifying with the actors.[105] For just as the prologue involves a cautionary warning against a monolithic vision, so, too, Welles's conception of the double further reorders the *fabula*. The "two-sided" character of Marlow/Kurtz, after all, helps to shape the film's self-consciousness, insofar as the audience is prohibited from experiencing any "realistic," Stanislavskian aesthetics. While we might say that just about all doubling in the classical Hollywood film occurs on the level of *fabula,* our experience of Welles's Marlow is shaped by the ironic reflection of Welles's Kurtz. We are instructed in the way that the "double actor" ironically conceives of itself: it is subversively non-mimetic in the *syuzhet/fabula* configuration. Here, once again, we are reminded of Brecht on the "alienation" effect in acting, the technique of which strives to "make the spectator adopt an attitude of inquiry and criticism in his approach to the incident," and in which "the actor does not allow himself to become completely transformed on the stage into the character he is portraying."[106]

After his experience with *Heart of Darkness,* Welles adhered more closely to the conventions of Hollywood cinema, but still inflected his own radical style. Welles's problems with Hollywood could have been intuited from the ambitions of his first screenplay, an echo that would find itself resounding throughout his career: "the overriding quality of his work is not its phenomenal realism but its distortion and excess. And the progress of his American films was to be a fairly steady movement away from the conventions of cinematic reality toward the bizarre and the surreal."[107] After 1940, Welles passed from his intimate relationship with the left-wing New York theater inspired by the populism of the New Deal. Some years later, the threat of fascism on the world scene had passed, and the subsequent stories in Welles's films exemplify what Naremore has calls "Welles's typical plot structure." The films begin as a retrospective, then show how the events transpired, then bring the story into a full circle.[108] But although the ordering principle of the *fabula* comes into greater prominence in Welles's later cinematic efforts, there are elements in *Heart of Darkness* that prefigure Welles's later work as well, as several critics have mentioned. Welles's interest in point of view and subjectivity in both radio adaptations and in *Heart of Darkness* anticipates *Citizen Kane*'s more elaborate and eloquent story and discourse, where multiple points of view share in a single event. As Richard Pells observes with regard to *Kane*, the technical fireworks served not only to awaken the audience to new conceptions of reality but also to illuminate the moral difficulties in passing judgment both on the character of Charles Foster Kane and the society out of which he sprang.[109] Indeed, *syuzhet* figures very prominently in *Kane* and much of the experimental narrative procedures in *Heart of Darkness* suggests a rehearsal for that film.

In many respects, *Kane* seems a tamer version of Welles's unproduced first film effort, or as Vincent Canby put it not too long ago, "more congenial movie material."[110] It might even be said that by the time of the appearance of *Citizen Kane* in 1941, Welles had become a better negotiator with American popular culture, while still maintaining his critical edge. Indeed, the experimentation with a subjective narration in *Heart of Darkness* becomes in *Kane* a multiple dramatic monologue; the seedy characters imagined in the Conrad story are transformed into vengeful and ruthless politicians like Boss Jim Gettys; and the discourse on the "primitive" is rendered comic: Charles's famously elaborate picnic sequence. Although Welles told Bogdanovich that there was no similarity between *Heart of Darkness* and *Citizen Kane*, there is a clear legacy of Kurtz's "fascism" in Charles Foster Kane, whose need to be loved and to control the media exemplify a sharp turn in the river into the continent of darkness. Kane is, in fact, a Kurtz without overt primitive savagery lapping at his heels. Both make tragic Xanadus for themselves away from civilization and are "trespassed" by inquisitive, aggressive cameras that burn away their own darkened, seemingly inaccessible hearts. Thus the "transformation" of *Heart of Darkness* into *Citizen Kane* is a marvelous example of how Hollywood managed to absorb and vitiate a more challenging modernist avant-garde.

Welles would later claim that he became disillusioned with subjective narration after one of the long point of view sequences in *The Magnificent Ambersons* (it was cut from the film). But it is easy to see that Welles's interest in narrative point of view was lifelong. The early preoccupation with subjectivity gave way to the more independently expressive camera in Welles's later work.[111] Indeed, in perhaps more than any other of Welles's later films, *Lady from Shanghai* replicates Welles's late-modernist interest in subjectivity, race, grotesque characters, anarchic, exotic cultures, and, indeed—Bertolt Brecht. As Barbara Leaming has noted, a major sequence in that film takes place in a Chinese theater, and Welles professed to be alluding to Brecht's famous essay on the "Alienation Effects in Chinese Acting."[112] The rhythmic juxtaposition of demonstrative detail with the more experiential character of first-person narrative haunts *Lady from Shanghai,* in which Michael's rather deliberately colloquial and experiential Black Irish manner seems at odds with the more expressively demonstrative camera work. Further, the particulars of the introduction in *Heart of Darkness* will appear in similar (albeit mutated) forms in later films. The adaptation of *Macbeth* is shot in an atmosphere that is "so intensely subjective, so much told from the central character's point of view, that at times the movie has a solipsistic quality"[113] The prisoner's plight in the introduction of *Heart of Darkness* looks forward to the entrapped, nameless victim in the protracted opening sequence of *The Trial* and its violent climax. In 1972, Jonathan Rosenbaum asked Welles in Paris at what point he had abandoned the *Heart of Darkness* project. Welles replied that "he never abandoned it—he still wanted to do it." And he told Peter Bogdanovich that he lamented that the adaptation of another of Conrad's novels, *Lord Jim* (Richard Brooks, 1965), did not pay closer attention to the book.[114] Coincidentally, Welles himself evidently had plans to adapt *Lord Jim* in 1964, but was prevented from doing so because of the proximity of the release of Brooks's film. Like Marlow himself, Welles was still searching for Kurtz.[115] Then again, Welles was also Kurtz who had come to Darkest Hollywood to expose its conventions rather than reveling in them.

In a certain sense, then, Welles never let go of *Heart of Darkness,* and the script appears to have had more than its share of rippling effects throughout the Wellesian corpus, even in those films that are not his own. Rosenbaum says that Carol Reed's *The Third Man* would have been "inconceivable without *Heart of Darkness,* and when Welles the actor stepped into his villainous part, a character analogous to Conrad's Kurtz—the unscrupulous exploiter from abroad, putting in his first, brief appearance an hour into the film—he knew from his theater experience as well as from his first screenplay that less from an actor could add up to more in terms of public perception."[116] Additionally, as Naremore has pointed out in his investigation of film noir film culture, there is a character called Kurtz in *The Third Man*.[117] Andrew Sarris's famous observation that "the dramatic conflict in a Welles film often arises from the dialectical collision between morality and megalomania" also describes Conrad's portrait of Marlow's encounter with Kurtz at the edge of the abyss, the *Heart of Darkness*.[118] Finally, if Welles's first days in Hollywood were already anticipating an auteur's alternative to the classical Hollywood narrative and its mythology of race and politics, then that blueprint was forged by a British modernist. Welles was indeed made for Conrad, but not for Hollywood—or its practices of film adaptation.

4

Filmed Theater

John Ford's The Long Voyage Home (1940)

For Bazin the space of theater was artificial,
conventional, and the space of film was the same as
the space of real life. Just as in real life we focus on
something while the rest of the world lies unseen, so in
a film the camera focuses on something while the rest of
the world lies implied in the space off screen.

—Gilberto Perez, *The Material Ghost*

Almost everyone has heard about the 1967 interview in which Orson Welles told *Playboy* that the film directors who appealed to him were the "old masters—by which I mean John Ford, John Ford and John Ford." He went on to say that, "with Ford at his best you feel that the movie has lived and breathed in the real world—even though it may have been written by Mother Machree."[1] Indeed, Welles drew a great deal from studying his favorite director, not least of which was sharing Ford's cinematographer, Gregg Toland, from *The Long Voyage Home* and *The Grapes of Wrath*, in *Citizen Kane*. Welles studied Hollywood studio directors whom Ford himself admired and who influenced him greatly, like F. W. Murnau. When it came to Ford, Welles treated his mentor's films like blueprints from a master architect to be memorized. "John Ford was my teacher. My own style has nothing to do with his, but *Stagecoach* was my movie text-book. I ran it over forty times."[2] But when he adapted Shakespeare in *Chimes at Midnight*, the battle scenes have a haunting evocation of a Ford western.[3] In retrospect, however, Welles's proposed project of appropriating Joseph Conrad for an RKO picture was vastly different from Ford's adaptation of American's greatest playwright. Indeed *Heart of Darkness* is almost completely antithetical to Ford's adaptation of Eugene O'Neill's four sea plays into *The Long Voyage Home*.[4] In *Heart of Darkness*, Welles deployed modernist invention to "defamiliarize," but in *The Long Voyage Home* Ford used a modernist style for conservative purposes, enhancing his reputation as one of Hollywood's few "arty" directors. If, as I have suggested in the previous chapter, Welles's work is a synthesis of Brechtian alienation and Gothic illusionism, he makes a formidable contrast to John Ford, who has been portrayed by Andrew Sarris as a regionalist painter. *The Long Voyage Home* ushers in a period in Ford's career deserving of Andrew Sarris's characterization of him as America's "poet laureate" of the visual.[5]

The contrasts between Welles and Ford are further exemplified in what they did with modernist technique in the 1930s. Welles used a version of savage, primitive modernism and experimental camera techniques to allegorize contemporary fascism and race relations in *Heart of Darkness;* that production, as we know, never saw the light of day for a variety of reasons. On the other hand, Ford's own assimilation of a modernist style allowed him to adapt prestigious literary properties and even imbue them with his own directorial style, which would eventually become more and more prestigious among Hollywood directors. Filmed in thirty-seven days for $682,495, in a partnership with Merian C. Cooper, Ford and screenwriter Dudley Nichols would tame Walter Wanger's and Argosy's production of *The Long Voyage Home* from O'Neill's brutal naturalism into a film that represents what Sarris refers to as "a conscious extension of the foggy expressionism of the Thirties into the programmed heroics of World War II."[6]

Not coincidentally, the artistic struggles Welles and Ford faced in 1930s Hollywood played out for most of their careers and became something like mirror images of each other. Welles was marginalized in the industry and, as everyone knows, often compelled to live and work outside the highly circumscribed parameters of the Hollywood establishment in order to finance his own movies. Ford, by contrast, worked extensively and almost exclusively in Hollywood and was conspicuous in his ability to negotiate political and artistic projects into bankable motion pictures. Ford's adaptation of Eugene O'Neill's *S.S. Glencairn,* one-act plays[7] about an ammunition-loaded British steamer's trip home from the West Indies, is a striking example of a Hollywood director making use of a cultivated, expressionistic art-house style, or what Bosley Crowther in his (October 9, 1940) review of the film referred to as "lean economy" and "muscular realism." With Joseph Conrad, Welles adapted a modernist novelist and radicalized the narrative in ways the Hollywood studios could never tolerate or middle-class audiences appreciate. On the other hand, Ford appropriated a modernist playwright and, by negotiating both a reputation and a directorial style, transformed O'Neill's plays into cultural capital for the studio. That symbolic capital, however, was not the "literary" property that had been so successful in adaptations over the previous decade, when such prestige productions flourished. Indeed, *The Long Voyage Home* was not a box office success, yet the film helped to further the aura of Ford as a prestige director. In some sense, *The Long Voyage Home* was a critically successful adaptation because it shifted attention from the source text to the cinematic auteur: it occurred at the precise moment when an interest in expressionistic film techniques, performative and arty style, and indeed, Ford's reputation, were at a high point. For by the time *The Long Voyage Home* was produced with Ford's newly developed company, Argosy, in conjunction with Walter Wanger, numerous ideological factors—the rise of a visually savvy audience, the emerging cult of directors, the interest in Hollywood "literary films"—would enable Ford to become the new author of O'Neill's plays. Even the way that the plays were gathered into a screenplay by Dudley Nichols and photographed by Gregg Toland reminds us that we are not dealing with a "play into film" as much as a radical transformation, a re-inscription of an author into a Hollywood auteur.[8] From the point of view of an investigation of adaptation of "theater into film," finally, Ford's production of O'Neill's plays managed to resolve what André Bazin referred to as the peculiar "dialectic between cinematic realism and theatrical convention."[9]

Filmed Theater

It is no secret that adaptation studies around the topic of "theater into film" have flourished nowhere near the extent of its prose counterpart over the years. But an essential understanding of the difference between the stage and cinema was crucially important to the evolution of film theory. In an early essay on film and theatrical aesthetics, Edwin Panofsky argues for a "basic nature" for film, simply to liberate it from the theatrical conventions.[10] At either end of the ideological spectrum, the two most celebrated theorists to write about theater into film were André Bazin and Sergei Eisenstein, both of whom related their insights to the broader spectrum of film form and style.[11] For both Eisenstein and Bazin, theater and its conventions were windows into film and their respective and divergent theories of montage and adaptation. Eisenstein came to cinema after a career in the theater, and his 1934 essay, "Through Theater to Film" (coincidentally published the same year as the first version of Panofsky's piece) retraces his transition from stage to screen, saying that any director should know the aesthetics of theatrical construction and the role of the *mise-en-scène*. This curriculum of stagecraft techniques, in fact, formed the first two years of the Course in Treatment in Eisenstein's course for directors at the State Cinema Institute, which emphasized theatrical principles. But Eisenstein himself was led to the cinema through a realization of the possibilities of "collectivity" in the "general structure and composition" that film offered, especially through montage.[12] Bazin, on the other hand, was writing not as an experienced theatrical director but as a philosopher and theorist at the edge of the French New Wave, where auteurists like himself rebelled against "filmed theater"—in a word, a photographed play—the cinema with too much chatty dialogue, and altogether too literary. Filmed theater for the auteurists fails to discover the visual language for adapting the play into cinema. Bazin takes the problems he sees in filmed theater a step further. In his essay on "Theater and Cinema," Bazin intends to free cinema from its illusionist legacy with the theater, and additionally and under the right circumstances to position cinematic spectatorship as the site that maximizes personal visual freedom and widens the choice of the spectator. The result is a realistic cinema that proceeds directly from the photographic image. Instead of resorting to either filmed theater on the one hand, or the camera overtaking the theater completely—forcing us to forget its conventions—Bazin suggests holding the two forms in a kind of unresolved tension. This strategy points to the de-illusionism of film because "the function of the cinema is to reveal, to bring to light certain details that the stage would have left untreated."[13]

In surveying the impact that the stage has had on cinema, then, Bazin regarded the theater as *une fausse amie:* "its illusory likeness to the cinema set the latter en route to a dead end, luring it onto the slippery slope of the merely facile."[14] Underlying Bazin's suppositions, of course, remains his heavily inflected interest in the philosophy of personalism and Christian humanism, influenced by Emmanuel Mounier, the founder of the journal *Esprit,* where "*Théatre et Cinéma*" was first published in 1951. For Bazin, the spectator's perception of the shot and his or her freedom underlie his aesthetics of deep focus and montage—and, indeed, or, as Bazin says in "In Defense of Mixed Cinema," "a new way of seeing things provided by the screen."[15]

According to Dudley Andrew, the early Bazin was passionate on the dominant and transformative role film should play in respect to theater: "The movie theater has often been criticized for the passivity of its public which is seen as both gregarious and individualistic, and this passivity is opposed to the communion of the theater throng before the actor's performance, a throng dominated by the chandelier, that luminous, crystalline, circular, and symmetrical object so dear to Baudelaire. In the movie theater, one hardly knows anything other than indirect lighting and that single long prism of rigid light—agile comet or moonbeam emanating from the projection booth—which carries within itself only shadows and fleeting illusions."[16]

For Bazin, film would rejuvenate the stage in a dialectical exchange, the result of which would be a cinematographic theater. In a historical retrospective of film history, Bazin traces "filmed theater" as far back as Melies, "who saw the cinema as basically nothing more than a refinement of the marvels of the theater."[17] Ultimately, Bazin would tie his speculations on theater and the cinema into larger theoretical suppositions. In one of his most significant essays, "The Evolution of the Language of Cinema," Bazin says that, "all you need to do is to compare two frames shot in depth, one from 1910, the other from a film by Wyler or Welles, to understand just by looking at the image, even apart from the content of the film, how different their functions are. The framing in the 1910 film is intended, to all intents and purposes, as a substitute for the missing fourth wall of the theatrical stage, or at least in exterior shots, for the best vantage point to view the action, whereas in the second case the setting, the lighting, and the camera angles give an entirely different reading. Between them, director and cameraman have converted the screen into a dramatic checkerboard, planned down to the last detail."[18]

Bazin clarifies his point of establishing a kind of cinema-theater hybrid when discussing the success certain auteur directors have had with adaptations of plays. "Cocteau maintains the essentially theatrical character of his play. Instead of trying like so many others to dissolve it in cinema, on the contrary he uses the resources of the camera to point up, to underline, to confirm the structure of the sense and their psychological corollaries. The specific help given here by the cinema can only be described as an added measure of the theatrical."[19] For Bazin, the great auteur directors accomplish the tricky resolution of the problem between theater and cinema. Bazin discusses directors like Cocteau, Welles, and Wyler in order to showcase the expressive possibilities in adaptation of theater for the stage. As I suggested in chapter 1, an understanding of adaptation relies heavily on the politics of authorship. In her insightful study of Shakespeare adaptations, for instance, Courtney Lehmann turns to a discussion of authorship, using some of the vocabulary of the auteurists of the 1950s and 1960s, "initiating a long-overdue process of theoretical adaptation that replaces the burning of historical bridges between the early and postmodern."[20] As is well known, Bazin pioneered auteurist issues related to adaptation and the politics of authorship in much of his central writings of the 1940s and 1950s in France, and "Theater and Cinema" recommends, once again, that certain auteurs were able to improve upon the theater and move it toward a kind of *"théâtre cinématographique,"* always insisting that *"le cinéma sauvera le theater."*[21] By linking the relationship between theater and cinema to the director, Bazin saw the current opportunities in the cinema by auteurs as a potentially rich improvement over the theatrical source text, while recovering its "spirit" in the adaptation. For him, Chaplin's mime became "more than the theater but only by going beyond it, by relieving it of its imperfections."[22] This faithfulness is paradoxical because theater requires that there will be "a certain artificiality, an exaggerated transformation of the decor . . . totally incompatible with that realism which is of the essence of the cinema."[23] According to Bazin, Laurence Olivier's *Henry V* (1944) handled the problem perfectly "by showing us, from the opening, by a cinematic device that we are concerned here with theatrical style . . . instead of trying to hide them, he relieved realism of that which makes it the foe of theatrical illusion."[24] Bazin maintains, then, that in the adaptation of the play a certain theatricality must be maintained: "the function of the cinema is to reveal, to bring to light certain details that the stage would have left untreated."[25]

The theater is limiting by itself alone, but cinema is capable of exposing its conventions so that the two media subsist simultaneously. The claim Bazin is making here obviously relates to the de-illusionism of theatricality for the sake of cinematic realism. Bazin often reveals himself as a phenomenologist distrustful of montage. In a related aesthetic, the very dynamics of cinematography, of long takes and deep-focus photography, provide the spectator a choice as a viewer, a freedom unavailable at the proscenium stage. He examines Hollywood directors in terms of their stylistic choices that invite spectatorial freedom in the shot, which has an obvious alliance with a preference for a dialogical relationship between theater and film: "The importance of depth of focus and the fixed camera in the films of Orson Welles and William Wyler springs from a reluctance to fragment things arbitrarily and a desire instead to show an image that is uniformly understandable and that compels the spectator to make his own choice."[26] Bazin will not favor routinely breaking up the space in montage for theatrical adaptation—that adds nothing to the theater—but widening the perspective in deep focus, clearly available in nontheatrical adaptations like Welles's *Citizen Kane*. In the famous Boarding House sequence from that film, which has received a great deal of critical attention, we see from a window of the boarding house the young Charles playing near a snowman in the distance, while Mrs. Kane and Mr. Thatcher look on. The camera pulls back, tracking Mary Kane, her husband, and Mr. Thatcher to a table in the foreground, leaving the young

Charles in the window frame still playing. As James Naremore notes, "By this means Welles deliberately avoids conventional editing techniques and lets each element—the actors and the décor of the home—reveal itself successively, until everything is placed in a highly symbolic composition. . . . The deep focus enables us to see everything at once, and the wide-angle lens slightly enlarges the foreground, giving it dramatic impact."[27] As Bazin suggests, the spectator is given optimal freedom here. For Bazin, *Citizen Kane* "is unthinkable shot in any other way but in depth. The uncertainty in which we find ourselves as to the spiritual key or the interpretation we should put on the film is built into the very design of the image. It is not that Welles denies himself any recourse whatsoever to the expressionistic procedures of montage, but just that their use from time to time in between sequences of shots in depth gives them a new meaning. Formerly montage was the very stuff of cinema, the texture of the scenario. In *Citizen Kane* a series of superimpositions is contrasted with a scene presented in a single take, constituting another and deliberately abstract mode of story telling."[28]

On the other hand, theater cannot be swallowed up in the cinema. Conventional Hollywood realistic editing, or the continuity system that disguises, gives us "the impression all the same of a continuous homogeneous reality. The insertion of a doorbell in close-up is accepted by the mind as if this were nothing other than a concentration of our vision and interest on the doorbell, as if the camera merely anticipated the movement of our eyes . . . classical editing totally suppresses this kind of reciprocal freedom between us and the object. . . . This utterly unaesthetizes our freedom."[29] Theater and cinema are to exist much like the famous image of the "twin stars" Bazin describes in discussing "fidelity" as a strategy in adaptation. As early as 1948, Bazin argued that it was necessary to keep the genres separate in adaptation criticism, because "The true aesthetic differentiations, in fact, are not to be made among the arts but within genres themselves: between the psychological novel and the novel of manners, for example, rather than between the psychological novel and the film that one would have from it."[30] From Bazin's perspective, then, theater inhibits freedom of perception, which can only be enlivened by the cinema. In contrast with the stage, which is "centripetal" and draws the spectator into its grasp "like a moth," the cinema is "centrifugal, "throwing that spectator out into a limitless and dark world which the camera constantly strives to illuminate."[31] Therefore, a mixed form of the genre, cinematographic theater, is a sure sign of maturity for the cinema and would optimally lead an audience to freedom when encountering the *mis-en-scène* in the adaptation of a production like Olivier's *Henry V,* Welles's *Macbeth,* or Wyler's *The Little*

Foxes. For Bazin, these directors find in the cinema "a complimentary form of theater, a chance to produce theater precisely as they feel and see it."[32]

Much like his theory of theater and cinema, Bazin's notion of adaptation would necessarily include *"un cinéma impur"*—a mixed cinema. His considerations on the dialogical relationship between the theater and the cinema in 1951 led Bazin, that same year, to an important extended essay in which he defined adaptation as resulting in "a restoration of the essence of the letter and the spirit."[33] Yet, as we have seen, Bazin was not only praising the cinema but the genius of the director for opening up perspective for the freedom of the spectator. Bazin saw the auteur as the hinge on which all successful adaptations would rest. "Certainly it would be better if all directors were men of genius," he says in "In Defense of Mixed Cinema"—"presumably then there would be no problem of adaptation."[34] The directorial choices that an auteur like Welles makes in adaptation from play to stage will certainly overshadow the theatrical production by sheer virtue of the expanse of freedom opened for the spectator in confrontation with the filmic *mise-en-scène.*

Bazin appears to intuit that cinematic, directorial authorship is at stake in adaptation throughout his writings. Claiming this authorship may be less of a struggle for a director who adapts a play than one who adapts a novel, because the source text is already cut free from the "literary" text and well into "performance" space. Obviously, Bluestone himself appears to be cognizant for the necessity of reworking the source text when adapting a novel, but does not quite want to credit the director as an author who brings his own unique (performative) style. "It is almost as if the film-maker must destroy the old medium in order to catch its essence in the new."[35] Capturing the "essence," or the essential aspects of the literary, remains the task for the director in Bluestone's analysis, but leaves little room for directorial claims to performance and authorship, certainly nothing like a dialogical arrangement of "mixed cinema" as envisioned by Bazin. Bluestone wants the director to become a *literary* auteur, a synthesizer of two media. But for the other auteurists of the French New Wave, who would take authorship in adaptation further than Bazin, the director seizes the work away from the author of the source text with deliberate performative, stylistic choices.[36] In sum, as Bazin sees the problem of adapting a stage play to the cinema, "the film is either the photographed play, text and all, in which case we have our famous filmed theater. Or the play is adapted to the requirements of the cinema and we are back with the composite that we spoke of above and it is a question of a new work."[37] Searching for a middle ground, Bazin has his own version of this *politique des auteurs:* that these directorial choices do not obliterate the source text completely but contribute dialectically to the kind of stylistics that aggregate toward cinematographic theater.[38] As I have suggested, Bazin's interest in the "impurity" of cinema sets the backdrop for his larger aesthetic concerns, not only with a theory of montage, but the ongoing development of the growth and maturation of cinema. "Bazin speaks from a long tradition of organicism when he suggests that cross-fertilization between the arts is necessary during the early stages of a new art, even while it is striving to individuate itself."[39] At the same time, though, Bazin's organicism plays out dialectically, in which two forms of theater and cinema appear to coexist in creative tension with each other.

We do well at this point to note the difference between Bluestone and Bazin. Bluestone's organicism led him to a metaphor of transformation and even insisting on the "predatory" features of film on the source text. Bazin's organicism, by contrast, is qualitatively different. In "*Le Journal d'Un Cure de Campagne* and the Stylistics of Robert Bresson" as well as "In Defense of Mixed Cinema," Bazin allows for the grasp of both media in dialectic tension rather than resolution, perhaps a bit more poetically realized in the original French: *Plutôt que de prétender se substituer au roman, le film se propose d'exister à côté: de former avec lui un couple, comme une étoile double.*"[40] This type of organicism is rather different from the kind used by Bluestone and the formalists during the same period in the 1950s; the Bluestone School would, one way or another, guard and protect the essential meaning of the literary text, and speak of adaptation as "the alchemist's firing pit," or "that metaphoric process which transforms pieces of fiction into new artistic entities."[41]

When it comes to Bazin's interests in *théâtre cinématographique,* one useful example that comes to mind is Hitchcock's adaptation of Patrick Hamilton's stage play *Rope* (1948). As is well known, Hitchcock deliberately shot it in a series of ten-minute-long takes, all of them stitched or "roped" together rather seamlessly one to the other. The result was a "play" that was conspicuously theatrical yet very cinematic: the camera's perspective was maintained constantly throughout, substituting for a theatrical production that formerly took place in a single room on a stage. At the same time, the set designs for *Rope* make it clear that we are, in fact, watching a stage play: the living room is cramped and confining; the city backdrop is obviously a flat matte piece, lit as it would be on the stage to suggest the passing of the day, and so on. Like Olivier's *Henry V,* the illusion of the theater is disclosed before us, deliberately highlighted. In many ways, then, the camerawork contributes to the theatrical dynamics of the play itself. Thomas Leitch says that the long takes "that are the principal innovation" in *Rope* "might be described as an attempt to be as faithful as possible to the claustrophobia of Patrick Hamilton's stagebound play."[42] The adaptation of *Rope* from stage to screen seems to suggest, once again, that an auteur can take possession of a source text in such a way that it results in a film that both draws from and contributes to the theatrical production. For Bazin, "cinema as digest" means that "one could also understand it as a literature that has been made more accessible through cinematic adaptation, not so much because of the oversimplification that such adaptation entails . . . but rather because of the mode of expression itself, as if the aesthetic fat, differently emulsified, were better tolerated by the consumer's mind."[43] Ultimately, the genius of the auteur provides the necessary medium for allowing film and theater to exist side by side. For Bazin, "Film theater is waiting for a Jean Cocteau to make it a cinematographic theater."[44] Or a John Ford.

Indeed Bazin's musings on the aesthetics of film and theater find an important resonance when John Ford and Dudley Nichols took over Eugene O'Neill's four plays of the sea. From our vantage point, it appears that the early part of Ford's career—the years that took him up to the beginning of the Second World War—was tailor-made for literary prestigious properties. He himself shared kinship with several of the very authors he adapted for the screen, perhaps no one so much as Eugene O'Neill. When *The Long Voyage Home* was screened at the University of Chicago in April 1968 at the invitation of the Student Documentary Film Group, he recalled how the project first began: "I was talking with Eugene O'Neill (he was a very dear friend of mine) about it, and he said, 'Jack, you must have seen my trilogy "The Long Voyage Home"'"[45] And I said I had. So he suggested combining them into a picture, and I said, 'That's a wonderful idea.' So we knocked it out. And after it was finished, United Artists set aside a projection room once a month and Gene would come and watch *The Long Voyage Home*. He loved it. And that's probably the greatest professional compliment I've ever had."[46]

Even in his twilight years, Ford was shrewd enough to maintain that praise from the author of the adapted source text never falls on deaf ears. Indeed, Ford had long been keenly aware of what was at stake in adapting classic literary property. By the time of his reflections on his most arty film in 1968, Ford had become the darling of auteurists like André Bazin at *Cahiers du Cinéma* and later Andrew Sarris, who ranked the director that same year among the "Pantheon" of masters in his book on American Directors. "*The Grapes of Wrath, The Long Voyage Home,* and *How Green Was My Valley* firmly established Ford as *the* Hollywood director despite the extraordinary challenges of Orson Welles and Preston Sturges."[47] By the 1960s, however,

Ford owed a great deal of his artistic reputation not only to Sarris and the auteurist critics but to a cadre of others devoted to a particular genre with which Ford shrewdly allied himself. Together with Frank Nugent, Michael Barkun, Lindsay Anderson, and Peter Bogdanovich, the critical appreciation for Ford was build on something other than the literary prestige productions that had boosted his reputation in the 1930s and early 1940s. It was, of course, these *cinéastes* who help to galvanize Ford's reputation, albeit not around adaptations of literary works but with the western. But that appreciation for the western really has auteurist roots. Bazin thought that with *Stagecoach,* Ford had brought film performance to perfection. According to Charles Maland, "Anderson, Barkun, Bogdanovich, and Sarris were thus crucial in helping to revise John Ford's public reputation in the 1950s and 1960s; he was no longer 'the man who directed *The Informer.*' He was no longer the socially conscious director of *The Grapes of Wrath.* He was, as he presented himself in the 1950 Directors Guild meeting, John Ford, who made Westerns."[48] But before his popular and critical connections with the western, John Ford adapted novels and plays—literary prestige, a well-known and trusted staple in the 1930s after the implementation of the Production Code. By the time Ford would direct his last great literary work, *How Green is My Valley* (1941) at the end of this period, studio head Darryl Zanuck assured the director that "this is going to be a masterpiece . . . not only a classical masterpiece but a masterpiece of surefire commercial entertainment."[49] Therefore it is mostly with literary adaptations that he established himself "as *the* Hollywood director" in the first part of his career through the early 1940s. *The Long Voyage Home* would help bring Ford to the crest of that particular portion of his career.

In Bourdieu's terms, the politics of authorship and cultural power are clearly available categories in Ford's span of work, fostered by his adaptation of literary projects. As Charles Maland has demonstrated very effectively, Ford spent years bestowing on himself an aura of symbolic capital within the matrix of the Hollywood institution. Maland asks how Ford's "reputation developed and what qualities were associated with that reputation over time."[50] That reputation is a hard position to tackle because Ford seems to have been many people in the course of his career. Maland tells us that

> he was sometimes considered an important realist or a gifted film stylist; at other times he was seen as an Irish genius particularly engaged in making films about Irish history, culture, or politics. *The Informer* (1935) was crucial in fashioning both aspects of Ford's image. In the late 1930s and early 1940s he occasionally received praise for making realist, even socially conscious,

films. From the war years on, he was sometimes the patriotic defender of traditional American values. But especially from the late 1940s on, he was the maker of westerns—"the Poet of the Western saga"—or "Pappy" Ford, the paternalistic Hollywood veteran who ruled his set during production with an iron hand but still managed to create a sense of community among the cast and crew.[51]

Moreover, Ford repeatedly reinvented himself, moving from a director of westerns to a high-art director of literary pieces and then to a director of more stylized westerns lionized by auteurists. He created something of an aura around his signature and was, at the very least, ambivalent about his origins and his identity. He changed his name (from Sean Aloysius O'Feeney) and was notoriously difficult to interview, so that the "bare facts of his birth and early years were shrouded in the mists of Celtic fancies."[52] There seems to be nothing short of mystique around Ford's authorship from the start. John Ford's movies are indeed what Sarris calls a "mystery" because, according to Lindsay Anderson, "Ford has delighted to indulge that fondness for mystification, that evasiveness, half mischievous, half poetic, which seems profoundly a part of the national temperament."[53] Although he did not seize a signature in the way that Hitchcock imprinted his films with cameo appearances and his comically ghoulish profile in his television series, it might be said that Ford invented himself as "John Ford" early on and, like his contemporary and fellow Irishman James Joyce, used a series of strategies in order "to forge the uncreated conscience" of their generation. Whether he was in dusty long-sleeve shirts and shaggy kakis in Monument Valley or holding a camera in a publicity shot for the War Department, Ford was in charge of his own image from the start of his career as a director, and seemingly worked to make sure that it worked for him. In a way, therefore, it is not hard to imagine that the creation of "John Ford" becomes analogous to the issues of authorship Ford would later explore in *The Man Who Shot Liberty Valance,* when Ransom Stoddard (James Stewart) asks a reporter if he is going to use the story about Tom Doniphon (John Wayne). Stoddard says, "You're not going to use the story?" To which the reporter replies, "It ain't news. This is the West. When the legend becomes the fact, print the legend."

Issues of authorship undoubtedly played into Ford's personal qualities and interests as a director. By temperament, Ford had a life-long hatred of any kind of authority and eventually made sure that he would have a great deal of control over his films. Throughout his life, he donated funds to support the IRA. He was notoriously cantankerous to interviewers who tried to create a thematic narrative out of his work, and was very clear about who owned his set. On the first day of shooting on *The Informer,* for instance, he gathered the cast together and, as one crewman remembers, took hold of the producer's chin and said, "This is Cliff Reid. He is the producer. Look at him now because you will not see him again on this set until the picture is finished."[54] But Ford's resistance to industry control extended beyond a mere personality trait; his power covered artistic vigilance, and carefully planned prefilm directorial observations reveal the beginnings of a fashioning of a reputation. In an article he published in the *New York Times* a month before the release of *The Informer,* Ford said that as he was leaving the RKO set, he saw some men dressed in "Black and Tan" costumes entering the sound stage, at the orders of a producer, to film additional scenes. The intervention on the part of the studio was enough to prompt Ford into his pioneering efforts at the Guild, and stimulated his emergence as a powerful director.[55] Ford's relationship with the Screen Director's Guild shows his interest in controlling every aspect of his films. In a speech to the Guild in 1933, for example, he said, "I don't think that we are stupid enough to deny that the picture racket is controlled from Wall Street. All right, last year, again I repeat, the most profitable year of all, this Guild was unrecognized. Big finance won the first round. Now they are going to try to win the second round. They are going to keep us unrecognized in bad times . . ."[56]

Despite his problems with authority, however, from the beginning of his career Ford showed his ability to collaborate and negotiate divergent aspects of the Hollywood industry. Ford's talent for vitiating various aspects of the industry into his own "Fordian" style started to emerge by the late 1920s, when he built his early reputation as a director of westerns at Universal at least in part on his relationship with the cowboy actor Harry Carey.[57] Ford helped to shape the big five-reel westerns at Universal, and then went on to play a major role in contributing to Fox's growth and prestige. That studio would also make Ford's own reputation. Fox gradually had been reorganizing its economic and artistic interests, typically playing to blue-collar audiences with films like the melodramatic *Over the Hill* (1920), which grossed an amazing three million dollars. But by the mid-twenties, Fox's audience had become much more diversified—including the Poli circuit, the Midwest circuit, and the West Coast theaters—so that by the end of the 1920s Fox would control more than five hundred houses.[58] According to Richard Koszarski, Fox's decision to expand into the upscale theaters meant that the studio no longer could rely on sentimental family budget westerns, which had previously made a great deal of money. Under the direction of Winfield Sheehan, the

West Coast operations were expanded to a new tract of one hundred acres in Beverly Hills.[59] Ford was able to capitalize on this situation. In 1924, he directed *The Iron Horse,* which was what Richard Koszarski calls "a prestige Western" inspired by Paramount's *The Covered Wagon* a year before.[60] *The Iron Horse* was one of the top-grossing films of the decade, and that film, together with Ford's later picture for Fox, *Four Sons* (1928), provided a blueprint for his subsequent features. As Sarris has observed, "*The Iron Horse* and *Four Sons* do happen to constitute in their obvious opposition a visual dialectic in Ford's style which was to remain unresolved to the end of his career [which is the] dialectic of day and night, sun and shadow, Manifest Destiny and Implacable Fate."[61]

The year 1927 was a watershed period for John Ford. "He began to make pictures on an altogether more ambitious level of artistry, the true characteristics of his mature work began to emerge, and, with smashing commercial success, his position at Fox became preeminent."[62] Ford's reputation as an aesthete began to flourish around this time as well, which occurred simultaneously at a portentous crossroads in the film industry in America. Hollywood's growing interest in the German expressionist art film in the mid-1920s, along with an expanding business capable of using studio expressionist lighting and a shadowy *mise-en-scène,* helped to bolster the industry—and Ford—considerably. Ford, then, gradually helped to assimilate a European art movement into American culture. This negotiation, together with the growing stratification of film audiences who were becoming more and more visually literate—and eventually interested in consuming more-complex photographic spectacle—enabled Ford to establish his reputation as a director of Hollywood art films.

A brief historical inquiry into Ford's encounter with this modernist movement will demonstrate that a goodly amount of his ability to combine politics and aesthetics was the result of his early stylistic absorption of German expressionism into mainstream Hollywood style and technology. In general, we might say that expressionism in art and literature emerged in Germany shortly before World War I and then declined in 1922, before disappearing by 1924.[63] As is well known, it was the German film of the 1920s that was most competitive with Hollywood. Indeed the very excesses of the moody German style would come to signify the art film for the cinematically educated audience and serve to distinguish "arty style" as uniquely different from Hollywood's massified and standardized conventions. But expressionism has a long history in Hollywood as well, beginning in the 1920s with such films as James Cruz's *One Glorious Day* (1922) and *Beggar on Horseback* (1923). According to Barry Salt, the German expressionist artistic movement was singular because "never before or since has an advanced artistic movement entered the commercial cinema so quickly."[64] Salt here is thinking in broad terms; the reception of the German film into Hollywood and its influence on directors like Ford is a bit more complicated. Nowhere does the sway of a modernist movement in America become more evident than in the historical reception of *Das Cabinet des Dr.Caligari* (1920). Michael Budd and Kristin Thompson remind us that while *Caligari* is often viewed as a somewhat avant-garde film, it is really rather similar to the conventional, classically standardized set of discursive practices operative in Hollywood by the 1920s.[65] According to Michael Budd, German cinema like *Caligari* "is systemically unstable rather than subversive."[66] On the other hand, although *Caligari* reminds us of a classical narrative structure, "too many disturbances remain for the film to become a fully efficient part of the commodity culture."[67] *Caligari* succeeded with a New York audience at the Capitol Theater, and then a few years later won canonization as a representative of the newly emerging "art cinema" in the United States and Europe, especially France. In fact, Thompson claims that although the film had its problems with a Los Angeles audience early on (because of either anti-German sentiments or a dislike of modernist style), it seems likely that *Caligari* was an overall success in the United States.[68]

Caligari's greater triumph a few years later owed to its aura as "a revival item springing up in the programs of the art cinemas that were in the cities in the second half of the twenties."[69] The rise of the art film in the United States—perhaps influenced by the rise of the cine-clubs in France, such as Jean Tedesco's *Théâtre du Vieux-Colombier*—would prove an important component to Hollywood filmmaking, and in Ford's career in particular. In America, Symon Gould organized the Film Arts Guild in 1925, eventually renting a small theater in New York, which drew large crowds. By all accounts, *Caligari* was among the largest money makers for these art houses. Moreover, by 1928, art cinemas were doing very well precisely because of revivals that turned films like *Caligari* into "classics" for an increasingly visually literate audience who would pay a bigger price and sit in smaller theaters for the privilege of viewing elite cinema. A Philadelphia newspaper reported on the "sensational trade" with *Caligari* in the newly opened Little Theater: "As far as the number of turn-aways, per patrons accommodated, is concerned, it was the Little Theater on Market Street, run by the Motion Picture Guild, which topped 'Dr. Caligari,' with a capacity of only 216 seats 50 and 75-cent scale, grossed about $5,000. . . . This has amazed local picture people, probably the Stanley company most of all. When 'Caligari' was first released Stanley would not touch it and it was finally booked in a neighborhood uptown."[70]

The success of *Caligari* and the art films with which it became associated did not go unnoticed by some of Hollywood's shrewdest executives interested in studio prestige and expanding the film repertoire for a more highbrow audience. William Fox may have been interested in increasing his own prominence by hiring F. W. Murnau at the exorbitant salary of $125,000 (which increased annually at $200,000). And even though Murnau's *The Last Laugh* (1924) had done miserably in the United States, the German director's presence allowed the studio's staff directors—Ford and others—to straddle "their own predilection for plastic realism with European notions of gestural and architectural stylization."[71]

There were a number of directors at Fox heavily influenced by Murnau's expressionist style, Raoul Walsh and Frank Borzage among them. After he saw *Sunrise* in a rough cut, Ford said that it would be "the greatest motion picture that has been produced [and doubted] whether a greater picture will be made in the next ten years."[72] As one of Ford's recent biographer's writes, "For Ford, Murnau's films were a revelation. Jack's pictures had tended toward a collection of medium shots with beautiful compositions as grace notes, but now he saw what was possible—that film was plastic, that light could be sculpted, and that the essence of cinema was rhythmic succession of striking images. If Universal and Harry Carey had been Ford's primary school, then Murnau constituted Ford's college."[73] Conversely, Murnau found himself positioned as one of Ford's big admirers. The German director loved *Mother Machree,* and he said that *Four Sons* would be "one of the greatest box office values that has ever been shown on the screen . . . I certainly congratulate you on the picture."[74] Appropriating something like a neo-expressionist style would suit Ford well when it came to literary adaptations. Indeed, as Scott Eyman observes, the film that so impressed Murnau, *Mother Machree,* "features stunning lighting, leagues ahead of most other directors. The deep chiaroscuro prefigures the overtly artistic lighting of *The Long Voyage Home,* as in a beautiful shot where a mother and son, unable to find a place to live because they're Irish, dejectedly descend a staircase in deep focus, moving away from the camera."[75] Ultimately, Ford would combine an expressionist technique with literary sources, and this more than guaranteed his reputation as America's "poet laureate," and the director of one of Hollywood's most avant-garde feature films.

At the same moment, Ford was also garnering and cultivating his reputation as a director associated with highbrow art. In an article he wrote for the *New York Times,* "Veteran Producer Muses" in June 1928, Ford speculated on the "Seven Wonders of the World." Maland argues that the article did a great deal to solidify Ford's reputation as something of an aesthete. Even though he would invest a good part of his career making a stylized modernist film technique available for middle-class audiences, "Ford presents himself as a creative artist, even something of an intellectual, as he 'muses' about the film industry. The somewhat elevated diction of the essay, as well as Ford's belief in the creative promise of the movies, presents an image that certainly contrasts with the gruff, informal pragmatist that we more often associate with the later Ford."[76] This would be the John Ford of the 1930s and 1940s, who learned to negotiate modernist aesthetics, making his reputation and career not from the western but from prestige literary properties.[77] *Stagecoach* is the only exception to this speculation, and that film is notable not only because it was Ford's return to the genre after ten years, but also because of the influence the picture had on Bazin and the auteurists. In a certain sense, it was a western with an arty edge, another "prestige Western" like *The Iron Horse,* the perfect symbol for a director who would bring Hollywood's arty feature film to American audiences a year later.

The Cultural Politics of Style

John Ford did not have a theatrical background, but his cultivated reputation, arty style, and collaboration with the urbane Dudley Nichols would help to make his Hollywood literary productions acceptable even to highbrow audiences familiar with authors like Eugene O'Neill. The most obvious example of this phenomenon was his work on RKO's production of an adaptation of Liam O'Flaherty's left-wing novel, *The Informer* (1925). When this film opened in New York City on May 9, 1935, it was a box office failure, but the Academy Awards ultimately helped to sell the film to a wider audience. Subsequently, *The Informer* was revived in 1936 and, according to the *New York Times,* became the "most substantial money maker" for RKO during that period; it would become the most prestigious film for RKO for many years and went into bigger and bigger revivals in the mid to late thirties.[78] According to Tag Gallagher, what delighted critics at the time was *The Informer*'s "single sustained mood, its heavy shadows and muffled sounds, its pedantic, heavy, slow tempos in acting and cutting. . . . *The Informer* stood out as new, different, and artistic, amidst Hollywood's assembly line product."[79] For Mike Cormack, RKO was able to market *The Informer* (and *Mary of Scotland* as well) as a prestige production precisely because Ford was invited as a guest director, with considerable liberty to make the picture. "The resulting stylistic variation became, in a sense, a proof of the films' quality, with the signifying codes of lighting and camera angle connoting, at a second-order level, artistic status."[80] Therefore, *The Informer* became a watershed for an appraisal of Ford, who was lavishly hailed by the critical and artistic establishment. Theodore Huff has described the picture as "much a landmark in the history of the sound film as *The Birth of a Nation* is in the silent era."[81] Even today, *The Informer* has been catalogued as the film that initiated a reputation of what Gallagher calls Ford's period of "idealism." Any art-house revival of Ford's work would be remiss without an inclusion of *The Informer*. Whatever the cause, the success of *The Informer* had nothing to do with O'Flaherty or fidelity to his text, or even, as George Bluestone suggests, endowing the grossest characteristics of the characters "with a nobility, honesty and reasonableness which the originals do not possess."[82] The production had everything to do with Ford's style to negotiate adaptation and his growing reputation as the director to handle such literary property.

After *The Informer*, Ford's reputation grew even more intensely, so that by the time of the release of *The Long Voyage Home* in 1940, he was catalogued by Lewis Jacobs together "with Vidor, Lang, von Sternberg, Mamoulian, Capra, Leroy and Milestone in a chapter of his pioneering film history titled 'Contemporary Directors'"[83] He was known, according to Maland, as Irish, informal, a careful stylist, and a social realist.[84] That combination made for a winning ticket for adapting American's most esteemed playwright, who was himself the son of Irish immigrants, an ingenious stylist and a social realist. Ford would appear to have been an ideal match to bring Eugene O'Neill's sea plays to the screen.[85] Like O'Neill, Ford was an Irish American Catholic who had an extensive interest in folk cultures, particularly those linked to the sea. Indeed, *The Long Voyage Home* may have been an attempt to recapitulate Ford's box-office smash about the sea's revenge on a small island community in *The Hurricane* (1937).[86] Ford's adaptation had an enthusiastic (and rare) endorsement by the author of the source text, Eugene O'Neill himself. O'Neill said that *The Long Voyage Home* was "an exceptional picture, with no obvious Hollywood hokum or sentimental love bilge in it."[87] In fact, after O'Neill first saw the film in July 1940, he sent Ford a telegram that said, "MY CONGRATULATIONS ON A GRAND DEEPLY MOVING AND BEAUTIFUL PIECE OF WORK. IT IS A GREAT PICTURE AND I HOPE YOU ARE AS PROUD OF IT AS I AM."[88] After the release of *The Long Voyage Home*, Robert Sisk suggested a stage revival of *The Hairy Ape* starring Victor McLaglen and to be directed by Ford. Whether or not the offer was made to Ford appears unclear, but he would have to turn the job down anyway, because he was in the midst of Darryl Zanuck's production of *How Green Was My Valley,* after which he left for the navy.[89]

O'Neill was no stranger to Hollywood, and it is often forgotten that the great writer of theater wrote screenplays for Hollywood. As early as 1915, he had sold a screenplay, which has apparently been lost, together with any other film scripts he may have authored.[90] Interestingly enough, O'Neill's biographer says that he "greatly admired" the *Cabinet of Dr.Caligari,* especially for its expressionist technique.[91] Perhaps for this reason, O'Neill was excited about doing a cinematic treatment of *The Emperor Jones.* His plays were adapted rather frequently in the 1920s—*Anna Christie* (1923 and 1930), *Strange Interlude* (1932), *The Emperor Jones* (1933), *Ah, Wilderness* (1935)— although he seemingly had little control over their transition to the screen. "O'Neill was fascinated by the stylized theatricality of filmic Expressionism, a style that would influence his dramatic work but would seldom be used in the film adaptations of his plays."[92] While intensely involved with film culture, O'Neill disdained what he called Hollywood's "hokum" and, according to John Orlandello, wrote *The Movie Man,* a one-act play that deals with an exploitative film producer who travels to Mexico to stage a revolution in order to film it.[93] In this regard, we should note that when he wrote his cycle of one-act sea plays, O'Neill himself was attempting a fusion of the theatrical and the cinematic, in the form of a new "language of the theater." Ernst O. Fink says that the sea plays require a stage director who sought "new ways of making his audience look and listen."[94] At the same time, that convergence of the new was precisely what Ford was accomplishing as a film director in appropriating European style into Hollywood conventions. In adapting O'Neill, Ford would use this expressionism to find a new language of Hollywood, even as O'Neill had experimented with a kind of cinematic theater. Here, once again, we are reminded of Bazin's dialectical interests in "theatrical cinema," or the way that the two media contribute and grow from one another, contributing to a theater that has learned from a filmic dialectic.

From a business perspective, Hollywood's interests in O'Neill were much less ambivalent, but the industry's interest in the theater began to play itself out in shaping a mixed cinema of its own. The movie studios' preoccupation with Broadway was especially keen after the coming of sound, and O'Neill's colorful language and skillful handling of dialects would make for interesting experiments in sound film's early stages. L. B. Mayer realized that he had to hire important playwrights from Broadway, and as early as 1928 sent Harry

Rapf to secure talent from New York.[95] *Anna Christie* (1930) was adapted by MGM as a Garbo vehicle, paving her entrance into the sound film. An award-winning, Broadway playwright by way of Provincetown, O'Neill represented prestigious property for a Hollywood searching for literary capital. He was, in fact, only a few years away from receiving ultimate prestige—the 1936 Nobel Prize for Literature. Ford undoubtedly was attracted to O'Neill because the two men explored similar themes in their work. For example, in his famous 1955 interview with Jean Mitry published in *Cahiers du Cinéma*, Ford explained why his pictures consistently deal with individuals tossed by chance into dramatic or tragic circumstances. Ford said that he wanted to make the characters "aware of each other by bringing them face to face with something bigger than themselves. The situation of the tragic moment forces men to reveal themselves, and to become aware of what they truly are. The device allows me to find the exceptional in the commonplace."[96] Similarly, a large body of O'Neill's work deals with a variation of "entropic" naturalism.[97] As one critic puts it, O'Neill remained "profoundly aware of the fact that whatever future the individual may plot for himself—future which implies a process of becoming—it is accompanied by an inevitable physical decline, a process of unbecoming. The reality of entropy is the one unambiguous fact about the future of any individual."[98]

O'Neill's sea plays reflect many of the themes present in his larger oeuvre: expressions of fatalism, or the devolution of the human subject, set adrift and alone. Mary Tyrone in *Long Day's Journey into Night* (1942) is a study of gradual fragmentation and disintegration, as she gradually slips into the darkness of addiction. In her pathetic physical and mental devolution, Mary propels the other characters in the play in motion toward their own entropic despair and alienation. The loss of community, humanity, and self-respect plagues O'Neill's characters as if all of them were set adrift, poised between memory and their irresistible fate. The shipmates on the *S.S. Glencairn* are docked off a West Indian island in *The Moon of the Caribbees* and in *Bound East for Cardiff*, and the crew of *In the Zone* are somewhere in the middle of the Atlantic. In the last of the plays, paranoia envelops the crew, who take one of their fellow shipmates prisoner for being what they think is a German spy, and who sadistically read his love letters to him. All the sea plays seem to involve us in the spectacle of an unmasking of the civilized subject, a Darwinian devolution into the "hairy ape." This preoccupation with the "primitive" is most evident in *The Emperor Jones* (1920) where, as Clifford Leech observes, "O'Neill takes his character progressively backwards into his personal history and then into the history of his people."[99] On another level, such a journey is also yet another example of a voyage into the heart of darkness, cloaked as a kind of entropic striptease. As part of a late-nineteenth– and early twentieth–century literary movement, O'Neill participated—during the 1920s especially—in an American version of naturalism derived in part from Ibsen. While many of his plays during the 1920s (perhaps, most obviously *The Emperor Jones*) experimented with the techniques of naturalism and expressionism, O'Neill saw himself as a character-driven playwright and, for instance, identified Yank of the sea plays as a particularly successful creation because the audience could identify with him.[100] Although *The Emperor Jones* was O'Neill's first expressionist play, he also seems to have had "two minds about Expressionism"; basically a classic realist, O'Neill even claimed that he did not believe that "an idea can be readily put over to an audience except through characters."[101]

Gypo Nolan in *The Informer* approximates an O'Neill character, and the story of a traitor who informs on his friends to collect a reward during the Irish Civil War of 1922 deals very naturalistically with the forces of fate, human choice, and tragic fall. With a foreboding sense of future doom surrounding them, characters in Ford and O'Neill resemble shipmates of the *Pequod* in *Moby Dick*: they are captives in a small, violent world that exposes their vulnerability and their humanity. In some ways, Ford's use of the individual's relationship to the community—so evident in his best features—functions also to reveal a restless and unprotected heart. Crucially, though, that damaged heart is revived, reanimated, and restored at the end of Ford's films. Redemption is still possible for Gypo. Consider *How Green Was My Valley* (1941), a story about the disintegration of a Welsh family of poor miners as seen through the eyes of a young boy; the tragic outcome of the film is somewhat redeemed by the boy's growth into manhood and his ability to make sense of a lost world through memory; it is a coming of age story shaped by a seemingly fatalistic environment. We might also recall the savage destruction of the Edwards family in *The Searchers* (1956), which ends with the racist Ethan's eventual repentance and Debbie's restoration to the (white) community. *The Long Voyage Home* shows that Ford performs similar narrational strategies, shaping savage entropy into heroic destiny in the context of community. At the very beginning of the film we sense the foreboding grip of fate that lies ahead for those who sail to the sea. The seamen are poised as if on a tinderbox, straddled between land and sea, life and death, as they skim along the dark ocean alert to any sign of a German U-boat. For both Ford and O'Neill isolation would be the test case for the human subject's alienation from and dependence on community. The ship's community in Ford's *The Long Voyage Home* is desperate, brutal, and even barbaric; but it is also courageous, and the mood of the film gradually shifts from ugliness to beauty. In a certain sense, Ford spent his career taming the "primitive" for Hollywood, and in his adaptation of the plays he manages to redeem O'Neill's desperate voyagers.

Ford would bring his own directorial and interpretive style to bear throughout the production of *The Long Voyage Home*, negotiating something like Bazin's idea of "cinematographic theater" in Hollywood. When Peter Bogdanovich asked Ford in 1967 if it was his intention to make *The Long Voyage Home* claustrophobic, the director said that "we purposely kept it in confined spaces—that was what the story called for. Life on a ship is claustrophobic, but you get accustomed to it."[102] Anchored off the coast in the West Indies, the all-male crew in *The Long Voyage Home* search off the bow of their ship for an irreclaimable world, not unlike the kind of Welsh utopia that the young Huw Morgan recalls in what Sarris calls the "past indefinite" of *How Green Was My Valley*. The opening of the picture thematizes the pain of absence during war in what we might understand as a "present indefinite." To the strains of "Harbor Lights" the film opens with the titles " . . . Men who live on the Sea never change—for they live in a lonely world apart as they drift from one rusty tramp steamer to the next, forging the life-lines of Nations."[103] When we meet the crew, we find that they are haunted by personal loss. The married, upper-class Brit called Smitty (Ian Hunter) keeps a cache of hidden letters from his family, and the lower-class Swede, Ole Johnson (John Wayne), longs to return home to his native country. By the end of the film we realize that the crew has been living only on memories because, as Sarris says, "the fog-shrouded London docks mark also the end of all the men's illusion of life on shore."[104]

The first half of the film involves the major action of O'Neill's *In the Zone*, and the second half lays a special emphasis on the one-act stage version of *The Long Voyage Home*. The film as a whole is structured around a community wrapped in complex personal and communal shadows. According to studio records, the conventional VLS was suppressed, and in its place was positioned a complicated and intricate process shot of an exterior "tropical black opening . . . with the background to be done in miniatures."[105] As Lindsay Anderson has observed, the *S.S. Glencairn* is haunted by a quality of isolation, something characteristic of the film's overall mood that it shares with *The Informer*. There is only one shot in the film of the ship actually at sail.[106] In the opening sequence, we see the native women in the foreground, dreamily and restlessly leaning against tropical trees and looking off in the distances toward a ship anchored in the horizon. The island women silently contemplate the distant music as the men of the ship look longingly into the night off the edge of the *S.S. Glencairn*. Rarely has there been a more eroticized opening in a classic Hollywood film, all the more so because of the heightening of tensions created by the disjuncture between land and sea, men and women, civilization and the "primitive." All of these exist within an expressive use of off-screen/onscreen relations that recalls Ford's *The Lost Patrol* (1934), which never shows the enemy on screen.[107] In *The Long Voyage Home,* the crew's sexual longing is depicted as empty space: as they look out in darkness, unsatisfied and lonely. The opening sequence remains a fascinating and stunning dialogue between light and darkness, seemingly without resolution.

Matthew Bernstein notes that during the first five minutes, information about characters and their motivations is withheld from us."[108] Not only is this a film about alienation—men without women, an Englishman without a family, a Swede without a home—but it is also a movie that keeps the audience at a slight loss, a bit alienated from the conventional Hollywood feature that communicates much more directly to the spectator. As Bernstein observes, "we see events whose significance remains ambiguous because we are denied a knowledge of their causes. Multiple interpretations of the sailors' actions suggest themselves. Perhaps they are restless to meet the island women, but the eyelines do not match in the alternating shots of the crew and the women. Perhaps the sailors' behavior expresses their general longing for the land, for liquor, or, as one critic has argued, for death."[109]

In isolating this particular segment of *The Long Voyage Home,* we are able to notice that Ford creates an extremely interesting interplay between the techniques of proscenium theater and the techniques of Hollywood movies. But this dynamic between theater and cinema extends well beyond Ford's adaptation of O'Neill and into his larger corpus, not only in a film like *The Lost Patrol* but especially in his westerns. Peter Lehman's analysis of three of Ford's best westerns is instructive in showing how Ford often exploits off-screen events for dramatic purposes. For Lehman, Ford's filmic space is structured around absence,[110] in much the same way theater uses "off-stage" material. Ford stretches out the off-screen space for a good while in the first part of the film, using the island music and its dramatic effect on the characters (Smitty is haunted by his memories from just listening to the sounds from the natives). On the thematic level, *The Long Voyage Home* is also an eloquent statement about absence and loss in the human heart, which affects all the characters on the ship. The gulf between onscreen and off-screen space becomes even further integrated into the plot and the characters, and in the case of the cultivated Brit, Smitty, part of his torment. As Cocky (Barry Fitzgerald) tells him "When a man goes to sea, he ought to give up thinking about things on shore. . . . Something on land has still got a hold of you." This sense of absence is reinforced not only by the off-screen/onscreen space but by Ford's characteristic emphasis on nostalgia and memory.

Eventually, we are given all the relevant information about the characters, but at first the technique is disorienting. Ford appears to be at pains not to engage filmed theater, to break up theatrical space with the camera and standard Hollywood shot/reverse montage conventions. According to the revised script, Ford even changed what Nichols had planned as a point of view shot of the sailors to the island women.[111] In modifying the traditional Hollywood convention of reverse-angle cutting, Ford expresses the condition of men who are caught in a harbor seemingly without much hope, captivated both by absence and desire. In a certain sense, he creates a cinema—indeed a theater—of loneliness longing for the restoration of coherence and community. The very absence of film conventions forces the audience to recognize that we are in a different theatrical space, perhaps something closer to a stage, yet well aware of its conventions. Therefore it seems that from the very start, Ford wants to, in Bazin's terms, relieve "realism of that which makes it the foe of theatrical illusion."[112] Loneliness and desire are approximated in astonishing gaps and not by the conventions of "filmed theater." Ford accentuates the theatrical aspects that O'Neill himself had in mind. At the end of *The Moon of the Caribbees,* O'Neill's stage directions say that, "There is silence for a second or so, broken only by the haunted, saddened voice of that brooding music, faint and far-off, like the mood of the moonlight made audible."[113]

Additionally, by tampering with the principles of Hollywood formal narrative structures in the film's opening sequence, Ford shows us what really is at stake in this O'Neill adaptation. The deprivation of information—the skewed continuity, the lack of a sutured closure (especially of eye-line matches), and reserved point of view—create a feeling of art cinema. In this context it is useful to recall the early shots of Gypo Nolan in *The Informer,* where Gypo stands outside a Dublin pub admiring the tenor singing a folk song. We expect a series of eye-line matches—because the strength of the film is largely its ability to account for the protagonist's subjectivity—but suddenly there is a long shot on the other side of the 180-degree line that distances us from Gypo.[114] The same technique is employed during the first ten minutes of *The Long Voyage Home* and, in similar fashion, there is a turn toward convention and resolution. As in *The Informer,* the film moves from art convention to classical convention, from fatalism to hope, from silence to speech. In a way, the island women depicted in the opening sequence resemble the O'Neill primitives in *The Moon of the Caribbees* or, for that matter, even the "real black type" that was to be Kurtz's lover in *Heart of Darkness*. At the same time, although this opening shot in *The Long Voyage Home* is a process shot, the composition hints at the kind of deep focus shot Bazin admired: there are really three separate "panels" of information: one of the native women in a three-quarter shot, looking toward the camera in shadow; there is another on the right in a long shot; between them both is the steamer. Clearly, the shot is meant to appear like deep-focus photography. Here, once again, is the Bazinian ideal, maximizing the freedom for the viewer, even as the feeling of loss overtakes the crew. With island music hauntingly sung in the background, displaced eye-line matches and ambivalent point of view only reinforce the expectation of the exotic world of the unknown, the native Other, the allure of the heart of darkness.

When the women are brought onboard the *Glencairn,* however, the form of the movie becomes less disorienting, but still uncomfortable for stylistic reasons. The opening sequence takes us from the drowsy, steamy world of silence, desire, and island primitivism to the civilized—and very cramped world—of the ship. The lonely space felt early on in the film is accentuated by the claustrophobic atmosphere on the ship, thanks to the compositions of the actors in close groupings (rather than shot/reverse shot sequencing) and art director's James Basevi's set pieces. That enclosed space is underlined by the British officers' harassment of the crew while they sleep, pointing a flashlight in their crowded sleeping quarters. The ceilings are low and the men are grouped together tightly in the compositions. When the women come onboard the ship, the sense of the small space seems almost overwhelming. Gregg Toland also sets the camera at low angles, often at floor level, allowing the characters to walk into deep shadows on the deck of the ship. In an interview for *The Screen Writer* (December 1947), Toland said that "*The Long Voyage Home* was a mood picture. Storywise . . . it was a series of compositions of the mood of the men aboard the ship. It was a story of what men felt rather than what they did."[115] The photography and editing add to the edgy feeling of the men trapped on a ship. In the first sequence on the *S.S. Glencairn* before it docks, each shot seems to lack conventional continuity altogether, not in any radicalized Eisensteinian way, of course—the *S.S. Glencairn* is not the battleship *Potemkin*—but the lack of eye-line matches and relative absence of the shot/reverse shots (especially in the early portions sequence that takes place on the ship), that were normative practice for

Hollywood editing, creates a relatively discontinuous, uncomfortable feeling to this portion of the film.

These expressionistic details eclipse our expectation of Hollywood realism: we are deeply confined to a space, rather like a stage where the camera only makes the area more intensely like a stage. In an effort to partner—and reveal—theatrical conventions, Ford appears to have deployed off-screen space on several occasions to intensify the realism of formal theatrical effects. Additionally, there are times in the film when the characters are positioned in such a way that off-screen space mimicks theatrical "stage right" and "stage left." For example, when the island girls board the ship, Smitty flirts with one of them. Ford keeps the camera static and photographs the characters in a centered, three-quarter shot. Yank comes into the scene as if from stage right, then leaves briefly and returns. During this time, the camera remains fixed, with no effort at a realistic, cinematic convention. As in a stage play, a three-dimensional space does not seem to exist around the characters.

Ford occasionally shifts to another kind of theatrical device as well. In one shot, for instance, Cocky is knocked to the ground as he struggles in a fight with another crew member. We catch the action of the fall at a peculiar angle, as if we were watching from our first-row seats in a theater, as he says, "You done that on purpose, you hairy ape!" There is another example of theatrical point of view toward the end of the film when the men enter a tavern and sing *When Irish Eyes Are Smiling*. Once again, the shot suggests a kind of first-row seat from the theater looking toward a proscenium stage. In a way, both of these scenes call our attention to the original source material and may even suggest a certain homage to O'Neill. In another sense, Ford is recalling theatrical conventions to make us aware, in the tradition of *Henry V,* that we are watching a play.

Once the ship docks in Baltimore, the cinematography shifts to a deep-focus style and presents us with a contrast to the ship's claustrophobic environment. In fact, the foggy shadows are the first place of refuge for Smitty, who tries to escape. Ford keeps the camera rolling as the man disappears into the infinite night, only to be captured later by police, who hastily return him to the ship before it is off again. The crew sails to England with a load of dynamite to be delivered there; they are jumpy at the thought of German U-boats. Even the night and fog cannot befriend or protect the crew, and they depart once again to face further claustrophobia from fear and then paranoia. Ford allows these tensions to build until the first real climax in the film: the confrontation with Smitty, who is falsely accused of spying for Germany. The sequence is shot in a series of intense close-ups, alternating with the reading of Smitty's letter from his wife, exposing his drinking problem and poignantly inviting him to return home. Suddenly, the crew realizes not only their shame, but the reason for Smitty's anxiety over returning to land all along. Soon after, the pathos doubles when Smitty is finally killed by German aircraft. In keeping with pre–World War II politics, *The Long Voyage Home* is almost exaggerated in its support of English heroics—the flourish of the Union Jack on Smitty's coffin becoming what British critics C. A. Lejeune and Lindsay Anderson described as "an unspeakably vulgar gesture."[116] At the same time, the camera's close-ups on the personal emotional details during this particular sequence suggest a marvelous contrast to the previous segment of the film, with its heavily drawn alliances to theatrical space. Ford's camera becomes a witness to the sinful entropy that occurs from paranoia and suspicion.

The rest of the film belongs to Ole Olson (John Wayne) and the crew's adventures on the docks in England. The fated devolution and inevitable decline that O'Neill forecast for his characters has already been suggested in the first part of the film: Smitty's descent into alcohol abuse and secrecy separates him first from his family, then the land, and eventually the community. Another kind of fate awaits the crew who run "free" on the London docks, only to discover the traces of their own entropic decline as well. Ole, long protected by the crew, is lured into a delay by a whore orchestrated by a dandified rogue hired to shanghai him to work on the *Amindra*. The innocent Ole unwittingly drinks too much and is carried away to the ship. Although he eventually is rescued from the *Amindra* by his shipmates, Driscoll (Thomas Mitchell) is himself captured and stowed away as crewmember. In the end we learn that while Ole did sail home to Stockholm, the *Amindra* was torpedoed and sunk in the English Channel. The discarded newspaper that floats down the channel with the unhappy headlines about the fate of the doomed ship—and Driscoll with it—reminds us that the crew has been in the grip of "Implacable Fate" all along, from the first moments of unquenchable desire in the "silent" first sequence.

Early on in this last portion of the film, we see a man begging for money on the London docks with a sign that reads: "I am totally blind." The man and his message stands as a fitting emblem for the trajectory of the film, which wants us to recognize the power of fated decline in the midst of entrapment and the constraints placed upon human freedom. Seemingly blind to their own destiny, the crew moves on, guided by instinct, bad choices, and fate itself. Toland's cinematography sets the mood and the technique for understanding what is at stake for the spectator in sharing the sense of the world of naturalism that inhabits *The Long Voyage Home*. The exterior shots later in the film open up a *mise-en-scène* that contrasts mightily with the earlier claustrophobic compositions on the ship. At the same time, the familiar Fordian interior shots allow the spectator, in Bazin's words, "to exercise at least a minimum of personal choice. It is from his attention and his will that the meaning of the image in part derives."[117] *The Long Voyage Home* sustains what David Bordwell calls a high degree of "frontality," or what he refers to as "several significant planes of depth, all in focus, [in which] there is an exaggeratedly enlarged foreground plane, usually a face [and] this has the effect of making the shot notably static: all the figures are visible from only one vantage point; any camera or figure movement would impede our sightlines."[118] In certain ways, the composition of the film allows the spectator to participate in the psychic space of the characters themselves, who are alternately cramped and liberated. The camera opens up a freeing space for the viewer that the theatrical production would have left to the world of illusion.

Yet in the midst of such visual freedom provided by the cinematography, we recognize that the fate that awaits all appears to be looming—drunkenness, capture, death. From the first moments of the film, we have been aware that human longing is wedded to the sea, chained forever to a vast chasm of desire. The caged parrot that the overly protected Ole conspicuously carries suggests the very lack of freedom that seems to be an illusion; he is protected from his fate by the community—until next time. Like the haunting streets themselves, the space only *appears* to be infinite, but the fog conceals the presence of rogues waiting for a deal or police patrolling at the margins marshalling behavior. Ford's camera has implicated the spectator in the very process of O'Neill's fated entropy: the film's dynamics allow us to sense that their fate is ours, their urgent longing our own. The only refuge for the crew at the end is community: Ole returns to his family, and the crew comes back to the ship, though scarred from loss.

The Long Voyage Home reflects, then, what Scott Eyman calls "O'Neill's aura of ordained doom."[119] But this alliance owes a great deal to the dialectic that Ford was able to bring to the sea plays. Indeed, in "In Defense of Mixed Cinema," Bazin says that "the differences in aesthetic structure make the search for equivalents an even more delicate matter, and thus they require all the more power of invention and imagination from the film-maker who is truly attempting a resemblance. . . . But one knows how intimate a possession of a language and of the genius proper to it is required for a good translation."[120] Ford's authorship of the film, implicitly endorsed by Bazin, was more explicitly made the director's own when the film was released. In 1940, Harry R. Salpeter wrote in *Esquire* that with *The Long Voyage Home*, "Art Comes to Hollywood."[121] Salpeter was referring to a series of paintings associated with the film that were featured in *American Artist*. According to Matthew Bernstein, producer Walter Wanger saw the opportunity to sell *The Long Voyage Home* as "high art," and "to appeal to 30 million well-educated Americans who refused to attend Hollywood movies" by associating it with a group of painters. He undertook an unusual publicity campaign designed to appeal to those thirty million well-educated Americans who refused to attend Hollywood movies: he spent $50,000 to commission nine canvases by contemporary regionalist painters. Thomas Hart Benton, Grant Wood, Raphael Soyer, Georges Schreiber, George Biddle, James Chaplin, Ernest Fiene, Robert Phillip, and Luis Quintanilla depicted scenes and characters from the film, which were exhibited in galleries in thirty-five cities around the country as the film went into exhibition.[122] The artists were given complete freedom of what to paint in the film, were provided with their own studios on the movie lot, and were allowed continual access to the sets and casts at any time.[123]

Wanger was certainly correct in seeing in Ford's films a kind of arty commentary on folk culture. *The Informer,* for example, is not much concerned with O'Flaherty's Nighttown Dublin, which is a "place of the forgotten ones . . . populated by degraded men and criminals, dope addicts, broken human souls."[124] Far from presenting a depressing landscape of poverty, the film depicts the folklorish and randy Irish in conflict with the police. Wanger's use of regionalist paintings to market *The Long Voyage Home* is consistent with Ford's populism, and it demonstrates the way in which the late 1930s were more and more informed by an ideology of left-wing realism. *The Grapes of Wrath,* a film that helped to shape *The Long Voyage Home,* suggests a window into Depression-era America as well, albeit stylized once again by Toland's cinematography and Ford's communitarian spirit. William Stott and others have reminded us of the very dramatic increase in a kind of populist-realist photography in the late thirties.[125] The perfection of the German minicam in the United States, together with faster film and more sophisticated lenses, allowed for an overall interest in greater depth of field and naturalistic detail. Such technological achievements no doubt account for the success of *Life* magazine and its photographers—Alfred Eisenstaedt, Tom McAvoy, and Peter Stackpole—all of whom used 35mm cameras for their candid shots, an important selling feature for the magazine.[126] Toward the end of the period, when Gregg Toland published his famous article on shooting *Citizen Kane* in *American Cinematographer* (February 1941), he was addressing not only his role in a particularly notable film, but a visual culture itself, fully formed. Toland appears to have intuited the growing collateral interest American film culture was having in realistic, deep-focus photography and documentary detail. He called his piece "Realism for *Citizen Kane*."[127] Toland said that in their discussion of preproduction planning, both he and Welles felt that "the picture should be brought to the screen in such a way that the audience would feel it was looking at reality, rather than merely at a movie."[128] Toland himself became a kind of celebrity in the mid-thirties, publishing articles later on how he "broke the rules." Those transgressive artistic codes that functioned in *Kane* were surely circulating in *The Long Voyage Home* as well, and available as we have seen from the first moments of the film. Indeed, the deep-focus photography that Bazin praised for allowing more ambiguity, or what Mike Cormack calls "complexity," had its ideological ramifications as well. "The increased autonomy of Hollywood in the late-thirties and early forties allowed deep focus to be used and its specific uses serve to take films another step away from the simplicity and clarity of the more restrained paradigm of the middle of the decade."[129]

According to Scott Eyman, United Artists "attempted to tie the picture's fate to the rising public profile of its director. 'John Ford gives your box-office drama with the kick of dynamite!' proclaimed the pressbook enthusiastically, if ungrammatically. 'The genius of John Ford becomes the business partner of your showmanship in realizing sweeping profits.'"[130] Despite Wanger's efforts, the film did rather poorly at the box office. It cost $689,459 to produce and lost $224,336. When seen from our own perspective, however, Wanger's and United Artist's problem in promoting the film appears to be a failure to realize exactly what they were selling. Deep-focus photography helped create a strange alchemy, a sort of literary-visual art. By this time, it is reasonable to say that the literary and the visually artful trafficked together in certain areas of American popular culture. Wanger seems to have capitalized on this development, but the attempt was in some ways unsuccessful in appealing to middle-class audiences more comfortable with standard Hollywood conventions. Then again, Wanger was counting on the folkloric quality of artistic regionalism to sell a film to an educated audience. Far from appealing to a cultivated segment of the American population, however, Wanger's exhibition—which Milton J. Brown of New York University called "the Wanger Circus"—only alienated them.[131] Even so, the film itself made some headway into the critical establishment. *Time* reported that *The Long Voyage Home* was "the best picture since *The Informer*." Several critics praised the film's artistry, particularly its cinematography. *The Hollywood Reporter* said that *The Long Voyage Home* was "about as high an art of motion picture as one would find in many days of looking at pictures."[132] By the 1950s, the film became important for some auteurists like Jean Mitry, who linked *The Long Voyage Home* together with *Stagecoach* as characteristic of Ford's movies that "exalte la solidarité humaine."[133] For later critics viewing the film as an adaptation, *The Long Voyage Home* became a chance to revisit the film/theater divide, principally examining the effective use of the *mise-en-scène* and related narrative issues. Frederick Wilkins begins his inquiry into the adaptation of *The Long Voyage Home* and *Long Day's Journey into Night* by saying that "neither the theatrical nor the cinematic method of adaptation assures a successful film. It is what the filmmaker does with the space, in terms of visual and aural images, that determines effectiveness."[134] But at the time, the film also seemed altogether too arty for middle-class audiences. In fact, Walter Wanger's secretary screened a postproduction version of the film and said that the opening titles helped "a lot in cleaning up the beginning and it does seem much shorter but you'll forgive me I think if I tell you I just can't like it. Perhaps it is too highbrow."[135]

That observation may be less of an estimation of Ford's success than a hint of an interest in another kind of feature film that would eventually dominate the industry, a mode of expression that would, in a way, bring O'Neill's fated entropy into the fore once again. With part of the world at war, the industry would find itself in the grip of something like "Implacable Fate," Sarris's expression once used to describe Ford's films. Indeed the interest in the literary, particularly the classics, that so dominated the era of the 1930s would begin to decline. In another sense, the language of the visual and an interest in another kind of performance style—much akin to *The Long Voyage Home*—would come to be the hallmark of the 1940s and 1950s. Ford would devote only one more feature to a literary enterprise—*How Green Was My Valley*—before his own entry into Fate's grasp at the start of World War II. Hollywood would then find itself decisively turning to documentary style, pulp fiction, and a new genre—film noir—which was not unlike the stylized, "ordained doom" already brought to the screen in the fated collaboration between Eugene O'Neill and John Ford.

5

Canon Fire

John Huston's The Red Badge of Courage *(1951)*

I can't do any more than make a picture that I
believe in and hope that there are enough like me to
want to see the picture too. I certainly don't have an
audience in mind. I am my own audience in a sense. The
very idea of trying to manipulate—even to entertain—an
audience when you get down to the specifics is quite
beyond me—or trying to imagine what an audience
would like. By God, I don't know what my best friend or
wife or son or daughter would like. I only know what I
like, and I hope that there are enough like me
to feel the way I do about it.

—John Huston on cinema

John Huston's original version of Stephen Crane's nineteenth-century, naturalistic Civil War novella, *The Red Badge of Courage*,[1] had every
chance of becoming one of the finest prestige pictures in the late studio era.
A fruitful discussion of *Red Badge* has already occurred with Lillian Ross's
shrewd production history, originally published in *The New Yorker* in 1952.[2]
But a distance exceeding fifty years has given us further insights. In retrospect, the film clearly belongs to one of the more turbulent periods in the
history of entertainment; it was made during the Korean War, at the height
of a Red Scare, when the old studio system was in deep economic trouble
because of the rise of television. Therefore *The Red Badge of Courage* straddles
two important cultural movements, one of them identified with New Deal
politics and the other with cold war anxiety about the Russian acquisition

of the atom bomb, leading to what William Graebner calls "a more sober and conservative male look."[3] The former attitude guided Huston's director's cut of *Red Badge;* the latter informed MGM's revision. Interestingly, the film on the fault line located beneath very shaky political ground—indeed it was literally broken up and then selectively reassembled by the producers. Huston's premier release print—which will be partially reconstructed here through existing archival script material—exemplifies the liberal, communal attitudes of the 1930s and 1940s, along with a strong indictment of war and ironic treatment of martial heroism. The revised (studio) version displays the conservative politics of the early 1950s; it presents the enemy as fearful and it uses the literary canon to reinforce patriarchal values.

As with literary adaptations, the film industry found historical films useful from the beginning, providing cinema with an aura of prestige and respectability. As we know, the early experiments with film were associated with recording pageants, theatrical spectacles, military formations, sporting events—occasions as mundane as a kiss between married couples or as exotic as a state funeral. As early as 1911, the Edison Manufacturing Company planned an "American History on Film" series that would deal with "the events immediately preceding the Revolutionary War and carry it to the present day."[4] Such films included a look at the historical past as a backdrop for important historical personages. These would include Napoleon (*The Price of Victory: A Story of Napoleon Bonaparte,* 1911), John Paul Jones (*The Star-Spangled Banner: The Life of John Paul Jones,* 1910) and Abraham Lincoln (*His First Commission: A Story of Abraham Lincoln,* 1911).[5]

In their study of Vitagraph's production of "historical qualities," William Uricchio and Roberta E. Pearson note that, unlike "literary qualities," "Historical films had no 'Ur-text' to point to as the ultimate authoritative source but derived instead from myriad and varied textual expressions associated with Washington and Napoleon . . . historical texts were circulated by many of the same institutions of cultural reproduction as literary texts, such as schools, the advertising industry, and uplift organizations. Historical texts also circulated through such other venues as museums, patriotic organizations, and public celebrations."[6]

These historical films would eventually morph into the prestigious "biopic" genre of the 1930s and 1940s. According to Marcia Landy, "historical films employed major stars and celebrated significant events in the forging of national identity. These films frequently served as a form of collective morality as well as source of morale. They were often produced on a grand scale in the mode of 'monumental history,' and they have been instrumental in establishing conventions about the commercial cinema's uses of spectacle in its treatment of the past."[7]

Undoubtedly, the Civil War has figured prominently in mass culture as a way to showcase the towering figure of Abraham Lincoln as a kind of folk hero and national savior, along with the Civil War itself as a landmark in the nation's identity. Jim Cullen has argued that there has been a long connection between American popular culture and the Civil War, which he describes as a very "reusable past." "Popular culture has played a critical role in preparing for, fighting, and remembering the Civil War; the two were entwined long before the war and long after it. The technological, economic, and social developments that made possible so many forms of popular culture—from religious tracts and dime novels to recorded music and film—were also the source of an often sharp debate over the nature, and future, of the nation."[8]

In this regard, historical films are part of the same discursive circulation of cultural reproductions as other institutions. Films about the Civil War that may be based on a historical novel form just one of the many textual expressions that operate not from a single source, but collaterally and intertextually from the circulation of a variety of sources streaming from that national event. In the language of Bakhtin, films about the war between the North and South are "subject to an artistic reworking" of other texts through a complex dialogue of past and present.[9] It is telling that two of the most influential—and controversial—historical feature films produced in the first half of the twentieth century both concern adaptations of historical novels set in the Civil War, and are linked with a legacy of American racism and misogyny.[10] The enormous popularity of D. W. Griffith's *Birth of a Nation* (1915) was based only in part on the celebrated success of its source texts (Thomas Dixon's *The Leopard's Spots*, 1903, and *The Clansman*, 1905, sold more than one million copies); the film tapped into deep-seated notions of race and sexual identity as well. According to Cullen, Dixon's historical fiction replaced Harriett Beecher Stowe's "moral indictment with a new master narrative."[11] The film's accomplishment almost certainly owed to the rise of the Ku Klux Klan during and after World War I and the rather universal, essentialist history of Reconstruction at the time, which portrayed the decades following the Civil War as "a never-ending picnic for African Americans."[12] Such racist attitudes were in place in the 1930s as well, when Griffith's film was rereleased in a synchronized version to sensational controversy and protests. As Donald Bogle has argued, Civil War black stereotypes pervaded popular culture and feature films in the Depression era, reinforcing a long-held prejudice. "Griffith's 'faithful souls' were shamelessly naïve representations of the Negro as Child or the Negro as Watered-Down Noble Savage. But these characters would make their way through scores of other Civil War epics, and they were to leave their mark on the characterizations of Clarence Muse in *Huckleberry Finn* (1931) and *Broadway Bill* (1934) and of Bill Robinson in *The Little Colonel* (1935) and *The Littlest Rebel* (1935)."[13]

Cullen notes that the circulation of post–Civil War attitudes made Margaret Mitchell's *Gone with the Wind* a phenomenal best-seller, and its adaptation the biggest blockbuster Hollywood had ever known, pulling in receipts that topped $20 million. Mitchell herself claimed a great debt to Dixon, writing in 1936 that she was "practically raised on your books, and love them very much."[14] Read from the perspective of the 1930s, *Gone with the Wind* mythologized the Civil War as a southern catastrophe and a vanished chivalric civilization. "Mitchell made slaveholding whites the true victims of the Civil War. In her rendition, the south was hounded by fanatics, cornered into defending a way of life, overrun by alien invaders, and forced to endure a harsh (and ridiculous) occupation."[15] Redeployed for a film audience in the Great Depression, Selznick's production of *Gone with the Wind* featured collective ideals about the survival of whiteness and wealth after the communal trauma of war. Scarlett O'Hara became a kind of icon, not only for the South, but for the American (white) woman who had risen from the economic dust heap to the promise of Reconstruction. When the film premiered in Atlanta on December 15, 1939, *Newsweek* reported that there would be a public holiday and that the Confederate banner would fly beside the American flag at the state capitol building.[16] Clearly, Selznick's promotion of the film included an invitation for the public to participate in the adaptation process itself, by running a contest in local newspapers vying for votes for a casting decision as to who should play Scarlett O'Hara. As Thomas Leitch has observed, *Gone with the Wind* extended its legibility well beyond its theatrical space, and long before the filming began, marketing synergy was in place. "Products marketed in connection with the film's release included paper dolls, collectible dolls, dress patterns, bonnets, hairnets, jewelry, perfume, postcards, board games and chocolates. . . . In a final twist the phenomenon of *Gone with the Wind* has become the basis of numerous tributes and critical studies that fans consume not as books but as 'collectibles.'[17] History, thanks to popular Hollywood adaptation practices with historical novels, does not get any more (re)usable.

If American film culture had accessed the Civil War before the Second World War, how would such a "reusable past" play out in the postwar period? Stephen Crane's 1895 novella about a young soldier facing cowardice during the heat of the Battle of Chancellorsville in May 1863 was itself undergoing a popular rediscovery by the early 1950s. By the time Huston proposed adapting the book to producer Gottfried Reinhardt in 1950, the novel had attained canonical status in the academy.[18] Although Stephen Crane never functioned with the kind of magical aura that possessed Charles Dickens in this country, the American author carried a certain cache at midcentury; his story of Henry Fleming's fateful dilemma in the face of wartime crisis potentially appealed to a wide audience. Ernest Hemingway wrote in 1942 that *The Red Badge of Courage* was the only enduring "real literature of our Civil War."[19] In 1950, John Berryman published the first critical biography of Crane, to wide acclaim.

It is well known that canonical fiction like *The Red Badge of Courage* was long esteemed as literary capital in Hollywood; it was even a potential prestige motion picture for MGM, a studio that was attempting to alter its direction under a new administration. "We must sell this picture as an important picture, in the great tradition," Reinhardt said. "Like *Mutiny on the Bounty.* Like *The Good Earth.*"[20] Furthermore, Crane's realism and penetrating interest in the human psychology of a young soldier were also appealing to the liberal Dore Schary, who had made his reputation by writing and producing social problem films at MGM, then briefly at RKO (as an outside producer). Now back at Metro, this time as vice president in charge of production, Schary said that he would make "good films about a good world," and produce five to ten "progressive" films per year.[21] He paid Howard Hughes $100,000 for the rights to produce a project he had already begun at RKO. The film eventually became William Wellman's *Battleground* (1949), a drama about the unfolding of the Battle of the Bulge that was hugely successful for Metro. According to Thomas Schatz, from Schary's point of view, *Red Badge* was *Battleground*'s natural successor.[22] Certainly, Schary was no longer interested in Mayer's dream machine, with its glossy reputation for glamour and stars. Moreover, by 1949 the combat film genre, in decline soon after the end of World War II, was making a comeback with films like *Task Force* and *Home of the Brave* and the *Sands of Iwo Jima.* Crane's realism depicted in *The Red Badge of Courage* seemed applicable for an audience who had faced the grim world of World War II and its aftermath. The rediscovered combat film in 1949 necessarily represented the solder from the perspective of a postwar reality: "Like the superior films from the late war era, particularly *The Story of GI Joe* and *They Were Expendable,* these focused primarily on the psychology and camaraderie of men at war and on the brutal responsibilities of leadership in combat. . . . *Battleground* and *Sands of Iwo Jima* both surpassed $5 million in domestic earnings, virtually ensuring the return of the combat film."[23]

This "third wave" of combat films persisted until the end of the 1950s and was accompanied by what Jeanine Basinger calls "a new cynicism toward war and those who plan it and lead it."[24] These observations and others are reinforced by productions about other wars. As Steve Neale looks at this genre, he says that these films lay bare the essential weaknesses that men encounter at war: "its effect is felt as much as on First World War films like *Paths of Glory* (1957) and on Second World War films like *Attack!* (1956) as it is on Korean films themselves, and it is preceded in the early years of the Cold War by films like *Twelve O'Clock High* (1949) and *The Caine Mutiny* (1954) which, like a number of contemporary novels and plays, focus sympathetically on the stresses, strains and values of command."[25] R. E. Shain's *Analysis of Motion Picture about War Released by the American Film Industry, 1930–1970* (1976) says that "the professional warrior" protagonist who functioned clearly as a stable force in combat films is succeeded by one who trades "long range political, social, and military goals in favor of immediate personal considerations."[26] What Schatz calls the prestige-level "male melodrama" emerging after 1946 often evoked a protagonist facing "post war angst to find himself."[27] Therefore Crane's fictional depiction of the psychological events of battle functioned as symbolic capital for a certain American audience who may not have been familiar with Crane but was conversant with the kind of noirish, realistic style that the novel evoked during the stress of wartime battle.

But that gritty style did not play at all well with Louis B. Mayer. Mayer was against realism altogether and, according to his biographer, questioned Huston's interest in that style in a pointedly earthy exchange about bathroom habits: "That's realism, John! It happens many times a day with every woman. So she locks the door, she keeps them out. That's what we do in our pictures. When something is ugly, we lock the door, we keep it out, because we don't want our customers to look at things that are ugly and say, 'Ugh, I don't want to see that!'"[28] Schary and Huston were adamant about making the picture, and the producer sent L. B. Mayer a somewhat "placating" memo stating that he believed that *Red Badge* "has a chance of becoming a highly important motion picture that will bring honor to the studio, plus every reasonable chance of making money . . . it is possible that it will be a classic . . ."[29]

Whether or not MGM would change from its former dream factory to a more socially conscious studio would not be Mayer's decision to make, anyway. The decision to film *Red Badge* ultimately came from Nick Schenck, the president of Loew's, the parent organization of MGM, who agreed with Schary. Shortly after *Red Badge* went into production, L. B. Mayer would be out of the studio at Schary's order and in "retirement." As Huston would later tell Gottfried Rienhardt, "we combined our efforts not only to reenact the Civil War . . . but we unleashed a civil war of our own at MGM. Louis B. Mayer was the first casualty."[30] But far from initiating what Schary and others hoped would be a new, liberal trend for Metro, *Red Badge* proved Mayer correct. There was indeed a deeply conservative mood in the country and the American audience would lack interest in an antiwar version of the Civil War. Schary had not counted on the problem of a vaguely allegorical antiwar film about the northern and southern conflict in America, when a civil war was raging in Korea with American troops at the helm. Because Huston had reframed Crane's novel into a kind of parable for the present, the Civil War became something like an *unusable* past for MGM. Therefore Schary's, together with Huston's, and almost everyone's expectations soon were crushed at the preview at the Picwood Theater: "When 'The Red Badge of Courage' flashed on the screen, there was a gasp from the audience and a scattering of applause. As the showing went along, some of the preview-goers laughed at the right times, and some laughed at the wrong times, and some did not laugh at all. When John Dikes, in the part of the Tall Soldier, and Royal Dano, in the part of the Tattered Man, played their death scenes, which had been much admired before, some people laughed and some murmured in horror."[31]

Bowing to economic interests and conservative cultural tastes, Schary's response was swift: the film was recut then released while Huston was in Africa shooting *The African Queen*. The original footage has been lost forever.[32] Along with the removal of key scenes (such as the Death of the Tattered Man and the Second Battle scene), Schary and MGM made other very significant changes, including a voice-over narration that not only excerpted portions of the novel, but also introduced Stephen Crane as an omniscient author of mythic, masculine superiority. According to the new framing narration added by the studio, "its publication made [Crane] a man." Therefore the story we see on the screen is an initiation into conventional manhood, not, as Huston imagined it, about the fragility of the human subject in crisis. Only sixty-nine minutes of Huston's original film has survived the original length (approximately 2 hours and 15 minutes). And even when the picture was finally released with all its changes in the summer of 1951, *Red Badge* would vanish in a matter of only a few weeks.

What went wrong in the adaptation of *The Red Badge of Courage* includes a number of factors, chief among them a maverick auteur bringing an unpatriotic novel to the screen during the Korean War, some years before the combat genre itself would be redefined. Huston's instincts anticipated a future trend of dismantling the "professional warrior" that would occur later in the decade, but in 1951 the "uncertainty about war aims and the necessity of leaving recently established homes and families to fight oversees" had not yet fully taken hold for American audiences.[33] Further, after World War II, the historical discourse of the Civil War and Reconstruction was no longer functioning as a communal lens to understand identity issues such as gender and race, as it once did for previous decades. Rather, in terms of shaping collective memory, George Lipsitz suggests that "when we look for broad categories capable of creating coherence out of the many kinds of stories told by Hollywood in the years since World War II, the five main themes that emerge do not seem sensitive to issues of change over time. These themes— the family in jeopardy, agonies of empire, corruption at the top, personal autonomy, and what literary critic Nina Baym (in another context) calls 'melodramas of beset manhood'—encompass an extraordinary number of Hollywood productions during this period."[34]

Lipsitz echoes what Thomas Schatz and numerous film historians read as the anxiety and insecurity present in feature films of the postwar period. As we will see, Huston's original adaptation of *The Red Badge of Courage* would become what Lipsitz calls a kind of "counter-memory" narrative that would challenge, rather than congeal, national identity and conventional constructions of masculinity.[35]

Huston's War

Huston had proposed *The Red Badge of Courage* to Dore Schary as the second of his two-picture arrangement with Metro (the other was the highly influential film, *The Asphalt Jungle*). In the context of the 1950s, Huston was a better match to adapt Stephen Crane's novel than he was to conform to MGM's changing politics. Major John Huston had experience both editing and writing *cinéma verité*–style films for the War Department whose focus, like that of Crane's young Henry Fleming, was the mental plight of soldiers. According to Lillian Ross, "Huston, like Stephen Crane, wanted to show something of the emotions of men in war, and the ironically thin line between cowardice and heroism."[36] Indeed, for some scholars, such as Donald B. Gibson, Crane himself was "redefining the hero."[37] Amy Kaplan observes that Crane departed from much of the chivalrous, mythological representation of the Civil War common in the 1890s by writing a revisionist history of the war that was antimilitary. "The novel implicitly contributes to and criticizes the contemporary militarization of American culture by focusing not on politics but on the problem of representing war. .... His war novel does more than parody either generic conventions or historical novels about the Civil War; it specifically parodies those narrative forms used to reinterpret the Civil War and to imagine new kinds of warfare in the 1890s."[38] The world Crane inhabits with Huston and American culture was a noirish one in which "dread and fascination are to a considerable degree shared by the narrator and reader."[39] Therefore Huston and Crane formed an important relationship in postwar Americana, precisely in their ability to explore the gritty realistic conditions behind human psychology and what produced them.

Trained as a journalist, Crane had written the book thirty years after the Civil War and three years before the Spanish-American War during the militarization of the 1890s. Joseph Conrad once said that Crane's novel was a masterpiece in part because of "the imaged style of the analysis of the emotions in the inward moral struggle going on in the breast of one individual."[40] Indeed, Linda H. Davis claims in her biography of Crane that the novelist pictured "Henry Fleming's battle as a psychological and spiritual crisis."[41] In 1965, a clinical journal published a long article on Crane's novel as "a study of anxiety-defense mechanisms working under pressure to establish some tolerable adaptation to a dangerous reality."[42] Crane's penetrating representation of a young Union soldier's profound fear in the heat of battle and his subsequent urge to free himself of that neurosis seemed like a prophetic utterance for post–World War II America fifty years later, considering that culture's growing interest in the psychodynamics of the human mind—particularly that of former soldiers. As Richard Jameson observes, in Huston's version of *The Red Badge of Courage,* "Henry Fleming virtually psychoanalyzed himself through a series of interviews with characters who either stood behind him, giving voice to his own thoughts and fears, or mused in foreground while he looked on anguished from behind."[43]

Gritty psychological realism was a common idiom Huston and other filmmakers used to interrogate the dark side of the postwar human consciousness. Guided by his documentary experience during World War II, when he had explored the spiritual terror of battle, Huston was a better choice to produce the work of an established American author than most Hollywood auteurs. Andrew Sarris said that Huston's "protagonists almost invariably fail at what they set out to do, generally through no fault or flaw of their own."[44] As James Agee recognized early on, Huston is "swiftly stirred by anything which appeals to his sense of justice, magnanimity or courage."[45] At the same time, Huston told Michel Ciment in a 1984 interview for *Positif* that he considers each case of adaptations separately in order to account for authorial intentions. *The Maltese Falcon* was "ready to be put into images. On the other hand, there were many original contributions in *The Red Badge of Courage* and *Moby Dick,* but I think and hope that the authors would have approved those additions."[46] Therefore while he was shooting *Red Badge,* Huston felt the film was to be the hallmark of his career and later told some friends that "this has got to be a masterpiece . . . or it is nothing."[47] In fact, when a Hollywood psychologist read the screenplay of *Red Badge,* he claimed that with a few alterations in the psychological *Zwischentone,* "the picture could be the outstanding one of the year."[48]

Undoubtedly, Huston's adaptation of *The Red Badge of Courage* gave him an opportunity to demythologize the American soldier. Even before the Second World War, Huston appears to have had an interest in exploring an unconventional look at soldiering. As a screenwriter, he was cocredited (together with Abem Finkel, Harry Chandlee, and Howard Koch) with adapting the diaries and stories of Sergeant Alvin York for the film that eventually became *Sergeant York* (Howard Hawks, 1941). But in an interview with Peter Bogdanovich, Hawks credited Huston alone as the author of the screenplay, saying that "Huston did it all. He just kept about two or three days ahead of me writing the scenes."[49] The story of a religious pacifist who becomes a hero during the Meuse-Argonne offensive during World War I is an interesting— and more optimistic—prelude to Henry Fleming's moral ambiguity in the face of battle. *Sergeant York* and *The Red Badge of Courage* make fascinating bookends, mirroring each other in different ways, even as they initiate two very different decades. As the director of the notoriously unchivalrous Sam Spade in *The Maltese Falcon* (1941), or the smoldering Dix Handley of *The Asphalt Jungle* (1950), Huston was never much impressed with what he called the "warrior myth" and its fictionalization in Hollywood, which, as we have seen, was at an all-time high in the late forties. By the time of the release of *Red Badge* in 1951 and the resurgence of the combat film in Hollywood, there were no fewer than thirteen such movies in circulation—only a few shy of those made each year between December 7, 1941, and 1945.[50]

In a certain sense, the myth of the returning soldier and his therapeutic healing becomes an icon of the postwar years in Hollywood, which itself was beginning more and more to appropriate vulgarized forms of Freudian narratives. Released at roughly the same time as *The Red Badge of Courage,* Stanley Kramer's *The Men* (1950), starred a moody Marlon Brando as a despairing, paralyzed World War II veteran brought back to psychological health by his faithful girlfriend. Similar "redemption narratives" surfaced in the years immediately following the war. In *The Pride of the Marines* (Delmer Davies,

1945), the blinded Al Schmid (John Garfield) undergoes extensive psychological treatment in order to adjust to a postwar world. Schmid gradually accepts his disability and his place in American culture and is rewarded for his domestication with Ruth Hartley (Eleanor Parker) and the Navy Cross. Even *The Best Years of Our Lives* (William Wyler, 1946), certainly one of the finest and most popular of Hollywood's films about the return of soldiers to America, manages to recapitulate the "warrior myth." The soldier may no longer be active, but he is still a man. Like Homer Parrish, he may no longer have hands, but if he struggles enough he can still get married. As Dr. Golden, the sympathetic psychiatrist says concerning his work with wounded soldiers in *Since You Went Away* (John Cromwell, 1944): "There's a whole, wide, broken world to mend."

A number of Dore Schary's most important productions concerned soldiering and its psychological ramifications. In *Till the End of Time* (Edward Dmytryk, 1946), a lonely Guy Madison returns to his parents' house after the war, only to find his mother shopping and his father playing golf. Like an abandoned child, the ex-Marine says that "it was kind of spooky coming home and finding no one around," yet, paradoxically, finds it difficult to adjust to a world in which his parents still tuck him in bed at night. Like *The Best Years of Our Lives, Till the End of Time* barely hints at the loss of virility that the war had provided for American men. The wounded soldier recovers, usually through a heterosexual union established at the end of the narrative. In the process, the returning veteran is often psychologically or physically reassembled. Similarly, Dmytryk's *Crossfire* (1947) was Schary's first production for RKO and dealt with a pathological soldier's (Montgomery, played by Robert Ryan) sadistic rage of antisemitism and its social implications. Montgomery is a vicious, bigoted murderer, with little chance of redemption in a postwar culture that does not reacclimate professional warriors to society. *Crossfire* represents the dark, psychotic side of the returning vet, but for others the problem of return was more protracted and therapeutic. The task of psychological integration that deals specifically with war injuries is the subject of *The Enchanted Cottage* (John Cromwell, 1945) and *I'll Be Seeing You* (William Dieterle, 1945), both produced by Dore Schary.

By contrast, Huston's controversial war documentary *Let There Be Light* (1946) did little to negotiate the cultural anxieties of what Dana Polan calls "the problem of placement" of returning veterans in postwar America.[51] I agree with David Desser, who says that "returning home, or finding a home once one has returned," is the crucial feature of Huston's theatrical and documentary films.[52] But those pictures tended to defamiliarize, rather than negotiate, American sensibilities. Just how Huston's feature films failed to vitiate postwar tension is evident in the reception of Huston's documentary. The War Department sent an armed guard to New York City after the initial screening of *Let There Be Light* in the spring of 1946 and pulled the film from its public exhibition at the Museum of Modern Art; it was suppressed for thirty-five years, and not until January 1981 did Vice President Walter Mondale secure the film's release.[53] The official response by the Defense Department was that the soldiers who were photographed during psychiatric interviews needed to sign releases. But *New York Post* critic Archer Winston wrote that the film had been hastily withdrawn, and that there was no release question because a commercial distributor offered to get a new set of releases from all the performers before showing the film.[54] It also seems that some individuals were deeply interested in reproducing the film commercially. According to studio records, a letter to Arthur L. Mayer from Colonel Charles W. McCarthy (August 12, 1946) indicates that the War Department would handle all clearances and if not, "[scenes] would be reproduced by professional actors."[55] Yet on September 9, 1946, the film was officially classified by the War Department "For Official Use Only."[56]

Huston is quite explicit about the incident in his autobiography and believed that the film was suppressed because its portrait of broken soldiers could adversely affect military recruitment. "I think it boils down to the fact that they wanted to maintain the 'warrior' myth, which said that our American soldiers went to war and came back all the stronger for the experience."[57] Huston dismantled the warrior myth no place more poignantly than in his other documentary for the War Department, *The Battle of San Pietro* (1945). Huston and photographers from the U.S. Army Signal Corps "produced one of the most harrowing visions of modern infantry warfare ever filmed: a documentary that conveys the raw, repetitive grind of battle and the grim vulnerability of the men who fought it with a respect and bitterness unprecedented in the history of film."[58] The film shows the factual record of the 36th "Texas" Division from the early winter of 1943.[59] In Huston's account, the hero of the war was not the triumphant warrior but the common man, the foot soldier. According to an unpublished memo of August 5, 1944, Huston discussed alternative titles for what was eventually titled *The Battle of San Pietro* with Frank Capra. And one of the options was simply *Foot Soldier*.[60] Clearly, the film is about the underdog and the lower classes—the ones, as he says, who could really use psychoanalysis but can ill afford it.

Because of disturbing scenes of the "battlefield dead," the film was not released to the public until May 21, 1945 (it was cut from four to three reels).

By that time, the war in Europe was over. Thus, *San Pietro* would herald the troubled production history of *Let There Be Light*—and, indeed, *The Red Badge of Courage*. Huston recorded the response to *San Pietro* in his autobiography: "The War Department wanted no part of the film. I was told by one of its spokesmen that it was 'anti-war.' I pompously replied that if I ever made a picture that was pro-war, I hoped someone would take me out and shoot me. The guy looked at me as if he were considering just that. The film was classified SECRET and filed away, to ensure that it would not be viewed by enlisted men. The Army argued that the film would be demoralizing to men who were going into combat for the first time."[61]

Huston wanted to include the frank voice-over discussions with the American soldiers at the very same time that we see body bags being taken away. He also wanted to incorporate interviews with survivors about the days to come and then disclose that they were, in fact, killed in battle. David Desser's analysis of the film is worth quoting at length:

> *San Pietro* relies on a deceptive simplicity in its basic structure, a chronological approach in which voice-over narration and shots of maps provide information. The voice-over situates us in space and time, and relates a little of the history of the small town and the valley in which it rest. The battle scenes are thus framed by images of peace: what the town was like up until the war and what it will return to after the victorious American troops depart. The battle scenes are, on the one hand, curiously passionate. Shot on the spot in the midst of actual combat, the film is not able to rely on standard Hollywood techniques to communicate the feel of battle: multiple angles, point-of-view shots, and dynamic montage are almost impossible. . . . On the other hand, their very documentary nature makes them gripping. Dispassionate single-take long shots of men falling from machine-gun fire or being struck by a burst of artillery show the dispassionate horror of war.[62]

Huston's deliberate dissonance with conventional Hollywood narration in his documentaries seems especially clear regarding representations of mythologies of masculinity. That demythologizing embraced his whole career. For David Desser, then, *Let There Be Light* inaugurates Huston's rethinking and revisioning of traditional American modes of masculinity and male behavior, which would reach fruition in such films as *The Red Badge of Courage*, *Moulin Rouge*, and *Fat City*.[63] Huston himself noted that what he thought was really behind the banning of *Let There Be Light* was that "the authorities considered it to be more shocking, or embarrassing perhaps to them, for a man to suffer emotional distress than to lose a leg, or other part of his body. Hardly masculine, I suppose they would say."[64] Clark's narrative in *The Battle of San Pietro* seems to smooth over the filmic dissonance and, therefore, operates as a signifier of stability in patriarchal culture. In Max Weber's terms, this is "charismatic authority" co-opted into "traditional authority."[65] Reading the film on a psychologically discursive, postwar contextual level, Clark's narrative functions as the voice of reassuring patriarch attempting to bestow stability and the law on its audience. Clark has a symbolic, paternal function in *The Battle of San Pietro,* insofar as he levels a patriarchal resolution by virtue of his military status—the "figure of the law" in the Oedipal culture—or what Jacques Lacan calls *"le nom de pere."*[66] But Huston's *noir* stylistics and interest in unglamorized psychological exploration in both *Let There Be Light* and *The Battle of San Pietro* suggest a very uneasy relationship with Clark's conservative order and cultural stability.

Huston's wartime films "can also be extended to include a number of Huston's later efforts, films not simply about war, or wartime . . . but films that grew out of Huston's personal experience of the Second World War, and the culture's experience of it as well."[67] Clearly, Huston allowed his experience of documentary filmmaking to inform his production of *The Red Badge of Courage.* Huston shares a documentary vision with Crane himself, who also allowed his journalistic background to inflect his fiction. Consider, for instance, Crane's description that occurs after the "first inconclusive engagement" in chapter 5 when Fleming notices "a flash of astonishment at the blue pure sky and the sun-gleamings on the trees and fields. It was surprising that Nature had gone tranquilly on with her golden processes in the midst of so much devilment." Howard C. Horsford draws our attention to Crane's novel and Huston's skillful directorial narration when he comments on this passage, saying that, "Huston and his cameraman capitalized on this double perspective. Especially in the battle scenes, the camera alternated between close attention to the principal actors and panning surveys of the battlefield as if from a distant height; in the event, the movement of men, the rush of flags, the flash of guns in the obscuring smoke became seemingly miniscule irruptions against the spring countryside."[68]

In Huston's case, *Red Badge* would face a censorship much as his documentaries did, calling our attention to the similar narrative dynamics operative in the nonfiction and the fiction film. Scott Hammen recalls the ways in which Huston's documentaries informed *Red Badge* when he says that, "the uncertainty and impatience of untried soldiers in the first part of Crane's book correspond to that pictured in *Report from the Aleutians.* The horror of actual combat that Crane describes later is captured by Huston in *San Pietro,* and finally, the inquiry into what happens to a man's spirit after exposure to such combat that is the novel's central subject is likewise that of *Let There Be Light*. It was as if Huston had already made a documentary version of *The Red Badge of Courage*."[69]

In this regard, much of Huston's work bears upon industry-related issues in the postwar period. Indeed, the interest in the correlation between the documentary and Hollywood was never greater than in the postwar years, obviously influenced by the trilogy of productions Huston himself had made for the War Department. There was a more general, contemporary (and international) drive toward neorealism, location shooting, and deep-focus photography. In fact, immediately following the war, in January 1946, screenwriter Philip Dunne took up this very question in a now famous article for the *Hollywood Quarterly* called "The Documentary and Hollywood." In some respects, we find Huston in the company of Orson Welles, whose celebrated send-up of the "News on the March" ten years earlier in *Citizen Kane* asks the viewer to reconsider the boundaries between truth and falsehood, and that "the gap between the two media is not so wide that it cannot be bridged."[70] Indeed, Huston's original version of *Red Badge* makes us aware of what it might be like not only to see men at war, but to be on the front as well. According to Huston's script additions for the "revised opening" dated May 3, 1950, the opening scene was to maximize and problematize the dominant metaphor of the "blind passage" for the audience as well as the soldier:

FADE IN:
Med. Long Shot—Embankment across a river—night.
Low fires are seen in the distance, forming the enemy camp. Trees and
  bushes. A low whistle is heard from across the river.

Med. Long Shot—The other side of the river.
Moonlight reveals some bushes and trees, and a sentry walking into
  view. Crickets sing in the still of the night. The low whistle is repeated. The sentry puts his rifle to his shoulder, stands staring into
  the gloom.

Close Shot—sentry—it is the youth.
THE YOUTH: Who goes there?

Med. Long Shot—across the river
SOUTHERN VOICE: Me, Yank—jest me . . . Move back into the shad-
  ders, Yank, unless you want one of them little red badges! I couldn't
  miss yeh standin there in the moonlight.

Close Shot—The Youth
THE YOUTH: Are you a reb?

Med. Long Shot—across the river
THE SOUTHERN VOICE: That's right—but I don't see much point in us
sentries shootin' each other, specially when we ain't fightin' no battle.

Close Shot—The Youth
THE SOUTHERN VOICE: So if yeh'll jest get out a' the moonlight I'll be
much obliged to yeh.

THE YOUTH (moving back): Thanks, reb.
THE SOUTHERN VOICE: Now, that's mighty polite of yeh, Yank, to
thank me.

Med. Long Shot—across the river
THE SOUTHERN VOICE: I take it most kindly. You're a right dum' good
feller. So take keer of yerself and don't go gettin' one of them little red
badges pinned on yeh.

Over the scene fades in:
"The Red Badge of Courage"

Background dissolves to:
Panoramic Shot of the entire Army Camp—over which follow the credits
As the credits FADE—the first light of dawn reveals the tents of an
army encamped on hills below which a river slowly circles. The fog is
clearing.

A title appears: "Spring 1862 . . . Tales of Great movements shook the
land, marches, sieges, conflicts—but for the untried army on the
Rappahannock war was simply a matter of waiting, of keeping warm,
and of endless drilling.

Med. Long Shot—new angle—Ext. Camp
The regiment is seen drilling in the distance. These soldiers do not drill
in the modern manner. Their steps are measured and they are not
always in step with each other.[71]

Although there is no such "silent prologue" in the novel, the opening sequence and its place at the beginning of the film are crucial to a consideration
to Huston's overall, formal design of the film and his adaptation insights into
Crane. The dominant issue from the start here is seeing the light, or rather,
being kept in the dark. For we do not see the Southern soldier, but, like the

Youth, only hear his voice. The audience is also kept in the dark (about the title of the film) until several scenes into the movie, when the title is finally announced. Thus, in *The Red Badge of Courage* Huston opens with the MGM lion's roar, accompanied by the sound of drums, which are dissolved in gunfire. Then there is the silent prologue, showing the Youth on sentry duty, followed by a harmonica playing the familiar folk tune "Kingdom Coming" as the name of the picture and all the credits roll.[72]

This sequence does indeed set the narrative stage and reminds us of James Agee's perspicacious observation that Huston's film "honors the audience," continually "opening the eye and requiring it to work vigorously; and through the eye they awaken curiosity and intelligence."[73] Lesley Brill believes that "facing the truth of one's existence or fleeing it" is characteristic of several of Huston's films, as diverse as *The Red Badge of Courage, Under the Volcano,* and *Freud.*[74] Like Welles's unproduced version of Conrad's *Heart of Darkness,* the issue of audience "liberation" arises in the prologue and occurs throughout the film; it surfaces in both directors in the stylized, literary, and neomodernist way in which they handle point of view.[75]

The inventive, subjective platform for *Red Badge* raised the problem of narration among the producers, as we might expect it would. After the failure at the first preview, Reinhardt told Huston that Spenser Tracy should record a narration and that the river-scene prologue ought to be cut because it was "puzzling." Reinhardt's motivation was, like the War Department's narration for *San Pietro,* to ensure a properly conservative tone. He said that he wanted to tell the audience, " 'Here is a masterpiece.' You've got to tell it to them . . . it might make the difference between life and death . . . the people must know this is a classic."[76] One of L. B. Mayer's biggest objections to the picture was what he regarded as Huston's inability to show the Youth's *thoughts.*[77] Huston was absolutely against any conventional voice-over narration in *The Red Badge of Courage.* Reinhardt said he preferred one, but he went along with Huston's more inventive strategy because "he loved John." As Reinhardt recalled, "John kept saying 'No narration.' Billy Wilder in *Sunset Boulevard* had the nerve; after the man is dead, he has him do the narration. Joe Mankiewicz uses narration. Narration is good enough for them but not for John."[78] In the end, they settled for "voice-over excerpts from the book itself, poetic evocations of what is going on in the Young Soldier's mind through an externalizing documentary device."[79] Eventually, a more "omniscient highly communicative style" became good enough for Dore Schary, who, together with the editors, altered the "silent prologue" considerably from what the preview audience at the Pickwood Theater experienced that opening night.

The scene of the Youth on sentry duty does not appear at the beginning of *Red Badge,* but after the Youth's tent scene. Needless to say, the change made the film much less challenging for audiences but more to Schary's liking as a standard adaptation of a literary property.

In his dismissal of a less conventional film style, Schary was exhibiting fairly predictable tastes, even if he said he admired Huston's first effort in *Red Badge.* In fact, Schary had expressed his concern with the music well before the preview. "I think all music in pictures has to be cliché to be effective," he said. "In Marine pictures, you play 'Halls of Montezuma.' In Navy pictures, you play 'Anchors Aweigh.' In this picture, the music that's effective is the sentimental-cliché music. It's a fact. Let's not debate it."[80] Schary's opinion about musical scoring was not necessarily the opinion of the industry, but his notions about music for films as "sentimental-cliché" is useful insofar as his observations suggest that he wanted to reposition the prologue to make the film altogether predictable.[81] Schary and others hoped that the music composed for the film—over Huston's objections—would help to fill-in what seemed missing in the first sequence. According to Ross, the producers hoped that the newly scored music for *Red Badge* by Bronslau Kaper "says what Crane says in the novel." As Reinhardt told Ross: "that was what was missing [was] what goes on inside the boy."[82] From the point of view of Roland Barthes, Schary is well within the boundaries of the classical narrative and configures the Hollywood musical score through semic connotations, which constructs the characters and ambience of narrative.[83]

To investigate the formal properties of the revised prologue further is to find even more evidence of Schary's deployment of *semic* codes, which rely on voice-over narration to redeploy Crane as a literary figure who bestows both cultural and masculine capital. The sequence begins with the shot of a novel, over which the following is inscribed,

> Stephen Crane's Great Novel of the Civil War
> The Red Badge of Courage
> A John Huston Production

According to Stephen Philip Cooper, this inscription on screen is an invitation "to conflate the novel with the book and figuratively to read the movie we are about to see."[84] A montage like the one introducing *Red Badge* is certainly not unique to Hollywood adaptive productions, which early on learned to advert to either a picture of a well-worn book or fairly recognizable textual quotations from the adaptive source. Nor are the shots that follow, in which the book opens and displays the credits, together with drawings of the Civil

War, unique. Illustrations such as these carry significant hermeneutic function, as J. Hillis Miller and others have noted. Artistic codes that evoke the cultural ambiance of the period are important, even crucial, to creating a cultural authenticity.[85] What is unusual about this particular sequence is the extra-diegetic voice-over that follows after the page turns, which constructs an "author" for the audience. A drawing of Stephen Crane appears, captioned "Stephen Crane." As read by James Whitmore, the narration begins: "*The Red Badge of Courage* was written by Stephen Crane in 1894. From the moment it was published, it was accepted by critics and the public alike as a classic story of war and of boys and men who fought war. Stephen Crane wrote this book when he was a boy of twenty-two. Its publication made him a man. His story is of a boy who, frightened, went into a battle and came out of it a man with courage. More than that, it is the story of many frightened boys who went into a great civil war and came out as a nation of united, strong, and free men."

From the very start, Schary saw his purpose in the revision process to bestow both prestige on the studio and to immobilize Huston's reading of the novel. "The big trick," according to Schary, "was setting up an outside voice saying, 'Look, this is a classic.'" [86] Sarah Kozloff has called our attention to the voice-over convention in Hollywood as "a last minute patchwork" for panic-stricken producers, which, in the case of *Red Badge,* has inflected a "heavy-handed and schoolmarmish" quality on to the production.[87] Kozloff hints here at the efforts of the film to strive for didacticism at the expense of a coherent narration. The film goes out of its way to tell us that we will hear a narration "of quotes from the text of the book itself." In fact, although the film strives mightily to conflate the novel and the film, the introduction of the "author" as prestigious and literary capital ruptures any contour of "novel into film": the "schoolmarmish" turn to "the author" constructs the canonical legibility of "Stephen Crane" as the writer of a "classic" whose publication of his Civil War novel, "made him a man."

In this regard, the early moments of *The Red Badge of Courage* invite comparison with the introduction to *David Copperfield,* discussed in an earlier chapter. The transition from novel to screen in both cases relies on the evocation and construction of the author in order to validate the prestige of the film about to be viewed. In the case of Charles Dickens, the author's own voice is a retrospective preface surveying a life's work; it asks the audience to remember that David Copperfield was his "favorite child," thereby endorsing the novel as the most endearing among many. With *The Badge of Courage,* the author's status is sanctioned for the sake of strengthening the aura of cultural capital.

Therefore Schary's revised version of Huston's film suggests what Robert Stam has identified as an intertextual and generic negotiation of a realistic novel and the *Bildungsroman,* or "novel of development," drawing from a variety of sources surrounding the source text that contributes to its legibility.[88]

Nothing much came of the authorial presence fictionalized in the film except further audience confusion. Although Huston reluctantly agreed to the strategy of altering the narration, the audience failed to realize that *The Red Badge of Courage* was a classic. A second preview was held at the Pasadena Theater and the result was worse than the first.[89] The only thing left to do now was to whittle the film down to its present sixty-nine-minute length.

The Reusable Past?

In a certain sense, the adaptation of *The Red Badge of Courage* is a marvelous example of how a Civil War novel becomes a kind of unusable Hollywood text during 1950s postwar America. Schary and MGM redeployed a "coming-of-age" novel so as to endorse the values of post–World War II patriarchy: Stephen Crane became a man, so did the Youth, so we can all become men. By extension, the Civil War operates vicariously for a contemporary audience: if these soldiers returned from their war as "men," so too must the Second World War and Korean War make men—that is "warriors"—of U.S. youth. Through a canonical novel, Schary makes Stephen Crane a kind of patron saint of masculinity, explicitly demonstrating what Barbara Herrnstein Smith's *Contingencies of Value* (1988) calls the very nature of the canon: to support the dominant ideology.[90]

From one perspective, then, it may appear as if the more socially conscious Dore Schary was returning to the conservative interests of L. B. Mayer, who turned out to be right about the audience's taste all along. In another way, both Schary and Reinhardt emerge here as representatives of the new liberal in 1950s America, eager to democratize a "classic" for educational (and moral) purposes. These producers echo the sentiments of Seymour Lipset, who remarked that the "market for good books, good paintings, and good music" ought to be expanded especially through mass culture.[91] Paul Lauter underlines this divergent use of canonical authority in his consideration of the canon and American literature when he says that, "it is, in fact, perfectly reasonable to include a work because it is historically representative or influential. Further, it is naive to assume that *nothing* but aesthetic quality goes into making even such fine works as Crane's *The Red Badge of Courage* or Faulkner's *Absalom, Absalom!* part of our literary canon while excluding Gilman's 'The Yellow Wallpaper' or Hurston's *Their Eyes Were Watching God*. Surely, the political system called 'patriarchy' is at some level involved in choosing works that focus on male experience and perspectives."[92]

Schary's more or less mythological reading of Crane's novel was not without precedent. A prevalent interpretation of *Red Badge* that guided the criticism of Crane in the early fifties was informed by New Criticism and popular forms of Jungian psychology, which rendered the novel as a kind of rite of passage. Critic John E. Hart viewed *The Red Badge of Courage* as a mythic process of self-discovery in manhood: "Following the general pattern of myth with peculiar individual variations, Crane has shown how the moral and spiritual strength of the individual springs from the group, and how, through the identification of self with group, the individual can be reborn in identity with the whole meaning of the universe."[93] Nevertheless, Schary and Huston were at absolute cross-purposes: as Schary's narrator tells us, writing *The Red Badge of Courage* made Stephen Crane a man. On the contrary, it seems that Crane, and Huston's efforts to redeploy him, had in mind the *un*making of a man and, more particularly, what it means to be a war hero.[94]

Besides removing the prologue from *Red Badge,* Schary also eliminated several other features of the film that had a noirish potential to be antimasculine. Here we are reminded of Huston's long history with such censorship by the War Department for precisely the same reason. One of these episodes is a key moment in the novel and what Huston regarded as a real jewel in the production. According to his script revisions (dated August 26, 1950), Huston had planned an elaborate scene to come after the death of Jim in which the Tattered Man would give long discourse that questioned the ability of a soldier to endure in the war, and would finally wobble off in the field and die. The Youth, now a deserter, would even abandon the poor man and go off to the edge of the woods. Although it appeared in the original release print, the entire scene was cut (except for some of the Tattered Man's opening observations), so that after the Tattered Man's first few sentences, the Youth suddenly finds himself alone in the woods.[95]

Close Shot—New Angle—Hillside

TATTERED MAN (in an awe-struck voice): Well, he was a reg'lar jim-dandy fer nerve, wa'n't he? A reg'lar jim-dandy. I wonner where he got 'is stren'th from? I never seen a man do like that before—. Well, he was a reg'lar jim-dandy.

He then takes his eyes off the dead man, turns to the stricken youth.

TATTERED MAN (swinging uncertainly on his legs): Look-a-here, pardner. He's up an' gone, ain't he, an' we ought as well begin t'look out fer ol' number one. This here thing is all over. He's up an' gon, ain't e? An' he's all right here. Nobody won't bother 'im. An' I must say I ain't enjoyin' any great health m' self these days.

YOUTH (turning slowly to the Tattered Soldier): You ain't goin' to—not you, too!

TATTERED MAN (waiving his hand): Nary die. All I want is some pea soup an' a good bed . . . Some pea soup . . .

They turn their backs on [Jim] the Tall Soldier and walk away, marching in the field, CAMERA DOLLYING with them.

TATTERED MAN: I'm commencin' t' feel pretty bad . . . pretty bad.

YOUTH (groaning): Oh, Lord!

TATTERED MAN: Oh, I'm not goin't die yit! There's too much dependin' on me fer me t'die yit. No sir! Nary die; *I can't.* Ye'd oughta see th' children I've got an' all like that. (He staggers drunkenly.) Besides, if I died, I would't die the' way that feller did. That was the funniest thing. I'd jest flop down. I would. I never seen a feller die th' way that feller did. Yeh know Tom Jamison, he lives next door t' me up home. He's a nice feller he is, an' we was allus good friends. Smart, too. Smart as a steel trap. Well, when we was a-fighten this afternoon, all-of-a sudden he bein t' up an cuss an beller at me. 'Yer shot, yeh blamed fool!' He ses t'me. I put up m' hand t' m' head an' when I looked at m' fingers, I seen, sure 'nough, I was shot. I give a holler an' started t' run. I run t' beat all. But b'fore I wuld git away, another one hit me in th' arm an' whirl me clean 'round. I cotch it pretty bad. I've an idee I'd a' been fightin' yit, if t' wasn't fer Tom Jamison. . . . There's two of 'em—little ones—but they're beginnin' t'have fun with me now. I don't believe I kin walk much furder . . .

They go for a moment in silence.

TATTERED MAN: Yeh look pretty piqued yerself . . . I bet yeh've got a worser one than yeh think. Ye'd better take keer of yer hurt. It don't do 't let sech things go. It might be inside mostly, an' them plays thunder. Where is it located?

YOUTH (turns on the Tattered Man like one at bay): Now, don't you bother me!

TATTERED MAN (a little accent of despair): Well, Lord knows I don't wanta bother anybody. Lord knows I've got a' nogh m' own t' tend to.

YOUTH: Goodbye.

He walks a little faster. The other pursues him unsteadily.

TATTERED MAN (in gaping amazement): Why, pardner, where yeh goin?

He, too, like the Tall Soldier, is beginning to act dumb and animal-like. His thoughts seem to be floundering about his head.

TATTERED MAN: Now—now—look—a—here, Tom Jamison—now—I woun't have this—here won't do—Where—where yeh goin'?

YOUTH (looks about vaguely): Over there.

TATTERED MAN (head hanging forward, words slurred.): Well, now look—a—here—now. This won't do, Tom Jamison. It woun't do. Yeh can't go trompin' off with a bad hurt. It ain't right—now Tom Jamison—It ain't—Yeh wanta leave me take keer of yeh, Tom Jamison. It din't—right—it.

He rambles on in idiot fashion. CAMERA DOLLIES AHEAD of the Youth as he runs, climbs a low fence, leaving the Tattered Man behind. CAMERA STOPS and the Youth disappears OUT OF SHOT.

TATTERED MAN (bleating plaintively): Look—a—here, now, Tom Jamison—You wanta leave me take keer a'yeh. It ain't right—.

The Tattered Man wanders about helplessly in the field.

DISSOLVE TO: Medium Shot—New Angle—Dusk—The Youth

At this point in the revised film we pick up The Youth, who wanders confused into the woods into the shot and sits down at the log. But according to the script material, there was an even more horrific climax planned for the Youth's encounter with the Tattered Man.[96]

Medium Shot—Edge of Woods

The Youth runs into the Shot, as if chased by furies. He stops by a tree breathlessly. As if haunted by the memory of the Tattered Man, he looks back in the direction from which he came, breathing heavily.

> Then he turns and gazes around, wiping the beads of perspiration off
> his forehead. Then, slowly he sits on a tree-stump, utterly crushed.
> He is a lost soul. OFF SCENE we hear rifle shots, which attract the
> Youth's attention and take him out of his daze. Slowly he rises an
> walks OUT OF SCENE.

For Huston, the Tattered Soldier was the most glaring example of the soldier in crisis and came to represent the plight of virile, bellicose America, represented here in psychological exhaustion—a theme repeatedly emphasized from his wartime documentaries through *Reflections in a Golden Eye* (1967). Not surprisingly, Schary was absolutely insistent on removing this particular sequence, which he judged to be altogether harmful to the picture. The audience reactions to the sequence did not help further its inclusion in the picture. When the preview audience saw Royal Dano play the scene, according to Ross, they "laughed and some murmured in horror."[97] Reinhardt, however, thought that the "Tattered Man scene" was "the greatest in the picture." But even though Reinhardt did manage to get Schary to restore the wounded man singing "John Brown's Body"—doubtless convinced, finally, of its potential as a musical "cliché" he so admired in war films—Schary revised it according to his own taste, which by most estimations utterly confused the logic of action in the picture.[98]

Pam Cook reminds us of the tension present here between Schary and Huston when she writes that the postwar era was filled with deep ambivalence about masculinity and the patriarchal social order that had long been sustained during the war.[99] But while Schary might have reflected the views of his contemporaries in offering a more or less mythological reading of the Civil War and *The Red Badge of Courage,* Huston appears to be closer to expressing what Crane himself would have wanted. In his famous description of the death of the Tattered Man, Crane could be describing the crisis of patriarchy as a World War II soldier faces death:

> As the flap of the blue jacket fell away from the body, he could see that the
> side looked as if it had been chewed by wolves. The youth turned, with sudden, livid rage, toward the battlefield. He shook his fist. He seemed about to
> deliver a philippic.
> "Hell—"
> The red sun was pasted in the sky like a wafer.

Neither Huston nor Crane idealized war or the human subject that encountered it; in fact, both made a career of subverting the dominant ideology.

While mythologizing the soldier was certainly a traditional way to interpret *The Red Badge of Courage* in the 1950s, Huston's reading of the novel was an avant-garde, more radical take. For more recent critics such as Amy Kaplan, for example, Crane's novel is not so much a novel about a mythological journey or remembering the Civil War, or even, as is commonly supposed, a recollection of fear and a reconstitution of manhood. "Crane is the master of forgetting . . . the novel looks back at the Civil War to map a new arena in which modern forms of international warfare can be imaginatively projected." Ironically, while Schary tried to get the film to resemble something like a coming of age novel, Crane, in fact, *parodied* the romantic tradition of the *Bildungsroman* and "subverts [Theodore] Roosevelt's interpretation of the battlefield as a crucible for redeeming primal virility."[100] Therefore the novel always seems to have invited a certain amount of ambiguity, and its final paragraphs continue to invoke a variety of criticism, questioning whether they are ironic or not.[101]

Huston accentuates this radical rereading of Crane even further in his production of *Red Badge* by foregrounding (anti)-masculinity through acting style, particularly by casting Bill Mauldin as Tom Wilson the Loud Soldier and, of course, Audie Murphy as the Youth, Henry Fleming.[102] Both men were famous World War II heroes. Mauldin was notable for his cartoons and Murphy was the most decorated soldier of the war, receiving twenty-four medals, including the Congressional Medal of Honor. After the war, he acted in a number of westerns, often cast as a daring outlaw—like Billy the Kid and Jesse James (whom he played twice). Murphy was even cast as himself in *To Hell and Back* (Jesse Hibbs, 1955), based on his exploits on the battlefield and his extraordinary rise from a private from a poor Texas sharecropper's family to a lieutenant in the army. Hollywood used him in western after western as if to recall his former military heroics as daring and spunky. Hedda Hopper probably spoke for millions of patriotic Americans when she headlined her column in the *Los Angeles Times* by saying that casting Murphy as Fleming was "the happiest and most appropriate casting of the year . . . for a change we'll have a real soldier playing a real soldier on the screen. It couldn't happen at a better time."[103]

The bulk of Murphy's work confirms his identity as a strong, masculine man's man, yet that quality is largely based on a paradox: his extraordinary status as a war hero conflicts with his seemingly boyish demeanor. And Huston knew exactly what he was getting. Perhaps Murphy was not a big movie star, but he did have an ambivalence that might be exploited. As John Ellis reminds us, "The star image is an *incoherent* image. It shows the star as an ordinary person and an extraordinary person. . . . The cinematic image (and the film performance) rests on the photo effect, the paradox that the photograph presents an absence that is present."[104] Therefore Huston wanted Murphy not because the ex-soldier was a movie star but because he was a boyish war hero, whom he referred to as "a gentle killer." *The Red Badge of Courage* continually works to exploit the paradox of stardom, even the performance frame. Ultimately, if Huston was trying to destroy the myths of heroism in war, he undercut the actor's (masculine) image as a hero by casting Murphy.

Our first glimpses of Murphy in *Red Badge* are anything but a validation of the manly man. A bewildered boy falters in the dark and then, soon after, is seen crying in his tent while composing a letter to his parents. That scene is especially moving because it recalls what Agee regards as Huston's technique at an unexpected close-up, which could "reverberate like a gong." The scene in the tent dissolves into a letter written by the Youth to his father explaining that if anything should happen to him, his dad should break the news to "Ma." Then, there is a very effective extreme close-up with the camera cramped in on the Youth, so that we see mostly his well-lit facial feature and tears. There is a cutback to the letter and then a head and shoulder shot of the Youth, followed by a fellow soldier (Jim) coming into the shot in the background. Henry wipes the tears away as he and Jim talk about bravery on the battlefield. The camera momentarily leaves the Youth again, only to return to the same head and shoulder shot. But this time Henry's face moves closer into the shot as he says, "Did you ever think that you might run too, Jim?" The camera leaves the Youth as Jim tells him that "I'd stand and fight. By Jimminy I would." The camera returns to a fascinating shot of a close-up of the Youth, reacting to Jim, still in the frame but with a third soldier between them. Recalling Agee's general observations about Huston's style, the close-ups that frame Henry again and again throughout the picture suggest not one "gong" but many, not a single bell but the tolling of several. In uniting form and content, the scene in the tent poignantly and disarmingly shows the pathetic fear of the Youth. These are the crucial scenes that will guide the ethical movement of the film, even as the camera emphasizes Henry's fear in a series of "gong"-like reverberations. As if to underline the ambivalence of what was supposed to be a tragic story, Huston took Murphy aside during the shooting and told him that there was a humorous aspect to the Youth's fear. "Fear in a man is something tragic or reprehensible . . . but fear in a youth—it's ludicrous."[105]

As we might expect, the preview audience was extremely upset about

Huston's characterization of Murphy, who at the age of nineteen and at the height of the worst part of the war had become identified as the most fearless of youths.[106] Interestingly, after Murphy's pictures appeared in *Life* magazine, the Hollywood establishment was quick to recognize that, in the words of one producer, he "could be photographed from any angle . . . with poise . . . spiritual overtones."[107] And so it is probably not a coincidence either that the studio cut almost three minutes (237 feet) from the potentially embarrassing tent sequence, perhaps to make Murphy more marketable in the future.[108]

There is a lot more to the studio's revision, which the specific alterations of the film only suggests. Let us briefly recall Schatz's insights about the way in which Schary viewed the film—as a happy successor to William Wellman's *Battlefield*. In that film, Holly (Van Johnson) has the briefest flash of doubt and runs momentarily from action. He is finally encouraged by his fellow soldiers—with no hint of their knowledge of his potential cowardice—at the Battle of Bastogne. Indeed, while Wellman lends a little personal psychological depth to the film, there is nothing very original, save for the insights provided by good acting and careful observation about group dynamics during wartime. In the end, *Battleground* provides an excellent example of Hollywood's efforts at postwar eclecticism: races, classes, and religious groups form together and unite against the other. Huston, however, has complicated the very notion of the wartime film by creating a prologue in which the enemy is portrayed as sympathetic: a young Southern Voice from beyond the river with understanding and empathy. Moreover, the depiction of the Tattered Man was a devastating portrait of the result of wartime "heroics" that faced the difficult issue of the largely uneducated infantry now in Korea. And, from what we have seen, it is hard to ignore that the Tattered Man scene seems to be a direct result of Huston's experience with wartime documentary and the "footmen," particularly, while working on *Let There Be Light*.

Like the Tattered Man, and, indeed, all the infantrymen in *Red Badge*, the returning soldiers in *Let There Be Light* are not only psychologically disoriented, but also blue collar, lower-class citizens guided by elite officers who give them no information. The Tattered Man's speech is a masterful construction of lower-class, regional dialect and, as such, he elicits our sympathy; he makes a point of telling us that he is together with others like him—Tom Jamison—who "lives next door t' me up home." In fact, as Murphy himself plays the Youth, he is a rather uneducated man. All the infantrymen are represented from the opening shots at the camp as workers doing their own laundry, who are guided by a destiny known only to the commanding officers. In a certain sense, Huston's representation of the Civil War as one fought by the lower classes was a painful reminder of the situation in Korea, where the lower classes were deployed to fight a war over the bourgeois panic of the Red Scare. Later in his career, Huston once again would adapt a novel about a previous war to critique a contemporary one. His adaptation of Carson McCullers's 1941 novel about a soldier in World War II, *Reflections in a Golden Eye,* reminds us of the turbulent issues at stake in Vietnam and the class stratification in the military. Both *Red Badge* and *Reflections* share a "dreamlike interrogation of power, delusion and violence."[109]

Huston's adaptation of *The Red Badge of Courage* shows his interest in linking (masculine) psychology to both class and politics. In a way, the Youth's flight from battle, his encounter with the Tattered Man, and his facing "himself" in the person of another soldier recall the complicated, difficult psychological agenda facing the soldier returning from World War II. Huston refuses to mythologize a returning veteran formed by violence and war; the past is always a haunting specter—a submerged, repressed memory that threatens to return. The uncut version of *Red Badge* reminds us of the best of the film noir tradition, a narrative that continually wants to come "out of the past," a mystery that may or may not lead to resolution. The Falcon surfaces like a curse that, even in the course of centuries, cannot be shaken loose because it is "the stuff that dreams are made of."

After the Youth runs from battle, it is the Tattered Man who confronts him (unknowingly) with the question, "War you hit?" That, of course, becomes the question for the rest of the film—the question of attaining the "red badge," of how to return to the center of the moral self. The Tattered Man's question is repressed, and the long scene Huston designed with the Youth and the Tattered Man only adds to the tension and the Youth's irascibility and avoidance of that question. Henry's flight from the Tattered Man, then, becomes a further flight from that same question.

In the next sequence, the Youth encounters a man running away from battle and asks him, "What are you running from?" At that point, the Youth struggles with another soldier and is wounded. The wound on Henry's head represents a psychological scar as well, earned from an encounter not with the other but with an existential encounter with himself. Furthermore, from the point of view of plot, the Youth has his chance to play out the former battle. But that skirmish, which might have signified a therapeutic "remembering and working through" for the Youth of the first battle, was also cut from the picture.[110] Like *Let There Be Light,* the dynamics of psychoanalysis invested the original version of *Red Badge* with a realistic view into human frailty and cultural blindness. Henry's "dark passage," initiated by a failure to recognize that the enemy is "within," becomes potentially illuminated for the audience. In the film's final version, all these narrative explorations have been significantly diminished.

Far from being an investigation of the formal comparisons that comprise "novel into film," this reconstruction of *The Red Badge of Courage* invites us to interrogate further a great deal of historical and cultural issues, not least of which are Hollywood studio politics. Huston and Schary present fascinating contrasts to each other. One was a director formed in the tradition of modernism, who worked to unmask the American dream—while working in the Hollywood Dream Factory. The other was a product of the liberal tradition of the social problem film, but attempted to negotiate the cultural contours of his age as a studio production chief in a changing movie industry. Nicholas Schenck even claimed that although he recognized that *Red Badge* would be a flop, he knew that the best way to help Schary was to allow him make a mistake.[111] Schary left MGM in 1956 for a career in the theater and as an independent producer. Huston fared much better, of course, with the other film he did for MGM, *The Asphalt Jungle*. Yet, as James Naremore has pointed out, *The Asphalt Jungle* would be the last of Huston's films that "resonated with the leftist satire of his earlier work."[112]

It is ironic that although the famous clash between Mayer and Schary caused the older studio mogul's ouster, it appears that the mighty studio chief who built MGM won at least one of the civil wars staged at Culver City. *Red Badge* might have been a brilliant allegory for the Left at the time of the blacklists; instead, the picture turned out to be a casualty of the cold war and a further indication that "an important movement in American cultural history was coming to a dark and destructive end."[113] Nevertheless, MGM's revision of Huston's *Red Badge* failed to bestow traditional, canonical prestige on the production, by stripping it of its psychologically disturbing, documentary texture. Perhaps the reason for the audience's outright dismissal of the original release print of *Red Badge* was because Huston gave the production not a mythology but a social consciousness. That story, about a failure of a young man in battle, was one American audiences could never face in the shadow of the war with Korea and the threat of communism. There might even be more in the film on the level of a political allegory. Hedda Hopper's readers may have been on to something when they fretted over the title of the film before its production and when she had to assure them, thoughtfully, that the adaptation of such a book by Crane could not possibly hold a menace to contemporary America. After all, she said, the book had been written many years earlier and had "absolutely no Commie implications."[114] Perhaps Hopper was a bit like a fidelity critic herself, failing to recognize the intertextual and historical interface between culture, Crane's novella, and the neomodernist director who would interpret both. In Huston's hands, though, *The Red Badge of Courage* was really about a redeployment of a timely narrative leveled at a civil war at home and abroad. We might even dare to speculate on the political signification of the "little red badge" of courage during the height of HUAC's fateful sweep of Hollywood, a historical moment that actually may have influenced the script for the film.[115] That was one badge of honor Dore Schary and MGM would have refused very happily.

Notes

Chapter 1. Is There a Novel in This Film? or The Cultural Politics of Film Adaptation

1. Thomas Leitch, "Adaptation Studies at a Crossroads," *Adaptation* 1, no. 1 (2008): 63. For a brief but superb introduction to the issues at stake in adaptation criticism, see James Naremore, "Introduction: Film and the Reign of Adaptation," in *Film Adaptation,* ed. James Naremore (New Brunswick, N.J.: Rutgers University Press, 2000), 1–16. Mereia Aragy's "Reflection to Refraction: Adaptation Studies Then and Now" nicely lays out the literature that has involved "novel into film" over the last several decades in *Books in Motion: Adaptation, Intertextuality, Authorship,* ed. Mireia Aragay (Amsterdam and New York: Rodopi, 2005), 11–34. See also Thomas Leitch, *Film Adaptation and Its Discontents: From "Gone with the Wind" to "The Passion of the Christ"* (Baltimore: Johns Hopkins University Press, 2007), Kamilla Elliot, *Rethinking the Novel/Film Debate* (Cambridge, U.K.: Cambridge University Press, 2003), and David L. Kranz and and Nancy C. Mellerski, eds., *In/Fidelity: Essays on Film Adaptation* (Newcastle, U.K.: Cambridge University Press, 2008).

2. There were sociological studies done in the early 1950s based on the little-mentioned work of Lester Asheim on "Books into Film." They are in four parts: "From Book to Film: Simplification," *Hollywood Quarterly* 5 (Spring 1951): 289–304; "From Book to Film: Mass Appeals," *Hollywood Quarterly* 5 (Summer 1951): 334–49; "From Book to Film: the Note of Affirmation," *Quarterly Review of Film, Radio and Television* 6 (Fall 1951): 54–68; "From Book to Film: Summary," *Quarterly Review of Film, Radio and Television* 6 (Spring 1952): 258–73. See Kyle Dawson Edwards, "Film Adaptation and Selznick International Pictures' 'Rebecca,' " (1940), *Cinema Journal* 45, no. 3 (Spring 2006): 32–58.

3. Linda Hutcheon, *A Theory of Adaptation* (New York: Routledge, 2006), 37.

4. See Dudley Andrew, "Adaptation," in Naremore, *Film Adaptation,* 31–34. See also Christian Metz, *The Imaginary Signifier* (Bloomington: Indiana University Press, 1977) and Keith Cohen, *Film Adaptation: The Dynamics of Exchange* (New Haven, Conn.: Yale University Press, 1979).

5. Leitch, "Adaptation Studies," 68.

6. Naremore, *Film Adaptation,* 8.

7. George Bluestone, *Novels into Film* (Baltimore and London: Johns Hopkins University Press, 1957), ix.

8. Bluestone, *Novels into Film,* 219. Robert Stam judges "parasitism" to be one of the eight sources of hostility to adaptation. See Robert Stam, "Introduction: the Theory and Practice of Adaptation," in *Literature and Film: A Guide to the Theory and Practice of Film Adaptation,* eds. Robert Stam and Alessandra Raengo (Oxford, U.K.: Blackwell, 2005), 3–8.

9. Bluestone, *Novels into Film,* 62.

10. Ibid., 216.

11. Naremore, *Film Adaptation,* 8.

12. Ibid., 7–8.

13. Robert Stam, *Literature through Film: Realism, Magic, and the Art of Adaptation* (Oxford, U.K.: Blackwell, 2005), 255.

14. Quoted in Stam, *Literature through Film,* 255.

15. John Ellis, "The Literary Adaptation: An Introduction," *Screen* 23, no.1 (May–June 1982): 3.

16. Naremore, *Film Adaptation,* 14.

17. André Bazin, "Adaptation, or Cinema as Digest," in Naremore, *Film Adaptation,* 26.

18. Naremore, *Film Adaptation,* 22.

19. Naremore, *Film Adaptation,* 10. See also Andrew, "Adaptation," 28–37.

20. Simone Murray, "Materializing Adaptation Theory: The Adaptation Industry," *Literature/Film Quarterly* 36, no. 1 (2008): 10.

21. Julie Sanders, *Adaptation and Appropriation* (London and New York: Routledge, 2006), 48. See also Leitch's observations on Sanders in "Adaptation Studies," 72–73, and Christine Geraghty, *Now a Major Motion Picture: Film Adaptations of Literature and Drama* (New York: Rowman and Littlefield, 2008).

22. See Jennifer M. Jeffers, *Britain Colonized: Hollywood's Appropriation of British Literature* (New York: Palgrave Macmillan, 2006). Leitch says that Jeffers's self-proclaimed title of "critical vigilante" "shows an impassioned determination to turn back the clock on cultural appropriation and implies a correspondingly conservative attitude toward adaptation far more backwards-looking" than most recent writing on the topic. Although she does not directly borrow the "parasite" metaphor from Bluestone as far as I am aware, the implication is clear: there is a kind of essentialist reading of writers like Shakespeare—"the very finest and noblest in the English language" which is in jeopardy through vulgarized entertainment. See Leitch, "Adaptation Studies," 73–74.

23. *Authorship in Film Adaptation,* ed. Jack Boozer (Austin: University of Texas Press, 2008), 21. See also *Film and Authorship,* ed. Virginia Wright Wexman (New Brunswick, N.J.: Rutgers University Press, 2003).

24. Thomas Leitch has categorized fifteen prevailing models in some recent writing on adaptation. See "Adaptation Studies," 65–68.

25. Leitch, "Adaptation Studies," 68.

26. Tom Gunning, "The Intertextuality of Early Cinema: A Prologue to Fantômas," in *Companion to Literature and Film,* eds. Robert Stam and Alessandra Raengo (Oxford, U.K.: Blackwell, 2004), 128–29. See also Gérard Gennette, *Palimpsests: Literature in the Second Degree* (Lincoln: University of Nebraska Press, 1997).

27. Elliott, *Rethinking the Novel/Film Debate,* 18.

28. Robert Stam, "Beyond Fidelity: The Dialogics of Adaptation," in Naremore, *Film Adaptation,* 66.

29. Stam, "Beyond Fidelity," 64.

30. See Robert Stam's helpful taxonomy of Gérard Genette's transtextuality in "Introduction," 27–31. Genette lists five: intertextuality, paratextuality, metatextuality, architextuality, and hypertextuality. See also Graham Allen, *Intertextuality* (New York and London: Routledge, 2000).

31. Ella Shohat, "Sacred Word, Profane Image: Theologies of Adaptation," in Stam and Raengo, *Companion to Literature and Film,* 43. See also Judith Buchanan, "Gospel Narratives on Silent Film," in *Literature on Screen,* eds. Deborah Cartmell and Imelda Whelehan (Cambridge, U.K.: Cambridge University Press, 2007), 47–60; and *Une Invention du Diable? Cinéma des Premiers temps et Religion,* eds. Roland Cosandey, André Gaudreault, and Tom Gunning (Laval, Qc.: Les Presses de l'Université Laval, 1992).

32. Pamala Grace, "Gospel Truth?: From Cecil B. DeMille to Nicholas Ray," in Stam and Raengo, *Companion to Literature and Film,* 46.

33. Erich Auerbach, *Mimesis: The Representation of Reality in Western Literature,* trans. Willard K. Task (Princeton, N.J.: Princeton University Press, 1946), 16–17.

34. David Morgan, *Visual Piety: A History and Theory of Popular Religious Images* (Berkeley: University of California Press, 1998), 122.

35. André Bazin, "Cinema and Theology," in *Bazin at Work: Major Essays and Reviews from the Forties and Fifties,* ed. Bert Cardullo, trans. Alain Piette and Bert Cardullo (New York: Routledge, 1997), 61.

36. Thomas Leitch, *Film Adaptation and Its Discontents: From Gone with the Wind to The Passion of the Christ* (Baltimore: Johns Hopkins University Press, 2007), 48.

37. Richard Maltby, "The King of Kings and the Czar of All the Rushes," in *Controlling Hollywood: Censorship and Regulation in the Studio Era,* ed. Matthew Bernstein (New Brunswick, N.J.: Rutgers University Press), 62. See also Felicia Herman, "The Most Dangerous Anti-Semitic Photoplay in Filmdom: American Jews and the *King of Kings,*" in *The Velvet Light Trap* 46 (2000): 12–25, and Richard C. Stern, Clayton Jefford, and Guerric DeBona, OSB, *Savior on the Silver Screen* (New York and Mahwah, N.J.: Paulist Press, 1999), 29–57.

38. Julie Sanders, *Adaptation and Appropriation* (London and New York: Routledge, 2006), 18.

39. Sumiko Higashi, *Cecil B. DeMille and American Culture: The Silent Era* (New York: Columbia University Press, 1994), 17. See also Robert S. Birchard, *Cecil B. DeMille's Hollywood* (Lexington: University of Kentucky Press, 2004).

40. Higashi, *Cecil B. DeMille*, 28.

41. The use of hymns is much more prevalent in the reedited 1928 general release print of *King of Kings* than in the 1927 road-show version.

42. Bruce Babington and Peter William Evans, *Biblical Epics: Sacred Narrative in the Hollywood Cinema* (Manchester, U.K., and New York: Manchester University Press, 1993), 118.

43. Higashi, *Cecil B. DeMille*, 185.

44. Babington and Evans, *Biblical Epics*, 119.

45. Leitch, *Adaptation and Its Discontents*, 52. Leitch's ingenious use of Bakhtin to account for the authority of the biblical adaptations is the best systematic account of interpreting the genre that I have yet seen. For an interesting essay on the role of the Bible as a cultural object in film history, see Gavriel Moses, "The Bible as Cultural Object(s) in Cinema," in Stam and Raengo, *Companion to Literature and Film*, 398–422.

46. Leitch, *Adaptation and Its Discontents*, 56. An interesting parallel in this regard might be the authoritative use of documentary footage inside a fiction film, as in Rene Clement's otherwise unremarkable *Is Paris Burning?* (1966). The documentary or newsreel footage clearly has an "authoritative" status and adds rhetorical authority to the fictive events with which it is in relationship. More recently, Gus Van Sant has also mixed documentary footage in his biopic, *Milk* (2008).

47. Kamilla Elliott, *Rethinking the Novel/Film Debate*, esp. 16–28.

48. Walter Benjamin, "The Work of Art in the Age of Mechanical Reproduction," in *Illuminations*, ed. Hannah Arendt (New York: Harcourt, Brace and World, 1968), 221.

49. Higashi, *Cecil B. DeMille*, 186–87.

50. Benjamin, "Work of Art," 221.

51. See Morgan, *Visual Piety*, 111–23.

52. Maltby, "The King of Kings and the Czar of All Rushes," in Bernstein, *Controlling Hollywood*, 70.

53. Morgan, *Visual Piety*, 122. The subjective point of view shots were enabled by the use of the newly developed Eyemo camera by Bell and Howell in 1925, and showcased as a production feature for *The King of Kings* in the 1927 issue of *American Cinematographer*.

54. Benjamin, "Work of Art, 222–23.

55. Higashi, *Cecile B. DeMille*, 192.

56. James Naremore, *Acting in the Cinema* (Berkeley: University of California Press, 1988), 158.

57. Naremore, *Film Adaptation*, 2.

58. Gerald Graff, *Professing Literature: An Institutional History* (Chicago: University of Chicago Press, 1987), 148–49. See also John Guillory, *Cultural Capital: The Problem of Literary Canon Formation* (Chicago: University of Chicago Press, 1993); John Frow, *Cultural Studies and Cultural Value* (Oxford, U.K.: Clarendon Press, 1995); *Politics and Poetic Value,* ed. Robert von Hallberg (Chicago: University of Chicago Press, 1987); Ava Preacher Collins, "Loose Canons: Constructing Cultural Traditions Inside and Outside the Academy," in *Film Theory Goes to the Movies,* eds. Jim Collins, Hilary Radner, and Ava Preacher Collins (New York: Routledge, 1993), 86–102.

59. See Guillory, *Cultural Capital,* 155–75. The overwhelming tendency not to historicize literary adaptation has its roots not only in formalism, but in publishing trends in English departments. See Robert B. Ray, "The Field of 'Film and Literature,'" in Naremore, *Film Adaptation,* 47.

60. Quoted in Herbert J. Gans, *Popular Culture and High Culture: An Analysis and Evaluation of Taste* (New York: Basic Books, 1970; rev. ed. 1999), 38.

61. Margaret Farrand Thorp, *America at the Movies* (New Haven, Conn.: Yale University Press, 1939), 23.

62. See, for instance, Bluestone's account of the Production Code, in *Novels into Film,* 36–45: "The film adapter, beyond understanding the limits and possibilities of his medium, must make a serious adjustment to a set of different and often conflicting conventions, conventions which have historically distinguished literature from the cinema and made of each a separate institution" (45).

63. See, for example, Steve J. Wurtzler, "David Copperfield (1935) and the U.S Curriculum," in *Dickens on Screen,* ed. John Glavin (Cambridge, U.K.: Cambridge University Press, 2003), 155–70 and chapter 2, below.

64. Thorp, *America at the Movies,* 254.

65. Ibid., 246 and following.

66. Pierre Bourdieu, "The Market of Symbolic Goods," *Poetics* 14 (1985): 16. See also Bourdieu's *Outline of a Theory of Practice* (Cambridge, U.K.: Cambridge University Press, 1977), 159–97, and *Language and Symbolic Power,* trans. Gino Raymond and Matthew Adamson (Cambridge, Mass.: Harvard University Press, 1991). The best survey of Bourdieu in English is David Swartz, *Culture and Power: The Sociology of Pierre Bourdieu* (Chicago: University of Chicago Press, 1997).

67. Pierre Bourdieu, *The Field of Cultural Production,* ed. Randal Johnson (New York: Columbia University Press, 1993), 108.

68. David Bordwell, Janet Staiger, and Kristin Thompson, *The Classical Hollywood Cinema: Film Style and Mode of Production to 1960* (New York: Columbia University Press, 1985), 161.

69. William Uricchio and Roberta E. Pearson, *Reframing Culture: The Case of the Vitagraph Quality Films* (Princeton, N.J.: Princeton University Press, 1993), 68. To see prestige productions in the context of other adaptations in the 1910s, see also Yuri Tsivian, "The Invisible Novelty: Film Adaptations in the 1910s," in Stam and Raengo, *Companion to Literature and Film,* 93–111.

70. Uricchio and Pearson, *Reframing Culture,* 69.

71. Eileen Bowser, *The Transformation of Cinema: 1907–1915* (New York: Charles Scribner's Sons, 1990), 42.

72. Uricchio and Pearson, *Reframing Culture,* 51 and following.

73. Lawrence W. Levine, *Highbrow/Lowbrow: the Emergence of Cultural Hierarchy in America* (Cambridge, Mass.: Harvard University Press, 1988), 52. For Levine, the use of Shakespeare by the dominant classes serves to foster further stratification and individuation from lower classes.

74. Uricchio and Pearson, *Reframing Culture,* 67.

75. Ibid., 65 and following.

76. Quoted in Uricchio and Pearson, *Reframing Culture,* 50.

77. Tino Balio, *Grand Design: Hollywood as a Modern Business Enterprise, 1930–1939* (New York: Scribners, 1993), 179.

78. Ibid., 180.

79. Charles Altieri, "An Idea and Ideal of a Literary Canon," in *Canons,* ed. Robert von Hallberg (London and Chicago: University of Chicago Press, 1984), 43. See also George A. Kennedy, "Classics and Canons," *South Atlantic Quarterly* 89, no. 1 (Winter 1990): 217–25; and Christopher Clausen, "'Canon' Theme, and Code," *Southwest Review* 75 (Spring 1990): 264–79.

80. Jane Tompkins, *Sensational Designs* (New York: Oxford University Press, 1985), 5.

81. Barbara Herrnstein Smith, *Contingencies of Value* (Cambridge, Mass.: Harvard University Press, 1988), 30. See also Frank Kermode, "Literary Value and Transgression," *Raritan* (Winter 1988): 34–53.

82. Bazin, "Adaptation, or Cinema as Digest," in Naremore, *Film Adaptation,* 22.

83. Balio, *Grand Design,* 180.

84. Pierre Bourdieu, *Distinction: A Social Critique of the Judgment of Taste,* trans. Richard Nice (Cambridge, Mass.: Harvard University Press, 1984), 6.

85. Bourdieu, *Distinction,* 176.

86. Bluestone, *Novels into Film,* 196.

87. See Michel Foucault's widely read, "What is an Author?" together with the other essays collected in *The Foucault Reader,* ed. Paul Rabinow (New York: Pantheon, 1984), 101–120; Roland Barthes is equally notable, "The Death of the Author," in *Image, Music, Text,* ed. and trans. Stephen Heath (New York: Noonday Press, 1977), 142–48; Dudley Andrew, "The Unauthorized Auteur Today," in Collins, Radner, and Collins, *Film Theory Goes to the Movies,* 77–85; James Naremore, "Authorship and the Cultural Politics of Film Criticism," *Film Quarterly* 44, no. 1 (Fall 1990): 14–22; Paisley Livingston, "Cinematic Authorship," in *Film Theory and Philosophy,* eds. Richard Allen and Murry Smith (Oxford, U.K.: Clarendon Press, 1999), 132–48. See also the essays in *Theories of Authorship,* ed. John Caughie, 1981 (New York: Routledge/BFI, reprint 1988); *Film and Authorship,* ed. Virginia Wright Wexman (New Brunswick, N.J.: Rutgers University Press, 2003).

88. Quoted in Boozer, *Authorship,* 21.

89. Roland Barthes, "The Death of the Author," in *Image-Music-Text*, ed. and trans. Stephen Heath (New York: Noonday Press, 1977), 142–48.

90. Timothy Corrigan, *Film and Literature: An Introduction and Reader* (Upper Saddle River, N.J.: Prentice Hall, 1999), 48–49.

91. Hitchcock quoted in Leitch, *Adaptation and its Discontents*, 238.

92. Leitch, *Adaptation and It Discontents*, 237. For a rather different take on Hitchcock and adaptation, see Richard Allen, "Daphne du Maurier and Alfred Hitchcock," in Stam and Raengo, *Companion to Literature and Film*, 298–325.

93. Leitch, *Adaptation and Its Discontents*, 239.

94. Quoted in Corrigan, *Film and Literature*, 51.

95. Quoted in Leitch, *Adaptation and Its Discontents*, 242–43. See also James Naremore, *On Kubrick* (London: BFI, 2007), 24–43. In terms of adaptation, Kubrick's use of what Naremore calls the "grotesque" allows for a modernist art cinema that suitably wrenches the literary into the visual and the performative.

96. Bourdieu, *Field of Cultural Production*, 16.

97. Bourdieu, *Field of Cultural Production*, 16–17. See also Swartz, *Culture and Power*, 117–42.

98. For John Frow, signature and brand are highly complex shifters, "markers of the edge between the aesthetic space of an image or text and the institutional space of a regime of value which frames and organizes aesthetic space." See "Signature and Brand," in *High-Pop: Making Culture into Popular Entertainment*, ed. Jim Collins (Malden, Mass.: Blackwell, 2002), 26–74.

99. Stam, *Literature through Film*, 257. Stam does a superb job in detailing the issues at stake in adaptation through the French New Wave. My scope here is necessarily limited.

100. Francois Truffaut, "A Certain Tendency of the French Cinema," in *Movies and Methods, Volume I*, ed. Bill Nichols (Berkeley: University of California Press, 1976), 232–33. For a discussion on authorship and adaptation in the French New Wave and Truffaut, see Richard Neupert, *A History of the French New Wave Cinema*, 2nd ed. (Madison: University of Wisconsin Press, 2002; 2007), 189–206.

101. Andrew, "Adaptation," 35.

102. Corrigan, *Film Adaptation*, 49.

103. Quoted in *Theories of Authorship: A Reader*, ed. John Caughie (London: Routledge and Kegan Paul, 1981), 9.

104. Jacques Rivette, "De l'invention," in *Cahiers du Cinéma: The 1950s, Neo-Realism, Hollywood and the New Wave*, ed. Jim Hillier (Cambridge, Mass.: Harvard University Press, 1985), 105.

105. Peter Wollen, "The Auteur Theory" in Nichols, *Movies and Methods*; Caughie, *Theories of Authorship*, 145.

106. Naremore, *Film Adaptation*, 6.

107. André Bazin, "*On the politique des auteurs*," in Hillier, *Cahiers du Cinéma*, 258.

108. André Bazin, "The Ontology of the Photographic Image," in *What is Cinema? Vol. I* (Berkeley: University of California Press, 1967), 13.

109. Andrew, "Unauthorized Auteur Today," 78.

110. Bazin, "Adaptation, or Cinema as Digest," 46.

111. Hillier, *Cahiers du Cinéma*, 10.

112. Alexandre Astruc, *"Qu'est-ce que la mise en scène?*, in Hillier, *Cahiers du Cinéma*, 268.

113. Thomas Elsaesser, "Two Decades in Another Country: Hollywood and the Cinéphiles," quoted in Hillier, *Cahiers du Cinéma*, 10.

114. Jacques Rivette, *"L'âge des metteurs en scène,"* in Hillier, *Cahiers du Cinéma*, 275–79.

115. Bluestone, *Novels into Film*, 164.

116. Vivian C. Sobchack, *"The Grapes of Wrath*: Thematic Emphasis through Visual Style," in Stam and Raengo, *Literature and Film*, 114.

117. Bluestone, *Novels into Film*, 168–69.

118. Hillier, *Cahiers du Cinéma*, 257. For another take on authorship and the auteur, see Charles J. Maland, "'Powered by a Ford': Dudley Nichols, Authorship, and Cultural Ethos in *Stagecoach*," in *John Ford's Stagecoach*, ed., Barry Keith Grant (Cambridge, U.K.: Cambridge University Press, 2003), 48–81.

119. Thomas Schatz, *Boom and Bust: The American Cinema in the 1940s* (New York: Simon and Schuster Macmillan, 1997), 80.

120. André Bazin, "The Evolution of the Western," in *Movies and Methods, Vol. I,* ed. Bill Nichols (Berkeley: University of California Press, 1976), 151.

Chapter 2. A Victorian New Deal

1. F W X Y Z S, "A Letter to Charles Dickens, Esq.," *The New World* 8 (January 6, 1844): 5–7.

2. See Lawrence W. Levine, *Highbrow/Lowbrow: The Emergence of Cultural Hierarchy in America* (Cambridge, Mass.: Harvard University Press, 1988), 249 and following. For a more general study of the influence of "Victorianism" on the contemporary age, see John McGowan, "Modernity and Culture, the Victorians and Cultural Studies," in *Victorian Afterlife: Postmodern Culture Rewrites the Nineteenth Century,* ed. Jon Kucich and Dianne F. Sadoff (Minneapolis: University of Minnesota Press, 2000), 3–28; and Jay Clayton, *Charles Dickens in Cyberspace: The Afterlife of the Nineteenth Century in Postmodern Culture* (New York: Oxford University Press, 2003), 146–65, and Daniel Walker Howe, ed., *Victorian Culture in America,* special issue of *American Quarterly* 27, no. 5 (December 1975).

3. Quoted in *Dickens: On America and Americans,* ed. Michael Slater (Austin and London: University of Texas Press, 1978), 8. See also William Glyde Wilkins, *Dickens in America* (Honolulu: University Press of the Pacific, 2005), a useful collection based on Dickens's 1842 tour of America.

4. Quoted in Sidney P. Moss, *Charles Dickens's Quarrel with America* (Troy, N.Y.: Whitson, 1984), 271–72.

5. Quoted in Moss, *Dickens's Quarrel,* 272.

6. Quoted in Moss, *Dickens's Quarrel,* 237.

7. Laurence Houseman was speaking in Sheffield on St. George's Day at a Shakespeare festival and is quoted in "Dickens the Low-Brow," *The Dickensian* 27, no. 217 (Winter 1930–31): 167.

8. Levine, *Highbrow,* 233.

9. Quoted in Slater, *Dickens,* 8–9.

10. Quoted in Levine, *Highbrow,* 233.

11. Dwight MacDonald, *Against the American Grain* (New York: Random House, 1962), 7. MacDonald seems really interested in advising us against Dickensian (popular) sentimentality. He provides us with another instance of how a highbrow intellectual might access Dickens.

12. James D. Hart, *The Popular Book: A History of America's Literary Taste* (New York: Oxford University Press, 1950), 103.

13. Sergei Eisenstein, "Dickens, Griffith, and the Film Today," in *Film Form,* ed. and trans. Jay Leda (New York: Harcourt, Brace, Jovanovich, 1949), 233–34. For a contemporary, formalist analysis of the influence of Dickens on Griffith, see Garrett Stewart, "Dickens, Eisenstein, Film," in Glavin, *Dickens on Screen,* 122–44.

14. Michael Pointer, *Charles Dickens on the Screen* (London: Scarecrow Press, 1996), 22.

15. Richard H. Pells, *Radical Visions and American Dreams: Culture and Social Thought in the Depression Years* (Middletown, Conn.: Wesleyan University Press, 1973, reprint 1984), 86, 96–150. Also, see Robert S. McElvaine, *The Great Depression: America, 1929–1941* (New York: Random House, 1984), 170–223.

16. Richard B. Hovey, "All the Things You Are," *Modern Age* (Summer 1993): 343.

17. Ruth Whittaker, "A Boom in Dickens," *The Dickensian* 30, no. 231 (Summer 1934): 157.

18. Quoted in Page Smith, *Redeeming the Time: A Peoples' History of the 1920s and the New Deal* (New York: Viking Penguin, 1986), 472.

19. Hart, *Popular Book,* 261.

20. Lawrence W. Levine, *The Unpredictable Past* (New York: Oxford University Press, 1993), 189–205. Levine qualifies his argument by saying that "Americans in the twenties, as before and a since, tended to turn to the past in their ideology and rhetoric more than in their actions" (205).

21. See Paul Davis, *The Lives of Ebenezer Scrooge* (New Haven, Conn.: Yale University Press, 1990). According to H. Philip Boulton's *Dickens Dramatized* (1987), from 1929 to 1941 there were no fewer than twenty adaptations of *A Christmas Carol* alone. Robert W. Paul filmed a 1901 version of *A Christmas Carol* in twelve tableaux. Scrooge or Marley's Ghost is described in detail in Michael Pointer, *Charles Dickens on the Screen* (London: Scarecrow Press, 1996), 8–14. In 1988, folklore expert and historian

Anne Rowbottom's research indicated that the English regarded a Victorian Christmas as the only "authentic" Christmas. See also *Functions of Victorian Culture at the Present Time,* ed. Christine L. Krueger (Athens: Ohio University Press, 2002).

22. Peter Ackroyd, *Dickens* (New York: HarperCollins, 1990), 34.

23. The first of these, *The Death of Nancy Sykes* (which recalls a famous scene from *Oliver Twist* that Dickens himself performed regularly on the stage), was shot in 1897 by American Mutoscope & Biograph Co. (later Biograph). See Graham Petrie, "Silent Film Adaptations of Dickens. Part I: From the Beginning to 1911," *The Dickensian* 97 (2001): 7–21; Mike Poole, "Dickens and Film: 101 Uses of a Dead Author," in *The Changing World of Charles Dickens,* ed. Robert Gidding (Totowa, N.J.: Barnes, 1993), 148–62. See also A. L. Zambrano, *Dickens and Film* (New York: Gordon, 1977). For a list of film and television adaptations, see Pointer, *Charles Dickens on the Screen,* 117–94, and Kate Carnell Watt and Kathleen C. Lonsdale, "Dickens Composed: Film and Television Adaptations 1897–2001," in Glavin, *Dickens on Screen,* 201–16.

24. Mary L. Pendered, "Dickens Plays and Films," *The Dickensian* 20, no. 1 (January 1924): 100.

25. Quoted in Pointer, *Charles Dickens on the Screen,* 13–14.

26. Production credits include: George Cukor (director); David O. Selznick (producer); Howard Estabrook and Hugh Walpole (writers); Oliver T. Marsh (cinematographer); Robert J. Kern (editor); Herbert Stohart (music); Cedric Gibbons (art director); Dolly Tree (costumes); Slavko Vorkapich (special effects); W. C Fields (Micawber); Lionel Barrymore (Dan Peggotty); Maureen O'Sullivan (Dora); Madge Evans (Agnes); Edna May Oliver (Aunt Betsey); Lew Stone (Mr. Wickfield); Frank Lawton (David as Man); Freddie Bartholomew (David as Child); Elizabeth Allan (Mrs. Copperfield); Roland Young (Uriah Heep); Basil Rathbone (Mr. Murdstone); Elsa Lanchester (Clickett).

27. Robert Stam, "Introduction: The Theory and Practice of Adaptation," in *Literature and Film: Guide to the Theory and Practice of Film Adaptation,* eds. Robert Stam and Alessandra Raengo (Malden, Mass.: Blackwell, 2005), 25. *David Copperfield* fits another intertextual element suggested by Stam, the *Bildungsroman,* or "novel of development."

28. Stam, "Introduction," 25.

29. Pierre Bourdieu, *The Field of Cultural Production* (New York: Columbia University Press, 1993), 7.

30. Ibid., 76.

31. Balio, *Grand Design,* 179. According to the *Motion Picture Herald,* there were four types of prestige properties: nineteenth-century literature; Shakespearian plays; best-selling novels and hit Broadway shows "acclaimed by the classes"; and biographical and historical subjects (179).

32. David Thomson, *Showman: The Life of David O. Selznick* (New York: Knopf, 1992), 179.

33. Thomas Schatz, *The Genius of the System: Hollywood Filmmaking in the Studio Era* (New York: Pantheon, 1988), 167–68.

34. Balio, *Grand Design*, 187. Balio says that the majority of these prestige pictures were at first biopics, but eventually included costume-adventure pictures, adaptations of literary masterpieces, and even class-A westerns (192).

35. Quoted in Schatz, *Genius of the System*, 252.

36. Thomas Doherty, *Pre-Code Hollywood: Sex, Immorality, and Insurrection in the American Cinema, 1930–1934* (New York: Columbia University Press, 1999), 289.

37. Quoted in Schatz, *Genius of the System*, 168.

38. Schatz, *Genius of the System*, 172.

39. David O. Selznick, *Memo from David O. Selznick,* ed. Rudy Behlmer (Hollywood, Calif.: Samuel French, 1989), 72.

40. Victor Shapiro, "Review of David Copperfield," *Motion Picture Daily's Hollywood Preview* (January 8, 1935).

41. Schatz, *Genius of the System,* 169. Fifty-four percent of the gross sales were from the United States and Canada and 21 percent from "other foreign." The budget for the film looked like this: Story/cont.: $69,457; Direction: $113,585; Cast: $46,769; Extras: $20,213; Cameramen: $33,608; Lighting: $19,062; Sets: $104,038; Props $42,019; Wardrobe: $33,544; Location: $ 4,348; Film/lab: $46,818; Sound: $31,864; Cutting: $9,566; Music: $ 45,914; General overhead: $171,726 (168).

42. Frank L. Dyer, "The Moral Development of the Silent Drama," *Edison Kinetogram* (April 15, 1910):11, quoted in Eileen Bowser, *The Transformation of Cinema, 1907–1915* (New York: Scribners, 1990), 200–201. It is worth pointing out that the first *David Copperfield,* a three-reeler produced by Thanhouser for Vitagraph, appeared only a little more than a year later. Eileen Bowser thinks that the 1911 production of *David Copperfield,* together with Vitagraph's *A Tale of Two Cities* (also 1911), helped transform early cinema into a prestige product.

43. Quoted in Richard Maltby, "'To Prevent the Prevalent Type of Book': Censorship and Adaptation in Hollywood, 1924–1934," in Naremore, *Film Adaptation,* 79.

44. Will Hays quoted in Maltby, "Censorship and Adaptation," 87. See also Gregory Black, *Hollywood Censored: Morality Codes, Catholics and the Movies* (Cambridge, U.K.: Cambridge University Press, 1994), 85 and following.

45. Maltby, "Censorship and Adaptation," in Naremore, *Film Adaptation,* 84.

46. Quoted in Balio, *Grand Design,* 189. Also see the excellent section on the Hollywood context for prestige productions, 179–211.

47. PCA Annual Report, February 15, 1935, quoted in Black, *Hollywood Censored,* 208. See also 203–217 for a full treatment of the production history of *Anna Karenina* and what Black calls "sex with a dash of moral compensation."

48. Quoted in Black, *Hollywood Censored,* 185.

49. See Leonard J. Leff and Jerold L. Simmons, *The Dame in the Kimono* (Garden City, N.Y.: Doubleday, 1990), 3–54. According to the studio records, the Confidential

Report of the Board of Censors approved *David Copperfield* without elimination in the following territories: Massachusetts (January 14, 1935); Ohio (January 17, 1935); Kansas (January 31, 1935); New York (January 31, 1935), and Pennsylvania (February 16, 1935). But the international community had reservations, and the following deletions were made: Hungary (August 2, 1935)—"Murdstone beating David"; Belgium (October 7, 1935)—"Truck drivers hard striking of David Copperfield's hand"; Sweden (February 6, 1936)—"Murdstone beating David," and the conversation between David and Mr. Dick on "the beheading of Charles I"; Latvia (April 8, 1936)—"David being beaten"; See "David Copperfield," in the George Cukor Collection, Margaret Herrick Library of the Academy of Motion Picture Arts and Sciences, Los Angeles.

50. Steve J. Wurtzler, "David Copperfield and the U.S. Curriculum," in *Dickens on Screen,* 156. Wurtzler also handles the more general use of film study guides in the 1930s as well, and says that in the same year that the study guide to *David Copperfield* appeared, there were also published guides to *Little Women, Alice in Wonderland, The Emperor Jones, Treasure Island, Great Expectations,* and *The Little Minister.* In 1936 study guides were available for *Romeo and Juliet* (with an introduction by Irving Thalberg and set design sketches by Cedric Gibbons), *Mutiny on the Bounty, A Tale of Two Cities, The Last Days of Pompeii, The Three Musketeers, Little Lord Fauntleroy, Les Miserables* (with an introduction by Darryl Zanuck and statements by director Richard Boleslawski and screenwriter W. P. Lipscomb), *Mary of Scotland, Scrooge (A Christmas Carol), A Midsummer Night's Dream,* and *The Shape of Things to Come* (159).

51. Wurtzler, "David Copperfield," 156.

52. Mary Allen Abbott, *A Study Guide to the Critical Appreciation of the Photoplay Version of Charles Dickens' Novel David Copperfield,* ed. Max J. Herzberg (Chicago: National Council of Teachers of English, 1935), 4.

53. Ibid., 5.

54. Ibid., 8–14.

55. Elizabeth Pollard Watson quoted in Wurtzler, "David Copperfield," 158.

56. Wurtzler, "David Copperfield," 158. See also Dana Polan, *Scenes of Instruction: The Beginnings of the U.S. Study of Film* (Berkeley: University of California Press, 2007).

57. Abbott, *Study Guide,* 4.

58. M. M. Bakhtin, *The Dialogic Imagination,* ed. Michael Holquist, trans. Caryl Emerson and Michael Holquist (Austin: University of Texas Press, 1981), 263.

59. Wurtzler, "David Copperfield," 170.

60. Eisenstein in Leda, *Film Form,* 232.

61. Brian McFarlane, *Novel to Film: An Introduction to the Theory of Adaptation* (New York: Oxford University Press, 1996), 21.

62. Robert Stam, "Introduction," 27.

63. Kamilla Elliott, *Rethinking the Novel/Film Debate,* 122. See also Rhoda L. Flaxman, *Victorian Word-Painting and Narrative: Toward the Blending of Genres.* Nine-

teenth-Century Studies. Series ed. Juliet McMaster (Ann Arbor: University Micro-films International Research Press, 1987). I am indebted to Elliott for this citation; and Joss Lutz March, "Inimitable Double Vision: Dickens, *Little Dorrit,* Photography, Film," *Dickens Studies Annual* 22 (1993): 239–82.

64. Elliott, *Rethinking the Novel/Film Debate,* 221.

65. Quoted in Elliott, *Rethinking the Novel/Film Debate,* 33. See also Michael Steig, *Dickens and Phiz* (Bloomington: Indiana University Press, 1978).

66. J. Hillis Miller, *Illustration: Essays in Art and Culture* (Cambridge, Mass.: Harvard University Press, 1992), 61 and following.

67. Angela Dalle Vacche, *Cinema and Painting: How Art is Used in Film* (Austin: University of Texas Press, 1996), 3.

68. David Bordwell, Janet Staiger, and Kristin Thompson, *The Classical Hollywood Cinema: Film Style and Mode of Production to 1960* (New York: Columbia University Press, 1985), 50. In discussing the *tableaux vivant* and its relationship with film production, Bordwell says that "post-renaissance painting provided one powerful model" for composition. Cinematographers and directors constantly invoked famous paintings as sources. Cecil B. DeMille claimed to have borrowed from Doré, Van Dyck, Corot, and one "Rubins." See Terry Castle, "Phantasmagoria: Spectral Technology and the Metaphorics of Modern Reverie," *Critical Inquiry* 15, no. 3 (1988): 26–31; also see Dalle Vacche, *Cinema and Painting.* J. Hillis Miller makes an important connection between iconography and representation in his discussion of Dickens and Cruickshank in "The Fiction of Realism: Sketches by Boz, Oliver Twist, and Cruickshank's Illustrations," in *Victorian Subjects* (Durham, N.C.: Duke University Press, 1991), 119–77, and *Illustration: Essays in Art and Culture* (Cambridge, Mass.: Harvard University Press, 1992). For an important discussion of the role of art direction on this topic, see Charles Affron and Mirella Jona Affron, *Sets in Motion: Art Direction and Film Narrative* (New Brunswick, N.J.: Rutgers University Press, 1995).

69. MGM went to great lengths to duplicate Victorian reproductions in nineteenth-century illustration for *David Copperfield.* The studio announced that the characters were made to look like Cruikshank, but the Dickensian was quick to point out that they were, in fact, based on Phiz's illustrations for *David Copperfield.* Phiz's original drawings were enlarged and then the characters made to pose to conform to them. In addition, the well-publicized month-long production trip that Selznick, Cukor, and others took to England in order to replicate the characters and settings in *David Copperfield,* the MGM's research department even consulted "street character types" in the *Illustrated London News* for 1844, 1846, and 1858 for the purpose of authenticating Dolly Tree's costumes and Cedric Gibbons's art direction. Finally, when Dodd and Mead published *David Copperfield* in 1935 as a tie-in with the film, the publicity stills replaced Phiz's nineteenth-century ink drawings. The Victorian art direction and costumes in the film were believed to be so authentic that Reginald B. Haselden, curator of the Huntington Library, sent a letter to Selznick saying that he was "very familiar with the Dickens period and Dickens London, and I think your most valu-

able achievement is the way in which you have reproduced the atmosphere of the book itself." (MGM correspondence file, Margaret Herrick Library of the Academy of the Motion Picture Arts and Sciences, Los Angeles).

70. Quoted in Gavin Lambert, *On Cukor* (New York: Putnam, 1972), 87.

71. Eisenstein's famous essay on Dickens as a kind of Ur-text for understanding montage and parallel editing is based not on *David Copperfield*'s first-person, semi-autobiographical form, but on the omniscient narrator in *Oliver Twist*. Brian MacFarlane believes the connection between Griffith and Dickens by theories of adaptation "has been overestimated and under-scrutinized." *See Novel to Film*, 1996), 8. Garrett Stewart notes certain blind spots in Eisenstein's essay and distinguishes between the "filmic rather than the cinematic elements" of Dickens's work. See, "Dickens, Eisenstein, Film," in *Dickens on Screen*, 122–44.

72. J. Hillis Miller, *Victorian Subjects,* 99.

73. David Bordwell, "Classical Hollywood Cinema," in *Narrative, Apparatus, Ideology: A Film Theory Reader,* ed., Philip Rosen (New York: Columbia University Press, 1986), 22.

74. Foucault, "What is an Author?" 107.

75. Gérard Genette, *Paratexts: Thresholds of Interpretation,* trans. Jane E. Lewin (Cambridge, U.K.: Cambridge University Press, 1997), 1.

76. Richard Maltby, *Hollywood Cinema: An Introduction* (Oxford: Blackwell, 1995), 327. For Maltby, an illustration of the paradigm is *The Pirate* (1948), with its movement from narrated introduction about the book (telling) to the world of the movie (showing).

77. Bordwell, "Classical Hollywood Cinema," 32.

78. A. Lindsley Lane, "The Camera's Omniscient Eye," *American Cinematographer* 16, no. 3 (March 1935): 95, quoted in David Bordwell, *Narration and the Fiction Film* (Madison: University of Wisconsin Press, 1985), 161.

79. Walter Allen, *The English Novel* (New York: E.P. Dutton, 1954), 165.

80. Thomson, *Showman,* 181.

81. Peter Brooks, *Reading for the Plot: Design and Intention in Narrative* (New York: Vintage, 1984), 123–24.

82. Matthew Arnold, *Culture and Anarchy* (Cambridge, U.K.: Cambridge University Press, 1932), 48.

83. Charles Eckert, "Shirley Temple and The House of Rockefeller," in *Star Texts: Image and Performance in Film and Television,* ed. Jeremy G. Butler (Detroit: Wayne State University Press, 1991), 187.

84. Arnold, *Culture and Anarchy,* 49.

85. James Agee, *Agee on Film* (Boston: Beacon, 1958), 18.

86. Arnold, *Culture and Anarchy,* 64.

Chapter 3. Into Africa

1. Orson Welles and Peter Bogdanovich, *This is Orson Welles,* ed. Jonathan Rosenbaum (New York: Harper Collins, 1992), 32.

2. Fredric Jameson, *The Political Unconscious: Narrative as a Socially Symbolic Act* (Ithaca, N.Y.: Cornell University Press, 1981), 236; see also Bill Nichols, "Form Wars: The Political Unconscious of Formalist Theory," in *Classical Hollywood Narrative: The Paradigm Wars,* ed. Jane Gaines (Durham, N.C., and London: Duke University Press, 1992), 49–77.

3. Robert B. Ray, *A Certain Tendency of Hollywood Cinema, 1930–1980* (Princeton, N.J.: Princeton University Press, 1985), 59.

4. The amount of attention that Conrad's novella has received over the last few decades owes in large part to the rise of postcolonial and cultural studies in the academy. Chinua Achebe challenged the conventional reading of Conrad's text as a "journey within" with his controversial essay, "An Image of Africa," *Massachusetts Review* 18 (1977): 782–94. That essay, subsequently revised, has become the touchstone of racial discourse concerning *Heart of Darkness,* a conversation that has been ongoing and significant. Also see Susan L. Blake, "Racism and the Classics: Teaching Heart of Darkness," *College Language Association Journal* 25 (1982): 396–404; Benita Parry, *Conrad and Imperialism* (London: Macmillan, 1983). For another position, see Peter Nazareth, "Out of Darkness: Conrad and Other Third World Writers," *Conradiana* 14, no. 3 (1982): 173–87; and Terry Collits, *Postcolonial Conrad: Paradoxes of Empire* (New York: Routledge, 2005), 105–23. For a readable summary of this debate, see David Denby, "Jungle Fever," *The New Yorker* 71, no. 35 (November 6, 1995): 118–29. The most recent edition of the text for the Norton Critical Editions (4th ed., 2006) exceeds five hundred pages, with Conrad's novella covering a mere seventy five. The Norton edition provides a good overview of the present discussion, including, for the purposes of adaptation, Louis K. Greiff's essay "Conrad's Ethics and the Margins of *Apocalypse Now,*" 484–99.

5. Albert J. Guerard, *Conrad the Novelist* (Cambridge, Mass.: Harvard University Press, 1958, reprint 1967); and Ian Watt, *Conrad and the Nineteenth Century* (Berkeley: University of California Press, 1979), 126–253. Watt characterizes Conrad's technique as "impressionism."

6. In contrast to canonical readings, *Heart of Darkness* has come to signify, as it does for Edward Said, in *Orientalism* (New York: Vintage, 1979), a colonial, "geographical appetite" in the guise of "moral neutrality of an epistemological impulse to find out, to settle upon to uncover—as when in *Heart of Darkness* Marlow confesses to having a passion for maps" (216). See also Marianna Torgovnick, *Gone Primitive* (Chicago and London: University of Chicago Press, 1990), 141–58; and Edward Said, *Cultural Imperialism* (New York: Knopf, 1993), 3–31. Under revisionist theory, Conrad's story becomes not a liberating mythic psychodrama but a late-nineteenth-century, Western imperialist obsession with "radical alterity," supported by modernist aesthetics, in which the primitive becomes a fetishized object to be consumed. See Patrick Brantlinger, "Heart of Darkness: Anti-Imperialist, Racism or Impressionism?" *Criticism* 27 (1985): 363–85. Brantlinger foregrounds Conrad in the context of British imperialism in *Rule of Darkness: British Literature and Imperialism, 1930–1914* (Ithaca, N.Y.: Cornell University Press, 1988), 255 and following.

7. Perry Meisel, *The Myth of the Modern* (New Haven, Conn.: Yale University Press, 1987), 229. Under revisionist theory, Conrad's story becomes not a liberating mythic psychodrama, but a late nineteenth century, Western imperialist obsession with "radical alterity," supported by modernist aesthetics, in which the primitive becomes a fetishized object to be consumed. See Brantlinger, "Heart of Darkness," 363–85.

8. See Ray, *A Certain Tendency,* 25–69.

9. Meisel, *Myth of the Modern,* 325.

10. Robert Sklar, *Movie-Made America: A Social History of American Movies* (New York: Random House, 1975), 195.

11. See, Michael Denning, "Towards a Peoples Theater: The Cultural Politics of the Mercury Theatre," *Persistence of Vision* 7 (1989): 24–38.

12. Robert L. Carringer, *The Making of "Citizen Kane"* (Berkeley: University of California Press, 1985), 3. Carringer has an indispensable chapter on *Heart of Darkness,* 1–15.

13. Welles and Bogdanovich, *This is Orson Welles,* 31.

14. Orson Welles, memo, September 15, 1939. I will be using the "Revised Estimating Script" for *Heart of Darkness,* which is dated November 30, 1939. All other unpublished material is from the Orson Welles Collection, Lilly Library, Bloomington, Indiana. See Box 14, File 16.

15. The introduction to *Heart of Darkness* recalls what James Naremore has noted about Welles's double-edged form of theatricality: "On the one hand, he was a brilliant practitioner of what John Houseman called 'magical effect,' and he was clearly indebted to a romantic or Gothic tradition of Shakespearean drama, grand opera, and stage illusionism; on the other hand, he was also a didactic, somewhat Brechtian storyteller whose cultural politics were shaped during the period of the Popular Front, and whose technique was visibly rhetorical, strongly dependent on direct address" (Naremore, "Director as Actor," 3; unpublished manuscript). As suggested here, Welles's attempts bring these two different aspects of his work into a synthesis: it is a blueprint for a dark, mysterious conjunction, all presided over by Welles's voice; but at the same time, it contains didactic elements that probe the dynamics of spectatorship.

16. Frank Brady, *Citizen Welles* (New York: Doubleday, 1989), 211.

17. See Jonathan Rosenbaum, "The Voice and the Eye: A Commentary on the *Heart of Darkness* Script," *Film Comment* (November–December 1972): 27–32; reprinted in Jonathan Rosenbaum, *Discovering Orson Welles* (Berkeley: University of California Press, 2007), 28–48.

18. David Thomson, *Rosebud: The Story of Orson Welles* (New York: Knopf, 1996), 76.

19. Marguerite Rippy, "Orson Welles and Charles Dickens, 1938–1941," in *Dickens on Screen,* ed. John Glavin (Cambridge, U.K.: Cambridge University Press, 2003), 146.

20. Quoted in Simon Callow, *Orson Welles, Vol. 1: The Road to Xanadu* (New York:

Penguin, 1995), 373. See also Paul Heyer, *The Medium and the Magician: Orson Welles, the Radio Years, 1934-52* (Lanham, Md.: Rowman and Littlefield, 2005).

21. Joseph Conrad, *Heart of Darkness* (New York: W.W. Norton, 2006), 33–34.

22. James Naremore, *More Than Night: Film Noir and Its Contexts* (Berkeley: University of California Press, 1998), 47–48.

23. Rippy, "Orson Welles and Dickens," 150.

24. Robert Spadoni, "Radio in Welles's Heart of Darkness," in *Conrad on Film,* ed. Gene M. Moore (Cambridge, U.K.: Cambridge University Press, 1997), 83–84.

25. Joseph Conrad, "Preface," in *The Nigger of the "Narcissus"* (New York: Viking Penguin, 1988), xlix.

26. Spadoni, "Radio in Welles," 84.

27. By 1950, Welles was listed as a participant in the National Citizens Political Action Committee, the Motion Picture Artists' Committee, the Negro Cultural Committee, the Theatre Arts Committee, the Hollywood Democratic Committee, the American Committee for Protection of the Foreign Born, the American Student Union, the Coordinating Committee to Lift the Embargo, the Exiled Writers Committee, the Friends of the Abraham Lincoln Brigade, International Labor Defense, and New Masses. See Joseph McBride, *Whatever Happened to Orson Welles?* (Lexington: University of Kentucky Press, 2006), 102. Naremore has shown that Welles was the subject of FBI investigation throughout the 1940s. See James Naremore, "The Trial: The FBI vs. Orson Welles," *Film Comment* 27, no.1 (January–February 1991): 22–28.

28. See Michael Denning, *The Cultural Front: The Laboring of American Culture in the Twentieth Century* (London: Verso), 1997.

29. Ricardo J. Quinones, *Mapping Literary Modernism: Time and Development* (Princeton, N.J.: Princeton University Press, 1985), 40.

30. See Judith E. Smith, "Radio's 'Cultural Front,' 1938–48," in *Radio Reader: Essays in the Cultural History of Radio,* eds. Michele Hilmes and Jason Loviglio (New York: Routledge, 2002), 214. Smith does a fine job in summarizing Denning's argument. See also Heyer, *The Medium and the Magician,* 15–43.

31. Quoted in Heyer, *The Medium and the Magician,* 31.

32. Quoted in Thomson, *Rosebud,* 76.

33. Smith, "Radio's 'Cultural Front,' " 214. MacLeish's other play, *Air Raid,* was also an antifascist story, and broadcast a few days before *The War of The Worlds.*

34. James Naremore, *The Magic World of Orson Welles,* rev. ed. (1978; Dallas: Southern Methodist University Press, 1989), 13.

35. Rosenbaum points out that in 1972, the recording that was generally available of *The War of the Worlds* was not the one broadcast on October 30, 1938. See "The Voice and the Eye," 31. But in 2001, Smithsonian released a "Legendary Performers" edition on CD starring Orson Welles. The original Mercury Theater on the Air broadcast of *The War of the Worlds* is available on this edition.

36. Jean-Pierre Berthomé and François Thomas, *Orson Welles at Work* (New York: Phaidon Press, 2008), 20.

37. Naremore, *Magic World of Orson Welles,* 13.

38. Smith, "Radio's 'Cultural Front,'" 214.

39. See Brian Neve, *Film and Politics in America* (New York: Routledge, 1992).

40. For the complete transcript of *"VooDoo" Macbeth* (1936) and *Julius Caesar* (1937), see *Orson Welles on Shakespeare: The W.P.A. and Mercury Theatre Playscripts,* ed. Richard France (New York: Greenwood Press, 1990), 29–168. Hereafter, this work is cited parenthetically in the text.

41. France, *Orson Welles on Shakespeare,* 30.

42. Ibid., 33.

43. Naremore, *Magic World of Orson Welles,* 137.

44. Ibid., 142.

45. Quoted in Naremore, *Magic World of Orson Welles,* 137.

46. Naremore, *Magic World of Orson Welles,* 138.

47. Quoted in France, *Orson Welles on Shakespeare,* 62.

48. Quoted in Naremore, *Magic World of Orson Welles,* 144.

49. Pells, *Radical Visions and American Dreams,* 254.

50. Barbara Leaming, *Orson Welles: A Biography* (New York: Viking Penguin, 1984), 338.

51. Callow, *Road to Xanadu,* 342.

52. Brady, *Citizen Welles,* 111.

53. Bertholt Brecht, *Brecht on Theater,* ed. and trans. John Willett (London: Methuen, 1982), 86.

54. France, *Orson Welles on Shakespeare,* 106.

55. Quoted in Willett, *Brecht on Theater,* 37.

56. Carringer, *The Making of "Citizen Kane,"* 3.

57. RKO "Studio Memo" on Orson Welles and *Heart of Darkness,* September 15, 1939.

58. Callow, *Road to Xanadu,* 464.

59. Callow, *Road to Xanadu,* 469.

60. Brady, *Citizen Welles,* 210. See also Callow, *Road to Xanadu,* for a more detailed summary of the introduction or prologue to the film. Callow also has an interesting summary of the production history of the script. Additionally, Jonathan Rosenbaum has reproduced the entire introductory sequence as an appendix to "The Voice and the Eye: A Commentary on the Heart of Darkness Script," reprinted in Jonathan Rosenbaum, *Discovering Orson Welles* (Berkeley: University of California Press, 2007), 43–48.

61. See, Sarah Kozloff, *Invisible Storytellers: Voice-Over Narration in the American Fiction Film* (Berkeley: University of California Press, 1988); and Edward Branigan, *Narrative Comprehension and Film* (London and New York: Routledge, 1992).

62. Mike Cormack, *Ideology and Cinematography in Hollywood, 1930–39* (New York: St. Martin, 1994), 24.

63. See the "Revised Estimating Script" for *Heart of Darkness,* November 30, 1939. Box 14, File 16, Orson Welles Collection, Lilly Library, Indiana University. All subsequent quotations are taken from this manuscript.

64. See Jakob Lothe, *Conrad's Narrative Method* (Oxford: Clarendon Press, 1989), 21–44.

65. Welles and Bogdanovich, *This is Orson Welles,* 32.

66. Joseph Conrad, "Preface," *The Nigger of the "Narcissus,"* xlix.

67. Carringer, *The Making of "Citizen Kane,"* 12.

68. RKO "Studio Memo" on Orson Welles and *Heart of Darkness,* September 15, 1939.

69. Quoted in Callow, *Road to Xanadu, 469.*

70. Jonathan Rosenbaum, "The Voice and The Eye," *Film Comment* (November–December 1972): 32.

71. Abdul R. JanMohamed, "The Economy of the Manichean Allegory: The Function of Racial Difference in Colonialist Literature," *Critical Inquiry* 12 (1985): 59–87.

72. Robert Young, *White Mythologies* (London: Routledge, 1990), 13.

73. Brantlinger, *Rule of Darkness,* 257.

74. See Jameson, *The Political Unconscious,* 225 and following.

75. Welles told Jonathan Rosenbaum that the contemporary political reference for him was Otto Skorzeny (1908–1975), an SS officer, and the then-recent activities in the Belgian Congo. See Welles and Bogdanovich, *This is Orson Welles,* 493.

76. Quoted in Callow, *Road to Xanadu, 457.*

77. Dita Parlo, a German actress who had just completed Jean Renoir's *Grand Illusion,* was supposed to have played the part of Elsa. A final decision never seems to have been made regarding Elsa, because Parlo had difficulty getting out of France (owing to her German citizenship), and Hollywood players such as Carol Lombard and Swedish actress Ingrid Bergman either declined or were fiscal impossibilities. Besides Welles as Marlow/Kurtz, the cast included: Everett Sloane (Stitzer), Norman Lloyd (Butz), Edgar Barrier (Strunz), Gus Schilling (Melchers), George Coulouris (Cams), Erskine Sanford (Schilman), Ray Collins (Blauer), John Emery (de Terpitz), Frank Readick (Meuss), Jack Carter (Steersman), and Vlaimir Sokoloff (Doctor).

78. Rosenbaum, "The Voice and the Eye," 29.

79. Welles and Bogdanovich, *This is Orson Welles,* 31.

80. Ibid., 493.

81. See Berthomé and Thomas, *Orson Welles at Work,* 34–35.

82. See *Hollywood Variety,* January 9, 1940. Simon Callow says that Schaefer got wind of the budget earlier, on September 1, 1939, just when Germany invaded Poland, and wired Welles, making a plea "to eliminate every dollar and nickel possible from heart of darkness script and yet do everything to save entertainment value." Callow also claims that "They returned to the original budget ceiling of $500,000 but Welles himself appears to dispute this figure when he told Peter Bogdanovich that "we couldn't knock $50,000 off the budget." See Callow, *Road to Xanadu,* 471 and Welles and Bogdanovich, *This is Orson Welles,* 31.

83. Welles and Bogdanovich, *This is Orson Welles,* 31.

84. Carringer, *The Making of "Citizen Kane,"* 12.

85. See Richard Maltby, "'To Prevent the Prevalent Type of Book': Censorship and

Adaptation in Hollywood, 1924–1934," in Naremore, *Film Adaptation,* 79–105. See also Thomas Doherty, *Hollywood's Censor: Joseph I. Breen and the Production Code Administration* (New York: Columbia University Press, 2007).

86. Brady, *Citizen Welles,* 215.

87. Welles's version of Conrad might be viewed within a larger cultural formation of antifascist art emerging in America between 1933 and 1945. See Cecile Whiting, *Antifascism and American Art* (New Haven, Conn.: Yale University Press, 1989).

88. Conrad, *Heart of Darkness,* 60.

89. Brady, *Citizen Welles,* 211.

90. See Donald Bogle, *Toms, Coons, Mulattoes, Mammies and Bucks* (New York: Continuum, 1973, rev. 1989), 35–100; Thomas Cripps, *Slow Fade to Black: The Negro in American Film, 1900–1942* (New York: Oxford University Press, 1977); and Ed Guerrero, *Framing Blackness: The African American Image in Film* (Philadelphia: Temple University Press, 1993.)

91. Richard Dyer, *Heavenly Bodies: Film Stars and Society* (New York: St. Martin, 1986), 116.

92. RKO "Studio Memo" on Orson Welles and *Heart of Darkness,* September 15, 1939.

93. See Jan Nederveen Pieterse, *White on Black: Images of Africa and Blacks in Western Popular Culture* (New Haven, Conn.: Yale University Press, 1992).

94. Franz Boaz et al., *The Genetic Basis for Democracy* (Washington, D.C.: American Committee for Democracy and Intellectual Freedom, 1939), 10.

95. See Christine Rosen, *Preaching Eugenics: Religious Leaders and the American Eugenics Movement* (New York: Oxford University Press, 2004).

96. Annette Kuhn, *Cinema, Censorship and Sexuality, 1909–1925* (London and New York: Routledge, 1988), 33.

97. Ibid., 34.

98. Brady, *Citizen Welles,* 215.

99. David Bordwell, "Classical Hollywood Cinema: Narrational Principles and Procedures," in Philip Rosen, ed., *Narrative, Apparatus, Ideology* (New York: Columbia University Press, 1986), 17–34.

100. Bordwell, "Classical Hollywood Cinema," 24.

101. Seymour Chatman, *Coming to Terms: The Rhetoric of Narrative in Fiction and Film* (Ithaca, N.Y.: Cornell University Press, 1990), 129.

102. Stephen Heath, *Questions of Cinema* (Bloomington: Indiana University Press, 1981), 122.

103. Brady, *Citizen Welles,* 216.

104. See Jean-Louis Baudry, "Ideological Effects of the Basic Cinema Apparatus," trans. Alan Williams, in *Movies and Methods, Vol. II,* ed. Bill Nichols (Berkeley: University of California Press, 1985), 531–42.

105. Welles's description of Elsa in the film script suggests his concern with acting and also hints at Brecht's own interests he expressed as "alienation." Rather than

"lose oneself in character," Welles conceived of the girl as a symbolic representation of human emotion: "Here is a chance for a real bit of what is popularly called 'great acting.' I guess great acting can only happen when an actor gets a chance to show one of the grand passions; well, here is one of them. Love is what it is called. This is the time when it really has got to be acted, and I mean ACTED. Because the girl hasn't got a love scene. She is just supposed to represent love and to make us believe she is in possession of that flame."

106. Brecht, *Brecht on Theater*, 136.

107. Naremore, *Magic World of Orson Welles*, 48.

108. Ibid., 176.

109. Pells, *Radical Visions*, 288–89.

110. Vincent Canby, "'Kane' at 50 Dazzles Yet with its High Spirits," *New York Times*, Sec. 2 (April 28, 1991): 1, 16.

111. See Rosenbaum, "The Voice and the Eye," 27–32.

112. Leaming, *Orson Welles*, 336–39.

113. Naremore, *Magic World of Orson Welles*, 141.

114. Welles and Bogdanovich, *This is Orson Welles*, 32.

115. Ibid., 493.

116. Jonathan Rosenbaum, "Welles in the Limelight: The Third Man," in *Discovering Orson Welles* (Berkeley: University of California Press, 2007), 264.

117. Naremore, *More Than Night*, 77.

118. Andrew Sarris, *The American Cinema: Directors and Directions, 1929–1968* (Chicago: University of Chicago Press, 1968), 79.

Chapter 4. Filmed Theater

1. The interview is reprinted in *This is Orson Welles*, eds. Peter Bogdanovich and Jonathan Rosenbaum (New York: DaCapo Press, rev. ed., 1998), 27.

2. Quoted in Tag Gallagher, *John Ford: The Man and His Films* (Berkeley: University of California Press, 1967), 152.

3. James Naremore, *The Magic World of Orson Welles*, rev. ed. (Dallas: Southern Methodist University Press, 1978; 1989), 226.

4. *The Long Voyage Home* was the first film produced by Ford's own production company, Argosy, with Walter Wanger Productions, and distributed through United Artists. Ford began shooting on April 17, 1940, and had its New York opening October 9, 1940. Along with Ford and Wanger, the production included Wingate Smith (assistant director); Dudley Nichols (screenwriter); Gregg Toland (director of photography); R. T. Layton and R. O. Binger (special effects); James Basevi (art director); Sherman Todd (editor); Edward Paul (musical director). The picture was filmed aboard the freighter *S.S. Munami* at Wilmington Harbor, California, with a cast that included John Wayne (Ole Olson), Thomas Mitchell (Driscoll), Ian Hunter (Smitty), Barry Fitzgerald (Cocky), Wilfrid Lawson (Captain), Mildred Natwick (screen debut as Frieda), John Qualen (Axel), and Ward Bond (Yank).

5. Andrew Sarris, *The John Ford Movie Mystery* (Bloomington and London: Indiana University Press, 1975), 91–123.

6. Ibid., 99.

7. *Bound East for Cardiff* (1914), *The Moon of the Caribbees* (1917), *In the Zone* (1917), and *The Long Voyage Home* (1917). The best edition of the plays to date is *Eugene O'Neill: Complete Plays. Vol. I: 1913–1920*, ed. Travis Board (New York: Library of America, 1990).

8. In fact, details of the productions were published at length by Ford himself. Ford and Nichols met to discuss the script of *The Long Voyage Home* before and after each draft. See John Ford, "How We Made The Long Voyage Home," *Friday* (August 9, 1940): 21–22. Ford and Nichols collaborated on *The Informer, Mary of Scotland, The Plough and the Stars,* and *The Fugitive*. Ford's biographer says that the Ford-Nichols pairing was "characterized by literary presence, theatrical value and heavy Germanic stylization." See Gallagher, *John Ford*, 465.

9. André Bazin, *What is Cinema? Vol. I*, ed. and trans. Hugh Gray (Berkeley: University of California Press, 1967), 87.

10. See Edwin Panofsky, "Style and Medium in the Motion Pictures," in *Film: An Anthology*, ed. Daniel Talbot (Berkeley: University of California Press, 1959), 15–32. Panofsky originally published the article in 1934 and then revised it for *Critique* 1, no. 3. (January–February 1947).

11. See Sergei Eisenstein, "Through Theater to Cinema," in Leda, *Film Form*, 1–18; Andre Bazin, "Theater and Cinema," in *What is Cinema? Vol. I*, 76–124. Also see Susan Sontag, "Theater and Cinema," in *Styles of Radical Will* (New York: Farrar, Strauss and Giroux, 1969), 99–122. More recently, the analysis of the place of theater in cinema has been interrogated much more systematically than in previous years. With the publication of Borwell's, Staiger's, and Thompson's seminal guide to classical Hollywood cinema in 1985, the interface between cinema and the stage has been increasingly revisited from a historical perspective. See, David Bordwell, Janet Staiger, and Kristin Thompson, *The Classical Hollywood Cinema: Film Style and Mode of Production to 1960* (New York: Columbia University Press, 1985), 50. See also Kristin Thompson's section in the same volume, "Novel, Short Story, Drama: the Conditions for Influence," 163–67, and Ben Brewster and Lea Jacobs, *Theater to Cinema: Stage Pictorialism and the Early Feature Film* (New York: Oxford University Press, 1997). Babak A. Ebrahimian, *Cinematic Theater* (Lanham, Md.: Scarecrow Press, 2004) is a more general and recent guide to the aesthetics of "play into film."

12. Eisenstein, "Through Theater to Cinema," in *Film Form*, 16 and following.

13. Bazin, *What is Cinema?*, 91

14. Ibid., 55

15. Ibid., 61.

16. Quoted in Dudley Andrew, *André Bazin* (New York: Columbia University Press, 1978), 63.

17. Bazin, *What is Cinema?*, 78.

18. Ibid., 34.

19. Ibid., 93.

20. Courtney Lehmann, *Shakespeare Remains: Theater to Film, Early Modern to Postmodern* (Ithaca, N.Y.: Cornell University Press, 2002), 24. See also Paisley Livingston, "Cinematic Authorship," in Allen and Smith, *Film Theory and Philosophy*, 132–47; and Andrew Bennett, *The Author* (New York: Routledge, 2005).

21. Bazin, *What is Cinema?*, 117 and following.

22. Ibid., 78.

23. Ibid., 86.

24. Ibid., 88.

25. Ibid., 91.

26. Ibid. 92.

27. Naremore, *Magic World of Orson Welles*, 32.

28. Bazin, *What is Cinema?*, 36. Brian Henderson notes that Bazin did not emphasize that "the long take rarely appears in its pure state" and that "the cut which ends a long take—how it ends and where—determines or affects the nature of the shot itself." Quoted in James Naremore, "Style and Meaning in Citizen Kane," *Orson Welles's Citizen Kane: A Casebook*, ed. James Naremore (New York: Oxford University Press, 2004), 135.

29. Quoted in Andrew, *André Bazin*, 126–28.

30. Andre Bazin, *Bazin at Work: Major Essays and Reviews from the Forties and Fifties*, ed. Bert Cardullo, trans. Alain Piette and Bert Cardullo (Berkeley: University of California Press, 1997), 49.

31. Andrew, *André Bazin*, 185.

32. Bazin, *What is Cinema?*, 124.

33. Ibid., 67 and following.

34. Ibid., 67.

35. Bluestone, *Novels into Film*, 68.

36. As Peter Wollen reminds us, "the director does not subordinate himself to another author; his source is only a pretext, which provides catalysts, scenes which fuse with his own preoccupations to produce a radically new work. Thus the manifest process of performance, the treatment of a subject, conceals the latent production of a quite new text, the production of the director as an auteur." Wollen, "The Auteur Theory," 541. The occasion for Wollen's observation is a longer study, in which he places the principles of structuralism at the service of auteurism. He notes that the director is not simply "in command of performance of a pre-existing text," and cites Don Siegal's adaptation of Hemingway's "The Killers" as an example (541). See also Peter Wollen, *Signs and Meaning in the Cinema* (London: Secker and Warburg, 1972), 102 and following.

37. Bazin, *What is Cinema?*, 83.

38. See Stam, *Literature through Film*, 252–306.

39. Andrew, *André Bazin*, 187.

40. André Bazin, *Qu'est-ce que le cinéma?* (Paris: Les Editions du Cerf, 2002), 124.

41. Bluestone, *Novels into Film,* 219.

42. Leitch, *Film Adaptation and its Discontents,* 238.

43. Bazin, "Cinema as Digest," 49.

44. Bazin, *What is Cinema?* 123.

45. This is a reference to four plays written between 1913 and 1917, *Bound East for Cardiff, In the Zone, The Long Voyage Home,* and *The Moon of the Caribbees.*

46. Quoted in Joseph McBride, *Searching for John Ford* (New York: St. Martin's Press, 2001), 318. For the full interview with the Documentary Film Group, see, *John Ford Interviews,* eds. Gerald Peary and Jenny Lefcourt (Minneapolis: University of Minnesota Press, 2001), 124–26.

47. Sarris, *The American Cinema,* 45. See also Charles J. Maland, "From Aesthete to Pappy: The Evolution of John Ford's Public Reputation," in *John Ford Made Westerns: Filming the Legend in the Sound Era,* eds. Gaylyn Studlar and Matthew Bernstein (Bloomington and Indianapolis: Indiana University Press, 2001) and "That Past, this Present: Historicizing John Ford, 1939," in *John Ford's Stagecoach,* ed. Barry Keith Grant (Cambridge, U.K.: Cambridge University Press, 2003), 82–112.

48. Maland, in Studlar and Bernstein, *John Ford Made Westerns,* 242.

49. Quoted in Thomas Schatz, *Boom and Bust: The American Cinema in the 1940's* (New York: Scribners, 1997), 85.

50. Maland, in Studlar and Bernstein, *John Ford Made Westerns,* 222.

51. Ibid., 223.

52. Sarris, *John Ford Movie Mystery,* 9.

53. Quoted in Sarris, *John Ford Movie Mystery,* 9. Ford earned a well-deserved reputation for being evasive and obscure during interviews. When, for instance, Bertrand Tavernier asked him why he made westerns, Ford told him in the 1966 *Paris interview,* "for health reasons. Westerns are a chance to get away from Hollywood and the smog." And again Tavernier: "Why did you become a film director?" Ford: "I was hungry." Ford became a master of an arty style, but was seemingly always at pains to deny that he made any efforts in that direction. See Bernard Tavernier, "Notes of a Press Attaché: John Ford in Paris, 1966," trans. Jean-Pierre Coursodon, *Film Comment* 30, no. 4 (July–August 1994): 66–75. See also Jean Mitry, "Interview with John Ford," *Cahiers du Cinéma* 45 (March 1955): 3–9.

54. Quoted in Bogdanovich, *John Ford,* 14.

55. Gallagher, *John Ford,* 339.

56. Draft of Ford's speech, dated 1933, quoted in Gallagher, *John Ford,* 340.

57. According to Tag Gallagher, Ford's successful relationship with Carey was typical of the director's ability to locate "an actor's eccentric traits and amplifying them into a screen personae." See Gallagher, *John Ford,* 24.

58. Richard Koszarski, *An Evening's Entertainment: The Age of the Silent Feature Picture, 1915–1928* (New York: Scribners, 1990), 84.

59. Ibid., 85–86.

60. Ibid., 86.

61. Sarris, *John Ford Movie Mystery*, 31.

62. Gallagher, *John Ford*, 47.

63. See Barry Salt, *Film Style and Technology: History and Analysis* (London: Starword, 1983; rev. 1992), 167.

64. Ibid., 167.

65. Michael Budd, "The Moments of Caligari," *in The Cabinet of Dr. Caligari: Texts, Contexts, Histories,* ed. Michael Budd (New Brunswick, N.J.: Rutgers University Press, 1990), 10.

66. Ibid., 25.

67. Michael Budd, "The Cabinet of Dr. Caligari: Conditions of Reception," *Cine-Tracts* 3, no. 4 (Winter 1981): 43.

68. Kristin Thompson, "Dr. Caligari at the Folies-Bergere, or the Success of an Early Avant-Garde Film," in Budd, ed., *Cabinet of Dr. Caligari,* 149. Thompson says that she could find only one instance in which the film received a negative reaction, other than the original Hollywood protest of the film by the American Legion outside Miller's Theater in Los Angeles in May 1921. The audiences hissed the following November in the Albany Theater in Albany, New York, and it was reported in *Variety* (December 2, 1921) as a seemingly unique experience for that film.

69. Thompson, *Cabinet of Dr. Caligari,* 149.

70. Thompson, *Cabinet of Dr. Caligari,* 160–61.

71. Koszarski, *An Evening's Entertainment,* 255.

72. Scott Eyman, *Print the Legend: The Life and Times of John Ford* (New York: Simon and Schuster, 1999), 106.

73. Ibid., 106.

74. Quoted in Eyman, *Print the Legend,* 106.

75. Eyman, *Print the Legend,* 107.

76. Maland, in *John Ford Made Westerns,* 226.

77. Ibid., 227.

78. *The Informer* garnered four Academy Awards: Best Director (John Ford); Best Actor (Victor McLaglen); Best Screenplay (Dudley Nichols); and Best Musical Score (Max Steiner). The film was also nominated as Best Picture, but lost to another studio who was having better luck with prestigious films than RKO, with *Mutiny on the Bounty.* The film had trouble with censors and was severely cut in Canada and banned in Peru. The British demanded 129 deletions, including any references to the Irish Republic and "Blacks and Tans." See Gregory D. Black, *Hollywood Censored: Morality Codes, Catholics and the Movies* (Cambridge, U.K.: Cambridge University Press, 1994), 297–98.

79. Gallagher, *John Ford,* 121.

80. Mike Cormack, *Ideology and Cinematography in Hollywood, 1930–39* (New York: St. Martin, 1994), 91.

81. Quoted in Lindsay Anderson, *About John Ford* (London: Plexus, 1981), 63.

82. Bluestone, *Novels into Film,* 77.

83. Quoted in Maland, *John Ford Made Westerns,* 228.

84. Maland, *John Ford Made Westerns,* 228.

85. *Bound East for Cardiff* (copyright 1914 *as Children of the Sea* and revised in 1916) was first performed at the Wharf Theater, Provincetown, Massachusetts, on July 28, 1916, and directed by O'Neill himself. *In the Zone* was first performed by the Washington Square Players, Comedy Theater, New York, October 31, 1917. *The Moon of the Caribbees* was first performed by the Provincetown Players, Playwright's Theater, New York, on December 20, 1918. The four plays are often revived together as either *The Long Voyage Home* or *S.S. Glencairn* and were done together for the first time by Frank Shay's Barnstormers in the Barnstormer's Barn, Provincetown, Massachusetts, in 1924.

86. That film shows the South Seas in turmoil and the protagonist Terangi literally adrift. The "primitive" here is a commercial lure insofar as it serves to show Hollywood's special effects (fabulously done by actual and miniature scales) and Dorothy Lamour in her sarong.

87. Louis Schaeffer, *O'Neill: Son and Artist, Vol. II* (New York: Paragon House, 1973; rev. 1990), 505.

88. Quoted in McBride, *Searching for John Ford,* 318.

89. Eyman, *Print the Legend,* 232.

90. John Orlandello, *O'Neill and Film* (London and Toronto: Associated Press, 1982), 11.

91. Schaeffer, *O'Neill: Son and Artist,* 76.

92. Orlandello, *O'Neill and Film,* 11.

93. Ibid.

94. Ernst O. Fink, "Audience Aids for Non-Literary Allusions: Observations on the Transposition of Essential Technicalities in the Sea Plays of Eugene O'Neill," in *The Language of Theater: Problems in the Translation and Transposition of Drama,* ed. Ortrum Zuber (New York: Pergamon, 1980), 81.

95. See Charles Higham, *Merchant of Dreams: Louis B. Mayer and the Secret Hollywood* (New York: Dell, 1993), esp. 146–51. Ironically, when *Anna Christie* was released in 1930 for Metro, it became famous less for O'Neill's dialogue than for Garbo's mimicking of silent pantomime and her by-now classic camp remark: "Gimme a viskey, ginger ale on the side . . . and don't be stingy, baby."

96. Quoted in Orlandello, *O'Neill and Film,* 89.

97. O'Neill was using certain naturalist techniques that were not only inherited from American authors such as Frank Norris and William Dean Howells, but also deployed by his contemporaries, such as John Dos Passos and Theodore Dreiser. See June Howard, *Form and History in American Literary Naturalism* (Chapel Hill: University of North Carolina Press, 1985).

98. C. W. E. Bigsby, *A Critical Introduction to Twentieth Century American Drama, Vol. 1* (Cambridge, U.K.: Cambridge University Press, 1982), 103.

99. Clifford Leech, *O'Neill* (Edinburgh and London: Oliver and Boyd, 1963), 39. See also Maida Castellun, "O'Neill's 'The Emperor Jones' Thrills and Fascinates," *New York Call*, November 10, 1920.

100. Schaeffer, *O'Neill: Son and Artist*, 76.

101. Quoted in Schaeffer, *O'Neill: Son and Artist*, 76.

102. Bogdanovich, *John Ford*, 78.

103. Producer Walter Wanger was responsible for engaging Gene Fowler in the opening and closing titles in order to clean up the beginning. See Matthew Bernstein "Hollywood's 'Arty Cinema': John Ford's Long Voyage Home," *Wide Angle* 10, no. 1 (1988): 38.

104. Sarris, *John Ford Movie Mystery*, 100–101.

105. See the John Ford Collection, Lilly Library, Box 16, f.16. The price of the process shot is listed as $400.00.

106. Lindsey Anderson, *About John Ford* (London: Plexus, 1981), 86.

107. See Bernstein, "Hollywood's Arty Cinema," (1988), 44, n. 18.

108. Ibid., 30.

109. Bernstein, "Hollywood's Arty Cinema," 30. See also J. A. Place, *The Non-Western Films of John Ford* (New York: Citadel Press, 1979), 258–61. Place discusses the longing for death in the film, and this wish is, perhaps, memory in its most fatal form.

110. See Peter Lehman, "Absence Which Becomes Legendary Presence: John Ford's Structured Use of Off-Screen Space," *Wide Angle* 2, no. 4 (1978): 36–42. Leman takes three of Ford's best westerns and shows how absence plays an effective role: *The Man Who Shot Liberty Valance* ("an absence which becomes a furious presence,") *She Wore a Yellow Ribbon* ("an absence which becomes a legendary presence"), and *The Searchers* ("an absence which becomes a confusing presence").

111. Bernstein says that the revised final script for the film (May 13, 1940) was planned and never photographed. See Bernstein, "Hollywood's Arty Cinema," 38.

112. Bazin, *What is Cinema?*, 88.

113. Quoted in Wilkins, "From Stage to Screen," 2.

114. This sequence is really an exception in *The Informer* because, as Bernstein points out, "Ford uses superimpositions extensively in order to reveal Gypo's thoughts. See Bernstein, "Hollywood's Arty Cinema," 35.

115. Quoted in Wilkins, "From Stage to Screen," 2.

116. Sarris, *John Ford Movie Mystery*, 100.

117. Bazin, *What is Cinema?*, 36.

118. Bordwell, Staiger, and Thompson, *Classical Hollywood Cinema*, 347.

119. Eyman, *Print the Legend*, 230.

120. Bazin, *What is Cinema?*, 67–68.

121. Harry R. Salpeter, "Art Comes to Hollywood," *Esquire* 14, no. 3 (1940): 65, 173–74.

122. Matthew Bernstein, *Walter Wanger: Hollywood Independent* (Berkeley: University of California Press, 1994), 166.

123. Unsigned article, "The Long Voyage Home as Seen and Painted by Nine American Artists," *American Artist* 4 (September 1940): 4.

124. P. A. Doyle, *Liam O'Flaherty* (New York: Twayne, 1971), 35.

125. See William Stott, *Documentary Expression and Thirties America* (Chicago and London: University of Chicago Press, 1973; rev. 1986) and F. Jack Hurley, *Portrait of a Decade: Roy Stryker and the Development of Documentary Photography in the Thirties* (New York: DeCapo, 1977).

126. John Tebbel and Mary Ellen Zuckerman, *The Magazine in America, 1741–1990* (New York: Oxford University Press, 1991), 230.

127. I am oversimplifying here, obviously, because "deep focus" will function within various stages and strategies within the classical paradigm. For a superb analysis of Toland, see Bordwell, Staiger, and Thompson, *Classical Hollywood Cinema*, 341–52.

128. Gregg Toland, "Realism for Citizen Kane," *American Cinematographer* (February 1941; reprint August 1991): 37.

129. Cormack, *Ideology and Cinematography*, 142.

130. Eyman, *Print the Legend*, 231.

131. Milton J. Brown, "Wanger Circus," *Parnassus* 12 (October 1940): 38.

132. *The Hollywood Reporter* (October 8, 1940): 3. See also Bernstein, *Walter Wanger*, 167. Bernstein says that "a former United Artist publicity executive remarked in April, 1941 that Ford's film was certain to be called arty.' " The film also became important in later venues for retrospective appreciations of Ford.

133. Jean Mitry, *John Ford* (Paris: Classiques du Cinéma, 1954), 23–38. Together with *Stagecoach*, *The Long Voyage Home* was an expression of human solidarity and individual liberty in the face of collective determinism.

134. Frederick Wilkins, "From Stage to Screen: The Long Voyage Home and Long Day's Journey into Night," *Eugene O'Neill Newsletter* 7, no. 1 (Spring 1983): 1.

135. Rosemary Foley, "Memo to Walter Wanger," September 13, 1940, quoted in Bernstein, "Hollywood's Arty Cinema," 44, n. 24.

Chapter 5. Canon Fire

1. *The Red Badge of Courage* (1951, MGM), producer: Gottfried Reinhardt; director: John Huston; screenplay: John Huston (from the Stephen Crane novella); adaptation: Albert Band; cinematographer: Harold Rosson; editor: Ben Lewis, supervised by Marguerite Booth; music: Bronislau Kaper; art director: Cedric Gibbons. cast: Audie Murphy (Henry Fleming, "The Youth"), Bill Mauldin (Tom Wilson, "The Loud Soldier"), John Dierkes (Jim Mauldin, "The Tall Soldier"), Royal Dano ("The Tattered Soldier"), Arthur Hunnicut (Bill Porter), Tim Durant (the General), Douglas Dick (the Lieutenant), Robert Easton Burke (Thomson), Andy Devine ("The Fat Soldier"), Smith Bellow (the Captain), Dixon Porter (a veteran). Voice-over commentary spoken by James Whitmore.

2. The two-part review in *The New Yorker* was brought out as a book the same year. See Lillian Ross, *Picture* (New York: Doubleday, rev. ed., 1993).

3. William Graebner, *The Age of Doubt* (Boston: Twayne, 1991), 17.

4. Edison Kinetogram, June 1, 1911, 13, quoted in William Uricchio and Roberta E. Pearson, *The Case of the Vitagraph Quality Films* (Princeton, N.J.: Princeton University Press, 1992), 51

5. Ibid., 54–55.

6. Ibid., 112.

7. Marcia Landy, "Introduction," in *The Historical Film: History and Memory in Media,* ed. Marcia Landy (New Brunswick, N.J.: Rutgers University Press, 2001), 8.

8. See Jim Cullen, *The Civil War in Popular Culture: A Reusable Past* (Washington and London: Smithsonian Institution Press, 1995).

9. M. M. Bakhtin, *The Dialogic Imagination: Four Essays* (Austin: University of Texas Press, 1981), 300. See also Dudley Andrew, "Adapting Cinema to History: A Revolution in the Making," in Stam and Raengo, *Companion to Literature and Film,* 189–204.

10. See, Melvin B. Tolson, "*Gone with the Wind* is More Dangerous than *Birth of a Nation,*" in *American Movie Critics: An Anthology From the Silents Until Now,* ed. Phillip Lopate (New York: Library of America, 2006), 140–44.

11. Cullen, *Civil War,* 70.

12. Ibid., 79. Griffith released his first sound picture in 1930, *Abraham Lincoln,* which also dealt with a Civil War theme.

13. Donald Bogle, "Black Beginnings: From *Uncle Tom's Cabin* to *The Birth of a Nation,*" in *Representing Blackness: Issues in Film and Video,* ed. Valerie Smith (New Brunswick, N.J.: Rutgers University Press, 1997), 20. See also Bogle's larger study, *Toms, Coons, Mulattoes, Mammies, and Bucks* (New York: Continuum, 1989).

14. Letter of Margaret Mitchell to Thomas Dixon, August 15, 1936, quoted in Cullen, *Civil War,* 70.

15. Cullen, *Civil War,* 80.

16. Balio, *Grand Design,* 210–11.

17. Leitch, *Film Adaptation and Its Discontents,* 146–47.

18. The film credits in *Red Badge* read "Adaptation by Albert Band." Band was functioning as Huston's assistant on the picture. Huston is credited in the screenplay and based on later interviews and recollections, the final "adaptation" belongs to Huston himself.

19. Quoted in Amy Kaplan, "The Spectacle of War in Crane's Revision of History," in *New Essays on The Red Badge of Courage,* ed. Lee Clark Mitchell (Cambridge, U.K.: Cambridge University Press, 1986), 106.

20. Ross, *Picture,* 129.

21. Schatz, *Boom and Bust,* 337.

22. Schatz, *Genius of the System,* 455.

23. Schatz, *Boom and Bust,* 368.

24. Jeanine Basinger quoted in Steve Neale, *Genre and Hollywood* (London and New York: Routledge, 2000), 130.

25. Steve Neale, *Genre and Hollywood* (New York and London: Routledge, 2000), 131.

26. Quoted in Neale, *Genre and Hollywood*, 131.

27. Schatz, *Boom or Bust*, 368.

28. Scott Eyman, *Lion of Hollywood: The Life and Legend of Louis. B. Mayer* (New York: Simon and Schuster, 2005), 436.

29. Interoffice memo, Schary to Mayer, June 9, 1950, quoted in Eyman, *Lion of Hollywood*, 434.

30. Quoted in Lawrence Grobel, *The Hustons* (New York: Charles Scribner and Sons, 1989), 39.

31. Ross, *Picture*, 184. Ross says that with the private audience, these scenes had been unanimously admired. But in the preview, some elderly ladies walked out, while "one masculine voice, obviously in the process of changing, called, out, 'Hooray for Red Skelton!'"

32. Metro asked Huston if he had a copy of the original print in 1975. He said, "It does not exist." See, John Huston, *An Open Book* (New York: DaCapo, 1994), 180.

33. Neale, *Hollywood Genres*, 130.

34. George Lipsitz, *Time Passages: Collective Memory and American Popular Culture* (Minneapolis: University of Minnesota Press, 1990), 165.

35. Ibid., 211–31. Lipsitz sees counter-memory as a challenge to the dominant historical consciousness, which is not "a denial of history, only a rejection of its false priorities and hierarchical divisions" (223).

36. Ross, *Picture*, 15.

37. See Donald B. Gibson, *Red Badge of Courage: Redefining the Hero* (New York: Twayne Publishers, 1988).

38. Amy Kaplan, "The Spectacle of War," in Mitchell, *New Essays*, 79, 84.

39. June Howard, *Form and History in American Literary Naturalism* (Chapel Hill: University of North Carolina Press, 1985), 98.

40. Joseph Conrad, "His War Book: A Preface to Stephen Crane's *The Red Badge of Courage*," in *The Red Badge of Courage*, ed. Sculley Bradley et al. (New York: Norton, 1976), 192.

41. Linda H. Davis, *Badge of Courage: The Life of Stephen Crane* (New York: Houghton Mifflin, 1998), 69.

42. Daniel Weiss, "The Red Badge of Courage." *Psychoanalytic Review* 52, no. 2 (Summer 1965): 32–52.

43. Richard T. Jameson, "John Huston," in *Perspectives on John Huston*, ed. Stephen Cooper (New York: G.K. Hall, 1994), 86.

44. Sarris, *The American Cinema*, 157.

45. James Agee, *Agree on Film* (Boston: Beacon Press, 1958), 325.

46. "Two Encounters with John Huston," in *John Huston Interviews*, ed. Robert Emmet Long (Jackson: University Press of Mississippi, 2001), 145.

47. Quoted in Agee, *Agee on Film*, 331.

48. Ross, *Picture.*

49. Peter Bogdanovich, *Who the Devil Made It* (Knopf, 1997), 318.

50. Jeanine Basinger reckons that, insofar as combat films are concerned, there were thirteen released in 1941–42; sixteen in 1943; thirteen in 1944; and sixteen in 1945. *The Red Badge of Courage* would figure here especially because its subject matter, like the ones indicated above, concerns *primarily* an instance in battle. See Jeanine Basinger, *The World War II Combat Film: Anatomy of a Genre* (New York: Columbia University Press, 1986), 281–94. There were, obviously, many more films in which wartime themes, but not battle scenes, played an important role.

51. See Dana Polan, *Power and Paranoia: History, Narrative and the American Cinema, 1940–1950* (New York: Columbia University Press, 1986), 193–249.

52. Desser also recognizes a split between the "therapeutic" films and the "noir" films of Huston as mirror images "in competition." I am suggesting something of a blurring of these distinctions, since it seems to me that there is a noirish element to therapy that Huston wants to convey. David Desser, "The Wartime Films of John Huston: Film Noir and the Emergence of the Therapeutic," in *Reflections in a Male Eye: John Huston and the American Experience,* ed. Gaylyn Studlar and David Desser (Washington, D.C.: Smithsonian Institution Press, 1993), 19–32.

53. *Let There be Light* was pulled from the program and replaced on the 3, 4, 5, and 6 of June 1946 with a British film, *Psychiatry in Action.* According to the museum's memorandum to the public, Iris Barry, curator of the Film Library at the Museum of Modern Art, regretted not being able to show "John Huston's profoundly human and valuable psychiatric picture." Other films were also changed during the same exhibition.

54. Archer Winston, "Let There Be Light," *New York Post,* June 2, 1946.

55. Letter, Colonel Charles W. McCarthy to Arthur L. Mayer, August 12, 1946. John Huston Collection, Margaret Herrick Library, Academy of Motion Pictures Arts and Sciences, Beverly Hills, Calif.

56. Letter of Kenneth C. Royall to Arthur L. Mayer, September 9, 1946. John Huston Collection, Margaret Herrick Library.

57. Huston, *An Open Book,* 125.

58. Lance Bertelsen, "*San Pietro* and the 'Art' of War," *Southwest Review* 74, no.3 (Spring 1989): 231. Eric Ambler, who would bring his own literary interests to the film, worked on *San Pietro* but is not credited.

59. The National Archives show that Ernie Pyle also interviewed the troops on December 16, 1943, and this was when Pyle was probably inspired to write "The Death of Captain Waskow." See Bertelsen, 231.

60. See Interoffice Memo, Major John Huston to Colonel Frank Capra, August 15, 1944, Huston Collection, Margaret Herrick Library. Alternative titles discussed were also *The Foot Solider and St. Peter* and *Foot Soldier at San Pietro.* Capra, who is often associated with the cinema of the "common man," favored *Foot Soldier,* but it was finally agreed that *Foot Soldier* would lead an audience to expect something about

the life of a foot soldier in battle—his ideas and psychology. Huston's attention to this issue is indicative of the importance he placed on the social and class function of his work. Moreover, *Let There Be Light* and *The Red Badge of Courage* both focus almost exclusively on the infantryman.

61. Huston, *An Open Book,* 119.

62. Desser, "Wartime Films of John Huston," 26.

63. Ibid., 29.

64. Quoted in Desser, "Wartime Films of John Huston," 29.

65. Max Weber, *The Theory of Social and Economic Organization,* trans. A.M. Henderson and Talcott Parsons (New York: The Free Press, 1947), 328.

66. See Jacques Lacan, *Écrits* (Paris: *Editions du Seuil,* 1966), 278.

67. Desser, "Wartime Films of John Huston," 19. See also the excellent essay by Gary Edgerton, "Revisiting the Recordings of Wars Past: Remembering the Documentary Trilogy of John Huston," in Studlar and Desser, *Reflections in a Male Eye,* 33–61.

68. Howard C. Horsford, "'He Was a Man'" in Mitchell, *New Essays on the Red Badge of Courage,* 113.

69. Scott Hammen, *John Huston* (Boston: Twayne, 1985), 57.

70. Philip Dunne, "The Documentary and Hollywood," in *Nonfiction Film Theory and Criticism,* ed. Richard Meran Barsam (New York: Dutton: 1976), 159.

71. "Revised Opening," May 3, 1950, MGM collection, Doheny Library, University of Southern California, Los Angeles.

72. Ross, *Picture,* 164.

73. Agee, *Agee on Film,* 330.

74. Lesley Brill, *John Huston's Filmmaking* (Cambridge, U.K.: Cambridge University Press, 1997), 86.

75. With the emphasis on a prologue that would in some sense function didactically, one is reminded of Welles's prologue to the unproduced screenplay for Conrad's *Heart of Darkness.* Chapter 3, above.

76. Ross, *Picture,* 189–90. It was only at this point that Huston agreed to try some narration, but after the second preview, in which only the scene of the veterans jeering at the recruits was cut, Huston left Hollywood immediately to make *The African Queen.*

77. Eyman, *Lion of Hollywood,* 434.

78. Ross, *Picture,* 165. Also see Gottfried Reinhardt, "Sound track Narration: Its Use Is Not Always a Resort of The Lazy or the Incompetent," *Films in Review* 4 (November 1953): 459–60.

79. Jameson, "John Huston," *Perspectives on John Huston,* 96.

80. Quoted in Ross, *Picture,* 182.

81. See Caryl Flinn, *Strains of Utopia: Gender, Nostalgia and Hollywood Film Music* (Princeton, N.J.: Princeton University Press, 1992). Flinn notes, on the one hand, that Nathan Levinson, a recording director at Warner Bros., said that "the score for each picture is written to suit the moods and tempos of the various scenes, and the

music found suitable for one picture is seldom, if ever, employed in another" (30). On the other hand, Roy Prendergast says that Hollywood was always "re-cycling" its musical scores (31). For Flinn, who follows Walter Benjamin here, Hollywood depends on an "aura," a new romanticism, for its musical authorship (13–50).

82. Quoted in Ross, *Picture*, 162.

83. Roland Barthes, *S/Z*, trans. Richard Miller (New York: Hill and Wang, 1974), sec. 28, 41, and 81.

84. Stephen Philip Cooper, "Toward a Theory of Adaptation: John Huston and the Interlocutive" (PhD diss., University of California, Los Angeles, 1991), 252. See also Gerard Genette, *Paratexts*, trans. Jane E. Lewin (New York: Cambridge University Press, 1997), 16–36.

85. J. Hillis Miller, *Illustration* (Cambridge, Mass.: Harvard University Press, 1992), esp. 9–60. Undoubtedly, it was Mathew Brady, the most famous photographer of the Civil War, who influenced the visual aspect of the film. Huston told Reinhardt that among his heirlooms was "a Brady" of his great-grandfather. See Ross, *Picture*, 66.

86. Quoted in Ross, *Picture*, 221.

87. Kozloff, *Invisible Storytellers*, 22. Another example of how narration was supposed to save a picture was Goldwyn's contemporary production of *Edge of Doom* (1950). See A. Scott Berg, *Goldwyn: A Biography* (New York: Ballantine, 1998), 453.

88. Robert Stam, "Introduction," 25.

89. Charles Whitting, *American Hero: The Life and Death of Audie Murphy* (Chelsea, Mich.: Scarborough House, 1990), 173.

90. Barbara Herrnstein Smith, *Contingencies of Value: Alternative Perspectives for Literary Theory* (Cambridge, Mass.: Harvard University Press, 1988), 51 and following.

91. Quoted in Richard H. Pells, *The Liberal Mind in a Conservative Age: American Intellectuals in the 1940s and 1950s*, 2nd ed. (Middletown, Conn.: Wesleyan University Press, 1989), 219. Pells provides a superb summary of the debates ensuing over "mass culture." See esp. 183–261.

92. Paul Lauter, *Canons and Contexts* (New York: Oxford University Press, 1991), 103–4. See also John Guillory, *Cultural Capital: The Problem of Literary Canon Formation* (Chicago and London: University of Chicago Press, 1993).

93. John E. Hart, "*The Red Badge of Courage* as Myth and Symbol," *University of Kansas Review* 19 (Summer 1953): 249.

94. From the moment the novel appeared, it was often viewed as satire of army life. In the April 1896 issue of *The Dial*, for example, U.S. Army General A. C. McClurg said that, "the hero of the book, if such he can be called, was an ignorant and stupid country lad without a spark of patriotic feeling or soldierly ambition . . ." In addition, "no thrill of patriotic devotion to cause or country ever moves his breast, and not even an emotion of manly courage." Quoted in Donald Pease, "Fear, Rage and the Mistrials of Representation in *The Red Badge of Courage*," in *Modern Interpretations: Stephen Crane's "The Red Badge of Courage*, ed. Harold Bloom (New York: Chelsea

House, 1987), 75. Pease's account of Crane in the 1890s sounds very much like Huston in the post–World War II years: "By driving a wedge between authorized versions of this war and experiences alien to them, Crane caused a fissure to form in the nation's self-conception, which not even the ideology of union would be sufficient to heal" (97).

95. According to the official document issued by MGM for production #1512, dated October 17, 1951, "The Red Badge of Courage" *Eliminations,* this cut corresponds to "Ext. Field-Hillside-Woods Sc. 172 to 178, with 232 feel eliminated (estimate cost: $5,635). I am indebted to Ned Comstock at the University of Southern California for bringing these script deletions to my attention.

96. There was a retake dated October 27, 1950. Scene 175 was OUT and replaced by 175x1. But a year later, according to the official MGM eliminations dated October 17, 1951, Sc. 175x1A was OUT.

97. Ross, *Picture,* 184.

98. Ross says that, along with the removal of the scene with the Tattered Man, the cuts had the effect of making the picture illogical. "The battle sequences added up to an entirely different war from the one that had been fought and photographed at Huston's ranch in the San Fernando Valley. The elimination of scenes accounted for part of the difference. The old man with the lined face who was digging was gone, the ragged veterans gibing at the recruits both before and after a battle were gone. Many small touches—brief glimpses of the men at war—had been trimmed, including a close-up of a wounded man berating an officer for 'small wounds and big talk.' The last shot in the picture—of the Youth's regiment marching away from the battlefield—which Huston had wanted to run long, had been cut to run short. . . . The revision had some odd results. Audie Murphy, who played the Youth, started to lead a charge with his head wrapped in a bandanna, rushed forward without the bandanna, and then knelt to fire with the bandanna again around his head." Ross, *Picture,* 226–27.

99. Pam Cook, "Duplicity in *Mildred Pierce,*" in *Women in Film Noir,* ed. E. Ann Kaplan (London: BFI, 1978), 69.

100. Amy Kaplan, "Nation, Region and Empire," in *The Columbia History of The American Novel,* ed. Emory Elliot et al. (New York: Columbia University Press, 1993), 249.

101. See, for example, Robert M. Richnitz, "Depersonalization and the Dream in *The Red Badge of Courage,*" *Studies in the Novel* 6 (Spring 1974): 76–87.

102. See James Naremore, "The Performance Frame," in Butler, *Star Texts,* 102–24.

103. Quoted in Ross, *Picture,* 73.

104. John Ellis, *Visible Fictions* (London: Routledge and Kegan Paul, 1982), 92. See also Dyer, *Heavenly Bodies*; and Naremore, *Acting in the Cinema.*

105. Ross, *Picture,* 73.

106. One person commented that "Audie Murphy is too good an actor to be stuck

in such a stinker as this." See Ross, *Picture*, 188, and A. H. Weiler, "By Way of Report: Information on Audie Murphy and His Role in Film," *New York Times*, October 14, 1951.

107. Whiting, *American Hero*, 175. The photos in *Life* were also responsible for calling James Cagney's attention to Murphy and bringing him to Hollywood.

108. According to the script eliminations, Int. Youth's Tent: scenes 15–23, was the first footage cut. See "Eliminations," MGM Collection, Doheny Library.

109. Stephen Cooper, "Political Reflections in a Golden Eye," in Studlar and Desser, *Reflections in a Male Eye*, 98.

110. The Second Battle, scenes 22–344, was by far the longest and most expensive sequence cut from the film. It ran 768 feet and cost $112,335. See "Eliminations," MGM Collection, Doheny Library.

111. Ross, *Picture*, 270

112. Naremore, *More Than Night*, 130.

113. Ibid., 130.

114. Eyman, *Lion of Hollywood*, 435.

115. Huston, in fact, revised his script for *Red Badge* after the Hollywood Ten were sentenced to a year in prison.

Index

Abbott, Mary Allen, 22, 47, 48, 49, 50, 51, 166
Achebe, Chinua, 65, 88, 169
Adapatation: and the art film, 27, 107, 108,
109; authorship, 6–11, 27–36, 81, 93, 96,
98, 101, 103, 104, 105, 121, 131, 161, 162, 177,
187; and canonical and classic texts, 5,
20, 27, 34, 126, 144, 145; and the canonical text, 1, 2, 5, 8, 10, 20–32, 44, 65, 129,
143, 144, 153, 169; and the Civil War, 10,
71, 114, 125, 127–33, 142–44, 148, 149, 151,
183, 187; and cultural power, 1–30, 33, 34,
36, 43, 45, 46, 59, 72, 81, 83, 86, 90, 96, 104,
125–27, 131, 135, 138, 142, 143, 152, 153, 156,
158, 169, 170, 174; and cultural value, 5–11,
20–29, 36, 45; and fidelity criticism, 1, 3,
4, 11–16, 20, 23, 27, 34, 35, 51, 80, 84, 100,
154; and formalist critics, 1, 3, 5, 6, 20, 21,
27, 31, 163; and illustration, 52, 167, 168;
and intertextuality, 5–20, 42, 51, 157; and
literary author, 5, 34; and mass culture, 2,
18, 20, 24, 26, 27, 69, 71, 127, 144, 187; and
MGM, 2, 8, 9, 10, 26, 37, 41–54, 58, 60, 63,
113, 126, 129–41, 144, 153, 154, 167, 168, 180,
182, 184, 186–89; and *mise-en-scène*, 4, 15,
33, 34, 35, 36, 52, 56, 96, 101, 107, 121, 124;
and modernism, 64–70, 76, 80, 88, 89,
95, 153; and montage, 4, 54, 56, 57, 96, 97,
99, 100, 102, 117, 137, 142, 168; and The National Council of the Teachers of English,
22; as the politics of redeployment, 2; and

the prestige production, 8–10, 20–29, 34,
35, 37, 42, 43, 44, 45, 46, 47, 77, 96, 104–13,
125–30, 143, 153, 159, 164, 165; and representations of African Americans, 85, 127;
and RKO, 9, 10, 44, 59, 64, 66, 67, 72, 77,
80–88, 94, 106, 110, 129, 135, 172, 173, 174,
179; and *tableaux vivants*, 13, 51, 52; use of
the Bible, 12–20, 25, 46, 158; and the uses
of narration, 9, 54, 55, 66, 67, 69, 71, 72,
76–92, 131, 137–44, 158, 166, 167, 168, 169,
172–74, 185–87
Agee, James, 62, 133, 141, 150, 168, 184, 186
Allen, Walter, 56, 168
America at the Movies (1939), 21, 22, 159
American Tragedy, An (1925), 46
Anderson, Lindsay, 104, 105, 115, 120, 180
Andrew, Dudley, 2, 31, 33, 97, 156, 160, 176, 183
Anna Karenina (1935), 44, 47, 165
Aragay, Mireia, 27, 155
Arnold, Matthew, 14, 20, 21, 35, 37, 42, 44,
58–62, 168; and *Culture and Anarchy*
(1867–68), 21, 58, 59, 168
Asphalt Jungle, The (1950), 132, 134, 153
Astruc, Alexandre, 4, 31, 33, 36, 162
Attack! (1956), 130
Auerbach, Eric, 157

Babington, Bruce, and Peter William Evans,
15, 158
Bakhtin, Mikhail, 12, 16, 50, 127, 158, 166, 183

GUERRIC DEBONA is a professor of homiletics and spiritual director at Saint Meinrad School of Theology.

The University of Illinois Press
is a founding member of the
Association of American University Presses.

———————————————————————————

Composed in 10.5/13 Adobe Minion Pro
with Frutiger LT Std display
at the University of Illinois Press
Manufactured by Cushing-Malloy, Inc.

University of Illinois Press
1325 South Oak Street
Champaign, IL 61820-6903
www.press.uillinois.edu